MW00721384

Spirituality, Religion, and Peace Education

a volume in
Peace Education

Series Editors:
Ian Harris, *University of Wisconsin-Milwaukee*
Edward J. Brantmeier, *Colorado State University*
Jing Lin, *University of Maryland*

Peace Education

Ian Harris, Edward J. Brantmeier, and Jing Lin, Series Editors

Spirituality, Religion, and Peace Education (2010)
edited by Edward J. Brantmeier, Jing Lin, and John P. Miller

Transforming Education for Peace (2008)
edited by Jing Lin, Edward J. Brantmeier, and Christa Bruhn

Dedication

I dedicate this book to my mother, Marge Hartmann.
Thank you for allowing me to choose my spiritual pathway.

Ed Brantmeier

I dedicate this book to global peace.

Jing Lin

I dedicate this book to all those teachers who bring compassion and
wisdom into their classrooms.

Jack Miller

Spirituality, Religion, and Peace Education

edited by

Edward J. Brantmeier
Colorado State University

Jing Lin
University of Maryland

and

John P. Miller
University of Toronto

Information Age Publishing, Inc.
Charlotte, North Carolina • www.infoagepub.com

Library of Congress Cataloging-in-Publication Data

Spirituality, religion, and peace education / edited by Edward J.
Brantmeier, Jing Lin, and John P. Miller.
  p. cm. -- (Peace education)
 Includes bibliographical references and index.
 ISBN 978-1-61735-058-0 (pbk.) -- ISBN 978-1-61735-059-7 (hardcover) --
ISBN 978-1-61735-060-3 (e-book)
 1. Peace--Study and teaching. 2. Peace--Religious aspects. 3.
Peace-building--Religious aspects. 4. Moral education. I. Brantmeier,
Edward J. II. Lin, Jing, 1962- III. Miller, John P., 1943-
 JZ5534.S65 2010
 201'.7273--dc22

                                                              2010018426

Printed in the United States of America

CONTENTS

PART II: PEACE EDUCATION, TEACHING AND LEARNING, AND SPIRITUALITY

ACKNOWLEDGMENTS

I would like to thank my co-editors, Jing Lin and Jack Miller for asking me to lead this project. Thank you to my family—Noorie, Noah, Ian—our journey together to India and to Nepal made the completion of this book possible. Finally, a deep thank you to all of my spiritual teachers—past, present, and future.

Ed Brantmeier

I would like to express my deep gratitude to Dr. Yan Xin, who opens the door of spiritual discovery and growth for me. I would like to thank my husband and my two daughters, my parents and parents-in-laws, and my sister-in-law, who always supports me and loves me unconditionally. I also deeply appreciate many of my teachers, students, and friends who have shared their inspirations and wisdom with me on our path of spiritual searching and enhancement.

Jing Lin

The editors would like to extend gratitude to Justyna Rucinska for indexing this book.

INTRODUCTION

Toward an Integrated Spirituality for Peace

Edward J. Brantmeier

Leaders have used religion to initiate and to sustain terrible acts of violence as religious ideology and doctrine have fueled countless wars and conflicts in the pages of history—and some of those violent pages have been purposely excluded or deleted from collective memory. Many people have given their lives for religion and many lives have been taken in the name of religion. On the other hand, religions and the spiritual paths that they provide also can bring out the best in human nature. Religions provided nurturance and meaning about how to live "good" lives to countless millions in multiple generations. This paradox of religion as both helping and harming needs to be acknowledged at the beginning of this book *Spirituality, Religion, and Peace Education*.

The purpose of this book is to explore how wisdom traditions can contribute to creating more peaceful individuals and a more peaceful world. Diverse cultural variations of the words peace, inner peace, and societal peace are explored through the lens of the vast wisdom and spiritual traditions of the world. Often times in these wisdom traditions there is a unity of inner and outer peace. The individual life is situated in a larger web of connective relationships: the individual to society; to humanity; to nature; to the world; and even the universe. Peace is pursued not only through religious teachings, laws, or institutions, but actively through personal cultivation of inner peace. Inner transformation leads to outer transformation—so the hypothesis goes. This book invites you to explore the philosophies, modes, and methods of both implicit and explicit education for peace within the context of wisdom traditions, religions, spiritual practices, and educational contexts.

This book *Spirituality, Religion, and Peace Education* attempts to more deeply explore the universal and particular dimensions of education for inner and communal peace. In several chapters, there is an explicit or implicit critique of modern education and the schooling systems that drive it. A critique of competition, consumerism, and materialism undergirds the exploration of education for wisdom, for peace, for balance, for a sense of the sacred, and for connection. Although practices vary, all these traditions place some emphasis on "actions," meditation being very important part of the process. Active work in blending oneself with the world in thought and deed, ethical orientations, energy, and spirit are rewarded with a more expansive world view and greater attunement to the needs of others. For example, Nathalie Kees has developed and teaches a course on contemplative practices in counseling and education at Colorado State University in the United States. In her chapter, she discusses an array of multicultural contemplative practices that she introduces to her students: the Buddhist practice of *tonglen* as a path to empathy and compassion; an indigenous Hawaiian practice of *Ho'oponopono* for forgiveness and conflict resolution; and pilgrimage and labyrinth walking for right action. Nathalie stresses the importance of the role of silence in contemplative, empathetic listening and how these silent spaces can lead to self and client healing.

When attuned to silence and inward knowing, individuals can become more loving, compassionate, forgiving, caring, respectful and engaged in social change as a result of these efforts. The impact that these individuals have on their communities and the institutions therein can be profound; people who pursue and cultivate inner peace can be catalysts for institutional and societal change. In their chapter Mary Lee Morrison and Ian Harris provide insight into the spiritual practices of the "inward teacher" and "clearness committee" of the Religious Society of Friends (Quakers). After doing so, they highlight the contributions of Quaker-inspired peace educators, scholars, and activists like Kathy Bickmore, Elise and Kenneth Boulding, George Lakey, Parker Palmer, and Priscilla Prutzman. In modern times, these people have helped to create the field of peace studies, several peace education programs, and have advance spiritual knowing and societal change. If we look at the life and work of people like Mother Theresa, Gandhi, Martin Luther King Jr., Chief Seattle, Thich Nhat Hanh, and other great voices for peace in history, we understand that each was grounded in a unique wisdom tradition and worldview that cultivates inner peace. From this connected place of peace, one is morally committed to act for the benefit of other people, animals, and ecosystems.

Premised on the assumption that there is a clear connection of the inner and outer worlds, this book situates and applies the insight of both spiritual and religious traditions to education broadly defined, to schooling, to community contexts, and to teacher education practices. The first section of this book focuses on great wisdom traditions and peace education. Confucius's virtues, Daoism, Judaism, Islamic Sufism, Christianity, Quakerism, Hinduism, Tibetan Buddhism, and Indigenous spirituality are examined in relationship to education for peace. In the second section of this book, various authors explore integrated spirituality that promotes stillness as well as enlivens, awakens, and urges reconciliation, connection, and wisdom cultivation in both teachers and students in educational contexts. Our understanding of education in this book includes and goes beyond the brick and mortar walls of schools; spiritual education is a process that connects people and the planet in intimate, purposeful, meaningful, and engaged ways. We hope this book will inspire both spiritual and religious people to examine the messages and practices of their own wisdom traditions. It is our hope that educators, both formal and informal, will benefit from an examination of these teachings, discourses, and educational practices for both inner and outer peace.

PURPOSES OF RELIGION

There are differences between integrated spirituality and religion as a social and political institution. Integrated spirituality is the connective, integrative, harmonizing force found within the lived teachings of great wisdom traditions. Religions serve as the vehicles for sustaining, propagating, and creating the cultural traditions associated with a particular religious worldview. In this sense, religions are the vehicle and spirituality is the lived message and process conveyed through religion. One is essence and the other is infrastructure. One is a tool and the other is both the process and outcome of the process. Religion is the tool to achieve spiritual attunement; this attunement can be the source of selfless action for the benefit of others in the world—an integrated spirituality in daily life.

What do religions do for people? Religions, as cultural formations, provide meaning, values, and frameworks through which people interpret personal and social experience and generate behaviors (Spradley, 1997). In the best case scenarios, religions help to heal wounds, to make sense of tragedy, to give purpose and higher meaning to life, and to provide a sense of higher or divine purpose. Authors in this book explore the history and

central teachings of Judaism, Christianity, Islamic Sufism, Hinduism, Daoism, and Tibetan Buddhism to present the pathways to peace established
by these globally impactful thought and belief systems. Through the
beliefs, values, and behaviors transmitted via religions, people make sense
and meaning of the world. Religions can elevate our understanding from
the everyday mundane to the transcendent sacred. They provide paths to
peace for practitioners, followers, or believers.

For some, analytical thought systems and meditative techniques provide a philosophy and practice for framing meaning and experience; they
help promote an awareness of reality and connectedness beyond the limited self. They can foster an understanding and experience of the radical
interconnectedness of all life. For example, in a chapter on the Tibetan
ethos and peace education, Jia Luo, a graduate student at the Ontario
Institute of Educational Studies in Canada, explores the Tibetan perspective of the causes of human conflict: desire, ignorance, and hatred. These
delusions can be analytically examined and the cultivation of wisdom
about the interdependence of all life, both human and nonhuman, can be
undertaken through meditation within a Tibetan praxis. Nonviolent,
compassionate action seems a logical extension from insight into interdependence.

Religions also provide moral codes for living life; they provide rules for
living the "good life"—though "good" can surely be culturally contingent.
The term religion is sometimes inadequate to depict a way of life, integral
to day to day meaning-making. In this sense, religion is not mere ritual or
timely observance of special days or occasions, but a day to day way of
making sense and meaning in the world via thought, feeling, and action.
Exploring more of a way of life than a religion per se, Jing Lin and Yingji
Wang provide an overview of virtues for actualizing the self and society as
taught by Confucius: *Ren*—love and compassion as human nature; *Yi*—
Selfless Help to Others: *Li*—Actions Leading to Social Harmony and
Peace; *Zhi*—Wisdom Cultivation; and *Xin*—Sincerity, Trust, and Faith. A
Confucian way of life integrates these in order to promote peace in the
self and society.

Religions provide day to day pathways as well as ritual, order, and
meaning in times of great stress such as death or natural disaster. They
also provide the same for births, marriages, as well as finding ones calling
in life. They encourage people to reach out to serve our fellow humanity.
The best aspects of religions provide hope, understanding, renewal,
inspiration, and meaning in this life and beyond. If we look to indigenous
spirituality as written about by Four Arrows or the place of spirituality in
the life and work of Ismaili teachers in Central Asia as written about by
Sarfaroz Niyozov and Zahra Punja in this book, we can see that spiritual
insight and wisdom hold a central role in both day to day work as well as

the understanding of the role of human beings in the wider world and cosmos.

How do religions provide these pathways of knowing for people? By establishing right conduct through sayings, paths, practices, disciplines, moral codes, commandments, laws, mores, mantras, religions provide frameworks for living the good life. In some cases, spiritual practices provided a connection to the spirit world for guidance, transcendence, and in some cases a non-linear view of time and life. Such practices are pathways to peace that allow adherents, in many instances, to be more peaceful and to create more peaceful societies. If aligned with means and ends for peace, perhaps the world's great wisdom traditions have the crucial answers to our questions about how to build a more peaceful world.

Religious Ideals Tempered With Realism

This idealistic portrayal of religion needs to be tempered with the harsh historical realities of religious hegemony used to mobilize, segregate, oppress, and in extreme cases, massacre millions of people. The worst face of religion can be understood in power structures institutionalized into stratified hierarchies that divide, oppress, conquer, and sustain dominance over others. Religions and "ways of life" can be and are used to stratify people in societies, to impose rules, and to impose an order that benefits the privileged elite. If arranged in a top down, hierarchical fashion, asymmetrical power structures are perpetuated and sustained among religious leaders and the followers of a particular religious tradition. Such differentials constitute division between the knowers and followers of a particular religious pathway.

Related in-grouping and out-grouping practices can sustain "us" and "them" identity constructs; discourses of "us" and "them," fashioned to promote conflict for specific political, economic, or social gains, are used to mobilize acts of violence against the "other." In some cases, limitations on material resources, the human spirit, freedom, and potentials to self-actualize are squelched via religious hegemony. In addition to bringing out the best in human nature, religions can also bring out ugliness in people and societies. It can be used to create and sustain deep "us and them" psychological barriers. A sense of self righteousness and group rightness can perpetuate everyday conflict and the need to convert or banish non-followers. If taken to the extreme, religious ideology can end in extremist violence against the other.

Despite all of this, this book aims to explore how religion and spirituality have in the past and might in the future contribute to create peaceful individuals and societies in positive, transformative ways. Because the focus in this book is to begin dialogue about peace education praxis, the tendency in most chapters is to focus more on the positive aspect of wisdom traditions rather than the negative aspects and historical complexities of violence and conflict as result of religious hegemony. The best, not the worst, is the focus of this book. However, many complexities of peace and violence as they relate to religion are explored in several chapters.

SPIRITUALITY AND WISDOM

Spirituality is not necessarily tied to a certain religion tradition or dogma. Spirituality can be an integral force inherent in vibrant peace and in life itself. As a process and force, spirituality is comprised of intuition, a sense of sacredness, of knowing, of connectedness, and of interdependence. One can be spiritual without being religious and one can be religious without being spiritual. One can also be both spiritual and religious. An integrated spirituality is a way of life, a lens from which to view and create reality with a sense of intuitive knowing and understanding of the connectedness and sanctity of all life. From this place of knowing and being, events in life take on new significance given an inherent reverence and equanimity about the processes of creation, sustenance, and destruction that comprise the continuum of time and space. An integrated spirituality is one that impacts one's knowing, feeling, and acting in the world and thus can transform the world if applied to the mundane necessities of day to day life. Spirituality can be enacted within oneself, within our homes, our communities, and the wider spheres of our influence and connection. There is an obvious connection between the spiritually attuned self and the impact this has on the relationships and institutions in which that individual works—just look at history or special people you know for validation of this truth claim.

Several chapters in this book speak to approaches to education that honor spirituality and wisdom. In William Timpson's chapter, he examines the role of reconciliation in peacemaking processes in his undergraduate honors peacemaking course at Colorado State University. A focus on the role of communicative acts to restore harmony and an awareness of our planetary connections and ecological interdependence to animals, plant, and mineral is nurtured. Four Arrows, an indigenous scholar and activist associated with the Fielding Graduate School, challenges the educational and cultural hegemony of the telling of indigenous history in attempts to raise consciousness of indigenous teachings of connectedness to nature and peaceful relations. Wisdom from his chapter reminds us that harm against others is harm against ourselves and that if we do not change our consumerist ways and thinking, "we are all in big trouble." If we all paid close attention to how we communicate, how we consume, as well as how we honor our relationship with the earth, perhaps we could bring about widespread social and ecological change.

If we integrated our spiritual knowing in our daily lives in deeper and more meaningful ways, deliberate action for the betterment of others and the planet might naturally be the result. Xin Li writes of humility and self-less service to others relayed in Daoist (Taoist) teachings about the positive, soft, and yielding qualities of water. This chapter asks how we can be selflessly beneficial to others with yielding humility and the self cultivation of unconditional goodness. Xin reminds us of how Daoist teachings about water exemplify some of these ideals. In the final heart and thought provoking chapter in this book, Jack Miller advocates for wisdom-based learning in teacher education that integrates a holistic approach and cultivation of the "thinking-heart" in both teachers as well as the students whose lives they touch. Jack communicates the need to counter current global economic and political trends with inner attunement in the teaching and learning process in order to actualize a more connected, balanced, and harmonious world. Educating for wisdom necessitates the cultivation of reflection, caring, and centeredness in our institutions of *higher* learning. An integrated spirituality centered in peace for peaceful outcomes could become the norm of day to day business.

TOWARD AN INTEGRATED SPIRITUALITY FOR PEACE

It is our hope that more intra-, interreligious dialogue and transdisciplinary scholarship about education for peace will emerge from reading this book.[1] We encourage readers to actively engage in discovery of the pathways to peace found in various religious and spiritual traditions represented here. Explorations into spirituality might lead us to an understanding of the sacredness of life and the radical interconnectedness of all life. Insight into interdependence may renew one's self-love and compassion for plants, animals, and fellow human beings who reside together on planet earth. This connected and grounded consciousness may provide a foundation from which spontaneous or deliberate compassionate action might build a more just and peaceful world. Acts of violence committed against the "self" or "other" seem particularly illogical and immoral from this place of knowing. Compassionate acts toward "self" reap positive merit for "others" and peaceful dialogue with "others" benefits the "self." These dialogic exchanges positively impact our homes, communities, and world.

How can we create society and global peace with agitated individuals and societies? To achieve a sustainable and vibrant peace, means and ends need to align. For example, protest of war, conflict, oppression, or other injustices, if violent and not guided by a spiritual and inclusive moral center, will indeed lead to continued violence. However, if activism is situated within a spiritual or wisdom perspective, dynamic, process-oriented, and vibrant positive peace is indeed possible.

A brief example of spiritually centered peace activism follows. As a graduate student at Indiana University-Bloomington in 2001-2003, I engaged in anti-war protests against United States policy that spear-headed military invasion in both Afghanistan and Iraq. As members of the Buddhist Alliance for Social Engagement, Jon Peters and I organized a few silent retreats, a workshop on spirituality, ecology, and sustainable living, and silent meditations at multiple antiwar protests. We, with a small number of other members, would sit quietly in a circle and meditate in stillness at the town square in Bloomington, Indiana. Other members of the anti-war protests would yell loudly, chanting all types of slogans and cheers such as "Support Our Troops: Keep Them Home" and later after invasion, "Support Our Troops: Bring Them Home." A few war support-ers would inevitably appear with signs that said, "Support Our Troops" and a handful of antiwar protestors would taunt and jeer at them, or even try to block their signs from public view from passersby in the central city square in Bloomington, Indiana. These oppressive actions seemed quite counterproductive to myself and fellow meditators given that our belief was that for a vibrant democracy to flourish, multiple perspectives and opinions were very necessary.

We understood that disagreement with opinions and policy need not be violent and that in order to actualize peace, we must first attune our inner selves with peace and then engage in peaceful action for societal change and transformation. Of course our protests did not reverse United States political and military policy in the aftermath of 9/11, however, engagement in one of the largest antiwar protests in U.S. history ener-gized us to commit to further social and political action. Personally, this engagement encouraged me to understand peace and nonviolence more deeply in my personal relationships, in my institutional capacities and affiliations, and in my engagement as a critical patriot and global citizen for peace and justice. I completed my dissertation studies on teacher engagement in an intercultural peace curricula development project at a high school in the United States where newcomer, transnational students were experiencing prejudice and discrimination (Brantmeier, 2007).

As a Fulbright-Nehru Scholar in peace studies at the Malaviya Centre for Peace Research at Banaras Hindu University in Varanasi, India in the Fall of 2009, I continued a lifelong journey to understand how to actualize inner and outer peace by reaching out to learn from some of the world's great wisdom traditions: Hinduism, Buddhism, and Islam to be specific.

Varanasi or *Benaras* (as referred to by many Hindus) is a spiritual center for many practicing Hindus around the world who make pilgrimages to the banks of the Ganges River to ritually bathe and purify negative karma. *Kashi*, the ancient name for this City of *Siva*, holds hope, renewal, and spiritual groundedness for many yogis, *saddhus*, ordinary Hindus, and wandering Westerner travelers alike. Both Hindu *mandirs* and Muslim mosques tower above the *ghats*. Not far from the heart of the city is *Sarnath*, the place where Buddha gave his first teachings on the four noble truths after he attained enlightenment in *Bodh Gaya*—just a few hours from Varanasi by car. Wandering holy men and women, water buffaloes, Mercedes, jewels, miniature palaces, oxen carts and absolute poverty-- Varanasi streets cradle all of life's processes of creation, sustenance, and destruction. This ageless city holds wisdom, a sadness, and beauty beyond measure. In the meantime amid all this life and energy, the Ganges waters, originating in the Himalayas, pass on through to someday merge with the ocean.

I was honored to participate in the Fulbright-Nehru Scholar program, a United States and Indian government sponsored program aimed at creating "mutual understanding" among scholars of these respective nation-states. The following words of Senator J. William Fulbright can be read on a poster outside the office of the Fulbright Commission of Nepal:

> The Fulbright Program aims to bring a little more knowledge, a little more reason, and a little more compassion into world affairs and thereby to increase the chance that nations will learn at last to live in peace and friendship.

Perhaps if the United States would redirect even a modest proportion of money used to fuel the military industrial complex toward exchange programs of this nature, the resultant citizen diplomacy efforts might prevent future international conflicts from arising around the world.

In a lecture I attended at the Malaviya Centre for Peace Research, Dr. Sanatkumar Sharma discussed "Yoga for Social Salvation in the Modern World." He suggested that "Achieving Excellence in Action is Yoga." With a translation of Yoga from the Sanskrit *yuj*, "to control," "to yoke," or "to unite," he urged our class, comprised of mostly Indian students, to unite their spiritual insight with excellence in social action. He urged them to explore the *Yoga Sutras* of *Patanjili* as well as the teachings in the *Bhagavad Gita*. His message focused on the importance of uniting personal spiritual knowing with social action for the mass welfare of Indian society and beyond.

Achieving excellence in action will arise with deep inner work from multiple practitioners of various religious/spiritual/wisdom traditions around the world. This inner work undoubtedly can be the catalyst for socially and environmentally responsible action that can transform our world—one individual, one community, one institution, one society, one country at a time. Our outer work can also bring inner peace. Please, let us never underestimate the power of words, of community, and of our individual and collective actions to transform our world into a place where all human beings can enjoy the peace of clean water, the peace of food, the peace of adequate shelter, the peace of medicine, and the peace of access and opportunity for educational and economic advancement. There are many people, plants, and animals whose sustenance is interwoven with our own consideration, kindness, and compassion. A slow rickshaw drive down the streets of Varanasi, San Diego, Rome, Sydney or any other city on the planet will undoubtedly affirm this.

In an exploration of the peacemaking, peacebuilding, and spiritual dimensions of 12 step programs in his chapter in this book, Brent Edward's asserts that the interrelationship of spirituality, religion, and peace education remains underexplored. The chapters in this book add to the dialogue and scholarship of this interrelationship. Inner peace education, as cultivated by various spiritual and religious traditions, needs to be the focus of deliberate, critical, and engaged scholarship in the field of peace education. Education for peace needs to incorporate wisdom from religious and spiritual traditions that have nurtured many people for thousands of years and that have given us hope and courage for peacemaking and peacebuilding. This book aims to rediscover and re-affirm wisdom in the religious and spiritual traditions of our world so that current and future generations of people, plants, and animals can survive, live, and prosper together. The invisible thread that connects all of these chapters is the promotion of selfless service to others for the sake of the greater good. "Others" here refers to both humans and the natural world of which humans are integral and consequential actors. If we enact the best ideals of wisdom traditions toward an integrated spirituality for peace, I am convinced we can transform our world for the betterment of future generations.

NOTE

1. It is important to note that the views expressed in these chapters do not necessarily express the views of the editors; individual authors provide unique snapshots of how their respective religions traditions and/or spiritual pursuits are connected to the larger project of building a culture of peace via educative means. Views in this book may or may not adhere to the respective wisdom traditions of particular practicing communities given the individual interpretations by the authors. The editors understand that the

texts themselves, an individual's interpretations of those texts, and a cultural community may vary widely in interpretation of a given religious idea or spiritual practice. Therefore, we acknowledge that this book represents a very small diversity of thought and interpretation and that many other interpretations may exist beyond the pages of this book. It is also important to note that we attempted to garner input from other indigenous authors (particularly from a Maori scholar from New Zealand and an Australian Aboriginal scholar), but schedules and conflicts in projects did not allow some scholars to contribute at this time.

REFERENCES

Brantmeier, E. J. (2007) Everyday understandings of peace & non-peace: Peace-keeping and peacebuilding at a U.S. Midwestern high school. *Journal of Peace Education*, *4*(2), 127-148.

Spradley, J. (1997). Culture and ethnography. In *Conformity and conflict: Readings in cultural anthropology* (9th ed., pp. 18-25). Boston: Little, Brown.

PART I

GREAT WISDOM TRADITIONS AND PEACE EDUCATION

CHAPTER 1

CONFUCIUS' TEACHINGS OF VIRTUES

Implications for World Peace and Peace Education

Jing Lin and Yingji Wang

INTRODUCTION

2,500 years ago, Confucius was born in the Lu State (552-479 BCE) in what is now Qufu city, Shandong Province in China. The time Confucius lived was characterized by warring states. States waged wars on each other and there was an enormous loss of life and disruption of the social order. Confucius believed that the Tao of Heaven must be followed in the human society. He traveled among the states to convince rulers that social order needs to be restored through virtue-based education. To him, peace is to be achieved by members of the society learning to live together and that eventually an ideal society will be realized on Earth. This ideal world is for the Good of All. In such a society, people are kind not only to their family members, but are also to others' children, elderly people, the weak, and

Spirituality, Religion, and Peace Education, pp. 3–17
Copyright © 2010 by Information Age Publishing

the handicapped. Able people have places to fully develop and utilize their abilities. People interact based on trust, kindness, selfless giving, and all members of the society contribute to the common good (*The Book of Rituals*). Hence for Confucius, the good world is not in the thereafter but it is here, and it is to be built through the efforts of the members of the society, exemplified by the deeds of *junzi*, or highly evolved beings.

In Confucius' mind, peace is achieved through harmony, and harmony is maintained by virtues, and virtues can be cultivated in every human being through education. The key virtues Confucius advocates are: *ren* (仁), or loving kindness; *yi* (义), or selfless giving; *li* (礼), or civility or actions of virtues; *zhi* (智), or acquisition of wisdom, and *xin* (信), the building of sincerity, trust and faith. He also advocates: *xiao* (孝), piety; *gong* (恭), respect; *qian* (谦), humility; *kuan* (宽), a form of all encompassing forgiveness, and *yong* (勇), courage. Confucius regarded it his mission to spread these virtues among state leaders hoping they would govern their countries with these values. He wished that he could cultivate leaders who could transform the lives of ordinary people by embracing the desired virtues. In his life time, Confucius had 3,000 students. He opened his door to all those who wanted to learn and sincerely believed everyone could be nurtured to be virtuous (教化) through education. Hence, education is for the transformation of individuals from the inside, by cultivating love and compassion in the heart, and by living in a virtuous state of being in daily life.

In this chapter, we will provide an analysis of Confucius' philosophy and discuss their relevance and implications to peace and peace education. We draw our insights from reading Confucian classics which contain his teaching. We look at the *Analects,* as well as other works such as *The Great Learning, The Doctrine of the Mean,* and *Mencius.* We draw fom these texts which are translated in a bilingual book by Legge, published in 1996. The most prominent text is the *Analects*, which is the collection of Confucius' conversation with his students, as well as descriptions of his deeds by the students.

Ren—Love and Compassion as Human Nature

In Confucius' mind, there are divine forces (*tian* (天), or heaven) that work in the human society; the divine force is not an external god or deity, but virtues exemplified through the heart and deeds of *junzi* (君子), or sages. Sages are human beings who have reached the highest state of virtues, who play a fundamental role in bringing peace and harmony to the society and the world. An ideal society would educate all people to become *junzi*.

In the *Analects*, the most central concept is *ren*. In the Chinese language, the word *ren* – 仁 , is the symbol of two people standing together, implying that human beings are always engaged in the reciprocal relationship of sharing kindness and love. This engagement is based on the notion that we always live in relationships. We are not independent but interdependent beings. The word *ren* can be translated into love, benevolence, or loving-kindness. When a student of his asked what *ren* is, Confucius says: to love people (*Analects*, 12.22). Confucius believed that benevolence is part of the innate nature of human beings. He states: People are born by nature to be kind; it is only the environment that makes people different. To have "*ren*" is to love people. This love is an all encompassing universal love with which we treat others as ourselves. With *ren*, one would not do harm to others, so Confucius instructs: "Do not do it onto others lest you do not want others to do it to you" (己所不欲，勿施于人). With *ren*, one places others in front of oneself, and treats other's success as one's own. Confucius says: "If you want to establish yourself, help others to establish themselves first; if you want to become prosperous, help others to achieve this goal first (己于立而立人，己欲达而达人)." This love, when extended to all people generously, can benefit the lives of the masses (博施于民而能济众). This ability for love, as the most basic in human nature, "is best understood as not a doctrine but a process, a continuing conversation and practice, whose highest aim is the realization of what it is to be human" (Conroy, 1988, p. 11).

Ren is in all of us. It is built into our system and wired into our neurological responses. Mencius, who expanded on Confucius' teaching in his book *Mencius*, illustrates this by an example. He notes that when we see a child crawling toward a well and is about to fall into it, we would instinctively reach out to help save the child. This spontaneous instinct, which he called *ce yin zhi xin* (恻隐之心), is our inborn nature to feel compassion and love for others. With this instinct, we can let go of our sense of separateness and connect ourselves to others, and the interconnections turn separate parts into an integrated whole (Lew, 2008).

For Confucius, *ren* needs to be integrated into the full spectrum of human social relationship. It should govern the relationship of leaders and subordinates, parents and children, and brothers and sisters. Based on a sense of responsibility for each other's well being, we perform our duty in support of each other. Every member of the society forms a reciprocal relationship that is mutually beneficial and responsible. Literally, *ren* is a verb, it has to be lived, cultivated, tested, and actualized.

Yi—Selfless Help to Others

The second principal concept in Confucius' teaching is *yi*, which is often translated as righteousness. Another translation in English can be "conscientious acts," which means "done according to one's conscience." In this chapter, we feel it is more appropriate to translate it as "selfless help to others based on our conscience."

Yi first points to the ability in humans to know what is right and wrong. Mencius (11.6) says, "*yi* is a sense of shame in doing wrongs." Further, *yi* implies that we have the obligation to help others. Members of a society should cultivate altruism regardless of personal gains. In the act of *yi*, people place others ahead of themselves without thinking about the fruit of action. *Yi* further means people do not take more than what they deserve but offer to give more to others rather than themselves. In the *Analects*, Confucius teaches that whenever a virtuous person gains some benefits, he/she will cautiously evaluate whether the gain is of virtuous means (16.10).

To help others regardless of one's own benefits requires virtue-inspired courage or boldness, which should not be mistaken with bold recklessness. Confucius says that if a virtuous person acts upon valor without conscience, he might recklessly upset the social order, and if a nonvirtuous person acts upon valor without conscience, he might commit robbery (17.23). Therefore, the righteous and conscientious people act with moral principles in mind.

Li—Actions Leading to Social Harmony and Peace

Li is another critical concept in Confucius' teaching. *Li* is close to being with Tao, the sage says. For Confucius, *li* is the acting out of *ren* in one's daily life. *Li* is vitally important for maintaining societal harmony and peace. Generally, *Li* is often interpreted as ceremonial rites or regulations. In fact, the word *li* should be treated as a verb. In reviewing Confucius' teaching, it is clear Confucius meant *li* to be civility and daily acts of respect, humility, care and kindness. *Li* requires a constant awareness of one's relationship with others. A person with true civility manifests *ren* in their every act of interaction with others. When one of Confucius' most famous disciple, Yan Yuan, asked what *ren* is, Confucius replies, "*Ren* is to refrain oneself (from nonvirtues) and to return to *li* (virtue-based actions)" (*Analects*, 12.1). Therefore, instead of regarding *li* as static rites, rituals or regulations, *li* is a dynamic expression of one's love, respect, and kindness.

In the tenth Chapter of the *Analects* many vivid examples are given of how Confucius sincerely respects all people he encountered, in accordance with *li*. When he entered the palace gate, he bowed deeply. When a gathering was over, he left only after the elders had left (to show deference and respect). Whenever he ate, even the simplest food, he would respectfully make offerings. When giving gifts to others, he had gracious and courteous manner. He urged his students to listen respectfully; speak courteously and act kindly. These examples indicate that *ren* is not an abstract term; it is incorporated into every moment of our daily life. Through performing these virtue-based actions with constant mindfulness, societal members can form harmonious relationships and peace is achieved.

Zhi—Wisdom Cultivation

For Confucius, the virtues of *ren*, *yi* and *li* need to be supported by *zhi* (智), which refers to the efforts to learn, to acquire wisdom, and to learn the Way of the universe. Enhanced by wisdom and knowledge, Confucius advises people to "cultivate the Way, abide by virtue, rest in loving-kindness, and delight in skills" (*Analects*, 7.6).

For Confucius, wisdom comes from learning. Learning can be for fun, but first and foremost, it is for the cultivation of oneself to become *junzi*. As mentioned earlier in the text, *junzi* are sages or moral/spiritual leaders who cultivate love for all humanity, seeking enlightenment through reflection, seeking knowledge from all people and taking engaged actions for social transformation for peace. For Confucius, those who are learned ought to be public intellectuals; they shoulder the responsibility to harmonize relationship in the family, the community, the country, and the whole world. To be able to fulfill their mission, they need to *gewu* (格物) or understand the physical world; *xiuxin* （修心） or cultivate their heart and mind. They need to be trustworthy, humble, loyal, and forgiving. They have achieved such a state of being that they are integral and whole inside and outside, in the private and public spheres. They maintain their integrity even when no one is watching, in the Chinese words, *shen du* (慎独), by knowing the law of virtues that produces reciprocal results in human society as well as in the universe. They exercise caution in their speech and actions. They seek to be well-rounded beings, being good also in poetry, rituals, music, shooting, and chariot driving (games of the past).

Seeking wisdom and knowledge and achieving enlightenment is a journey. Confucius outlines his life as a journey in this way: at 15, he establishes his goal to learn and acquire wisdom; at thirty he established himself and began to be recognized for his service to the society; at 40, his doubts about life were reduced for he has found many answers through life experiences; at fifty, he knows what heavenly providence is, knowing that one can make efforts but not force the results which one desires; at sixty he can hear any criticism, having let go of arrogance and greed, and knowing the benefits of all opinions; at seventy, he has achieved freedom, living in a state of being wherein he acts according to his heart without breaking the law of virtues. He is his true Self- body, mind, and spirit.

In another dimension, Confucius recognizes although we aspire to learn, we do not all learn in the same way. Hence he guides his students to learn according to their traits and abilities. He had a student who was very brave and had little fear, hence he tried to discourage the student from his bold recklessness and recommended caution. He had a student who was timid and he encouraged this student to go and try out his ideas. He accepted his students who wanted to be great leaders of a state, as well as those who just wanted to govern a community, or those who prefered living a life enjoying communion with nature disregarding fame and wealth.

Confucius urges humility and curiosity in learning, for he says "when three people are walking together, you can definitely find something to learn from at least one of them." Ultimately, learning is for lofty goals, that is, learning is not for one's sake but for the betterment of the world. One should have the courage to: "establish heart/mind for Heavens and Earth, shape the destiny of the common people, continue on the teaching of the sages of the past, and bring peace for the thousands of generations to come" (Zhang, 1978, p. 376).

Xin—Sincerity, Trust, and Faith

In Confucius' teaching, the virtue of *xin* (信), or sincerity, trust, and faith, is also paramount. It is the gateway to universal wisdom and to the building of genuine human relationship. *Xin* is often used together with the word *Cheng* (诚) to form the term *Chengxin* (诚信), which implies that internally we should cultivate sincerity and faithfulness and externally we should be trustworthy when relating to others (内诚于心、外信于人). *Xin*, as sincere engagement and trustfulness, helps one to feel the divinity of the cosmos and help human society to develop true brotherhood and sisterhood. To have *xin* is to arrive at *tong* (通), which means an unimpeded connection with the heart and soul of people, and the heart and soul of Heaven and Earth:

It is only he who is possessed of the most complete sincerity that can exist under heaven, who can give its full development to his nature. Able to give its full development to his own nature, he can do the same to the nature of other man. Able to give its full development to the nature of other men, he can give their full development to the natures of animals and things. Able to give their full development to the natures of creatures and things, he can assist the transforming and nourishing powers of Heaven and Earth. Able to assist the transforming and nourishing powers of Heaven and Earth, he may with Heaven and Earth form a union. (Legge, 1996, p. 49)

FROM SELF-TRANSFORMATION TO WORLD PEACE

For Confucius, virtues crystallized in *ren, yi, li, zhi, xin*, represent the Way of the universe. If human beings treat seriously the cultivation of virtues as true science, there would be no conflicts or violence in the world. In Confucius' teaching, the hope for a peaceful world is not first based on external sources, rather it is achieved through one's dynamic and active cultivation of inner virtues which leads to a highly evolved virtuous self. This virtuous self is cultivated in social relationships. As Tu (1985) eloquently pointed out, the Confucian self is the dynamic center of relationships, the path to community, and a dynamic process of spiritual development. Wang pushes it further by saying that the self-transformation is to become a spiritual and universe being: "Through attuning itself to the spirit of the universe, the self is simultaneously dissolved and enlarged by participating in the transformation of the ever-expanding cosmos. The self becomes a part of the creative cosmic processes" (Wang, 2004, p. 63). Confucius uses the concept of Tao and divine destiny to highlight this aspect of the cosmic self in all of us. Hence, we live in this world with a divine purpose.

Self-transformation for social change is an active and integral process. The Confucian concept of *ren* is interpreted by Hongmei Peng (2007) as *junzi*-in-the-making, meaning that *ren* is love in action. Similarly, selfless help to others (*yi*) and virtue-based actions (*li*) are all proactive actions in self-transformation and social transformation.

However, self-transformation for social transformation also means that one knows the context in which one lives in, and one judges correctly as to what to do and what not to do given the conditions of the time. One should not push for changes if the time is not right. Confucius says: When Tao prevails in the world, the *junzi* comes out to serve the world; when Tao is lost and not being upheld, the *junzi* recedes into the background to continue his cultivation. In fact, this state of serving or not serving the world is not absolute. When one is in a nonactive state, or not being in public office shouldering societal duties, one can take the opportunity to improve oneself and also enlighten others. This is what Confucius did. He travelled among the warring states for 16 years, trying to convince state leaders to follow the law of virtues to no avail. When he realized that the time was not right, he came home and began to focus on compiling books and teaching students. His latter efforts had an even greater impact in China and the world, as his teachings were transmitted from generation to generation, inspiring countless people to follow his example of cultivating peacebuilding virtues and transforming the world through actions.

In order to comprehend the relationship between self, social relationship, and the world, it would be helpful to understand Confucius' worldview of dynamic interdependence. In the following section, key concepts in Chinese worldview such as *Qi*, interconnectedness, and harmony are introduced.

Qi, Interconnectedness, and Harmony

In Chinese ancient philosophy, including both Confucianism and Taoism, our world is formed of an invisible form of energy, called *Qi*, which permeates the universe creating myriads of things and beings. *Qi* flows in our body as the life energy that propels the heart to beat and the organs to function harmoniously and in accordance with the rhythm of the outer environment. *Qi* is within every existence on earth, and fills the universe. *Qi* is "the underlying unity of life that is simultaneously moral and physical, spiritual and material" (Tucker, 1998, p.191). We are supported by *Qi*, and we can also proactively control and direct *Qi* if we act according to the principles of virtues. *Qi* can sustain human life and the earth, and can fill the space between Heaven and Earth (*Mencius*, 3.2). In this philosophical and ontological perspective, harmony is a balanced state of *qi* working among people and things. When people harbor *ren*, help each other with *yi*, and acquire the wisdom of life and the universe, *qi* works harmoniously, the human society as well as nature will prosper. Harmony is a state in accordance with the working of Heaven, or Tao. To strive for social harmony is to strive for the Tao.

Harmony as a peaceful state in the human world enables the *qi* of people and things to support each other. *Qi* is energy, which is also physical, spiritual and informational all at the same time (Lin, 2006). In nature, there are myriads of things that support each other with *qi*, each with their distinctness but work for a common goal. In human society, there will be differences, but people should work together to live in harmony emulating the law of the universe.

Harmony does not mean the denial of differences. Diversity and unity, consensus-building and respect for difference, are all embraced in the concept of *he er bu tong* (和而不同), literally translated as "harmony but not sameness." This harmony hence is rich and diverse; it means the recognition and acceptance of differences, and in an atmosphere of respect and acceptance, people work to achieve common goals. Hence, in Confucius teaching, harmony and diversity coexist.

Harmony requires a sense of balance. In the *Doctrine of the Mean* (cited in Legge, 1996), Confucius talks about the notion of Equilibrium, referring to the dynamic center, not being out of balance towards either side. When our world is resting in this dynamic equilibrium, there is harmony. "Equilibrium is the substance of Harmony. Both are interdependent and are the two sides of a coin. Equilibrium and Harmony work together as a wheel" (Chen, 2000, p. 10). For Confucius, equilibrium and harmony are in accordance with the Way of the universe. Confucius says,

> Equilibrium is the great root from which grow everything in this world, and Harmony is the universal path which should be practiced. Let the states of equilibrium and harmony exist in perfection, and a happy order will prevail throughout heaven and earth, and all things will be nourished and flourish. (*The Doctrine of the Mean*, p. 1)

The concept of harmony sums up the goals of cultivating and acquiring virtues. Education is for creating social harmony, for harmony enables creation of all forms of life and existence, and harmony enables the state and society to coexist. In Confucius' teaching, this is not merely some moral doctrine, but a universe law. Hence if a person wants to be successful or a state hopes to become prosperous, constructing harmonious relationship with each other and maintaining harmony with nature are preconditions and necessary mechanisms.

REFLECTIONS ON CONFUCIUS' TEACHING AND WORLD PEACE TODAY

Cultivating Peace With Others

The greatest challenge today is to shorten the distance between people in heart and mind. Although, we have technology that allows for instant communication, values are needed so that we use the technology in our advantage to build global understanding and respect. The idea of mutuality and reciprocity based on virtues, enhanced by instant communication through technology, can help us realize our interconnected wellbeing and destiny.

Adopting Confucius' teaching about interpersonal relationships, harmony should be chosen over conflict and cooperation over destructive competition and domination. Harmony is not a static state but a dynamic living process. Harmony is active and creative because it "is grounded not in conformity, but in dynamics set in motion by difference and multiplicity shifting in a network of creative imagination" (Wang, 2004, p. 172).

Confucius says when we relate to others, if we always look for some good quality in others from which we can learn, we will naturally treat them with respect. This is still true today. When we truly care about and respect others, we break down the divisive walls supported by social class, race, gender, cultural background, or political ambitions. We need a new understanding that we share the same root, and the same kind of basic nature. Acknowledging our underlying interconnection should lead to the understanding that respecting others is equivalent to respecting ourselves.

Confucius' teaching of compassion and humility carry great relevance today. When we meet people who have committed wrong doings or who have conflicting ideas with our own, Confucius advises us to reflect on ourselves whenever we see others' nonvirtuous behaviors (*Analects*, 4.17). Mencius (7.4) elaborates on this point, saying that if we are treated unkindly while we have been kind to others, instead of blaming others, we should always reflect on our own actions—Is my love sincere and unconditional? Through constant self-reflection, forgiveness, and reconciliation are achieved first through our own effort.

On the other hand, being respectful does not mean total conformity. Confucius says that a virtuous person would find harmony while embracing differences (Analects, 13.23). He also says that for those people who did wrong things, there needs to be justice. Wang (2004) explains,

> Harmony means negotiating between the Way and current circumstances, with balance at heart.... Harmony is contrary to, rather than compatible with, conformity. Harmony is not achieved by agreement, rather, criticism is necessary for reaching harmony. For Mencius, overthrowing a government that violates the will of the people is achieving harmony. For Confucius, the purpose of criticizing rulers is to urge them to follow the Way of harmony. (p. 61)

Hence, harmony is achieved through negotiations and proactive actions and social interventions. Harmony is often the result of struggle by individuals and the society for dynamic balance.

In Confucius' mind, love, kindness, respect, forgiveness, mildness, frugality, and deference are needed to maintain good relationships among people. He is against arrogant language and warns of speaking too much when our actions do not match our words.

Cultivating Peace Among Nations

Confucius' teaching can help us put forward a new paradigm for international relations. His assumption on human kindness and altruism —that we are born to be kind—could help us to change our current paradigm of fear of "others" and work on building our common bondage. Adopting Confucius' teaching of harmony, we should strive at an inclusive, cooperative and collaborative paradigm—from oppositional relationship among nations to a new framework in which we become "us" for the common good.

In terms of peace among states, Confucius maintains that people should employ politics with the virtues as outlined above (*Analects*, 2). *Analects* (13) describes that when the leader engages in virtue-based actions, the people will become respectful; when the leader is righteous, the people will listen and rely on her; when the leader is trustworthy, the people will put their hearts into living virtues as well. Consequently, a virtuous leader does not need to command orders, yet people will follow her naturally, and those who win the hearts of his people through virtues will gain the whole world. Therefore, for a national leader, the most important job is not to rule or to dominate, but to cultivate her own virtue so that she can set up an example for the whole country. Instead of forcing obedience onto the people, it is only through exemplary acts of kindness and trust that a leader can naturally win the hearts of people.

In Confucian texts, there are many examples of how to be a nation's leader. When powerful countries relate to smaller countries, they should treat the smaller nations with genuine care, allowing their own development and benefits to come to their citizens. In this way, smaller countries will respect the powerful countries.

Confucian wisdom has provided valuable insight in establishing new international relation theories and attempting to create a new world order of harmony and peace. If we sincerely engage ourselves in cultivation of virtues and relate to others and our world with loving-kindness, respect, humility, and forgiveness, we would eventually be able to develop harmonious relationships among nations.

REFLECTIONS ON PEACE EDUCATION IN THE TWENTY-FIRST CENTURY

Incorporating Confucius' ideas into current peace education effort would be a highly valuable process. Through teaching our students how to cultivate peace within themselves, with others, and how to act as future leaders of peace, we can help our students become pillars for global peacemaking.

Currently, our education system has an overwhelming focus on competitiveness and skills acquisition to the neglect of cultivation of virtues and wisdom. The school reform rhetoric caters to the pressure of market force and focuses mainly on boosting the competitive edge of students. Abilities to embrace people with love and respect, to handle human relationship with wisdom, to resolve conflicts through harmonizing social relationship are not current priorities in education.

Confucius' teaching about the role of education as nurturing whole humans with virtues has direct implication for today. For Confucius, peace comes from respectful and compassionate human beings, and education is the vehicle for fostering the future citizens. Education is about relational coexistence.

Today, an educators' role is not helping students to become whole. In Confucius teaching, education is for strengthening the inner ability of ourselves to help others and serve the world. This is a dynamic process of self-transformation for social improvement. This process is to let go of the small self and work for the common good through virtue-based action. There is no individual success per se if there is no collective success. Peace starts from the self to family, to community, to country, and to the world. For Confucius, education for peaceful relationships is to take place everywhere, in the family, the community, and the larger world. Teachers need to be good examples, and so should our leaders. The macro environment of the society can shape the traits and characters of everyone in a positive way.

In terms of addressing the escalating violence in this world, our education system has mainly promoted conflict resolution skills. But this is not enough, for the roots of conflicts are not effectively dealt with or eradicated. *Confucius' teaching tells us where to build peace so that conflicts do not even arise.* It is not merely enough to have knowledge, in Confucius' mind. Peacebuilding is inherent in every act of our daily life and in the whole of the learning process. Hence, we suggest that peace education should permeate family life, the schooling process and societal influences including the media and government policies. Our media today spreads too many violent images and messages, which are not conducive for children to see others as trustworthy human beings. Hence peace education is never meant just to be for schools.

The current functionalist paradigm that treats students as objects to be labeled, graded, degraded, and screened for the differential, unequal social hierarchy can no longer serve us. It is time for a paradigm shift in education—from merely focusing on knowledge acquisition, accountability and competitiveness, to cultivating deep human connection based on virtues of love, service, giving, humility, respect, among others. Instead of engendering a spiritual void, rendering students to feel empty, meaningless, and disconnected through the destructive competition, we need to rediscover and recover our true nature as loving social and moral beings. We need to empower our inner virtues and abilities, to enable students to open their hearts to see one another as connected by our common humanity and become messengers of peace in the world.

We need a new sense of self based on our interconnected and interdependent relationships, and "the quest for one's own personal knowledge must be understood as an act of service to the community as well: 'A humane person, wishing to establish his [or her] character, also establishes the characters of others and wishing to enlarge himself [or herself], also helps others to enlarge themselves' " (Tu, 1993, p. 41). If we want peace, we should take initiatives to give peace to others first; if we want love, we should love others first. If we truly understand that we are all connected, we should realize that it is impossible to enjoy individual freedom and happiness while others are in pain or suffering. Therefore, peace education must endow students with a sense of mission for the world, that is, the world's problems are not out there far away from me; they are right here in our surroundings and within our hearts. We need a sense of urgency to take action to extend our love to larger and larger circles of being. Just as *The Great Learning* states:

> Their thoughts being sincere, their hearts were then rectified. Their hearts being rectified, their persons were cultivated. Their persons being cultivated, their families were regulated. Their families being regulated, their States were rightly governed. Their States being rightly governed, the whole world was made tranquil and happy. From the emperor down t the mass of the people, all must consider the cultivation of the person the root of everything. (Legge, 1996, p. 5)

Therefore, in peace education, teachers themselves should continuously cultivate virtues. They should encourage students to be of service to others and the world. When students take concrete actions and see in teachers and other adult actions as examples of how to handle conflicts, they can envision and take leadership to build a world with peace, love, and harmony.

In sum, Confucian wisdom provides us with valuable insights into peace education. Three aspects need to be given special attention. First is the focus on self-cultivation because true peace must be created from within. Second is the cultivation of self through relationships, because we are all interconnected and interdependent. Last and most importantly is the emphasis on love, kindness, respect, service, wisdom, humility, and harmony, because it is the way of the universe. If peace education can realize these three essences in practice, a peaceful and harmonious world is at hand!

Reflection and Conclusion

In this chapter, we have focused Confucius' teaching of virtues. They are:

- Benevolence, kindness, love or compassion
- Daily action of respect and deference, to live in a state of *ren*;
- Service and help to others without thinking of benefits to one's self;
- Wisdom be guided by the Tao or universal law
- Sincerity: Be sincere, truthful, and faithful in all you do.

In Confucius' mind, these are heavenly virtues reflected in the human society. The harmony of the human society is achieved by people embracing virtues and living a virtuous life in daily interactions. The ones who have achieved perfection in virtues are called *junzi*, who exemplify perfect kindness and compassion. When they have arrived at this state of virtuous being, they have thorough integrity both with others or when they are alone. A *junzi* with perfect virtues are mild, kind, deferential, frugal, yielding, forgiving and trustworthy (温，良，恭，俭，让，宽，信).

Confucius treats *ren* as central in human society. Human beings all have the seed of *ren*, but it needs to be nurtured and cultivated through education and self efforts. Cultivating the trait of love and kindness requires one to study, understand, reflect upon, seek answers and establish goals to live the true meaning of *ren*. In Confucius' teaching, peace education is living a life of *ren*. One needs to reach the level of taking all people as belonging to One Family, as illustrated by *junzi* who accept both the "good people" as well as the "bad people" (唯仁者能好人，能恶人).

Fundamentally, Confucius does not treat virtues as simply moral choices per se, but as the organizing principles of human life and society, emulating the virtues of Heaven and Earth. Virtues are the foundational mechanism for humans to establish themselves and for any governments to remain strong and long-lasting. It is the way to build a harmonious society. Ultimately, the ideal world is one for the Common Good, where everyone treats each other as members of one family, the talented people use their potentials to the utmost, the young and the elderly are taken care of, and the handicapped are treated with compassion and love. It is a peaceful and loving world.

REFERENCES

Chen, G. (2000, November 9-12). *The impact of harmony on Chinese conflict management*. Paper presented at the annual meeting of the National Communication Association 86th, Seattle, WA.

Conroy, F. H. (1988). *Learning to be human: Confucian resources for rethinking general education*. Princeton, NJ: Princeton University Mid-Career Fellowship Program.

Legge, J. (Trans.). (1996) *The four books: The great learning, the doctrine of the mean, the Confucian analects, the works of Mencius* (bilingual) Changsha, China: Human Publisher.

Lew, K. K. (2008, Jan. 24-25). *Confucianism and cognitive, moral, aesthetic and senate intelligence*. Presentation at Symposium on Contemporary Significance of Confucianism: Implications for Harmonious Society, Sustainable development and World Peace, at Library of Congress and University of Maryland.

Lin, J. (2006). *Love, peace, and wisdom in education: Vision for education in the 21st century*. Lanham, Maryland: Rowman & Littlefield Education.

Peng, H. (May, 2007). *A conversation between Confucius and Dewey on individual and community—A hope for human unity*. Unpublished dissertation. Knoxville, TN: University of Tennessee.

Tu, W. (1985). *Confucian thought: Self-hood as creative transformation*. Albany, NY: State University of New York Press.

Tu, W. (1993). *Way, learning, and politics: Essays on the Confucian intellectual*. Albany, NY: State University of New York Press.

Tucker, M. (1998). The philosophy of ch'i as an ecological cosmology. In M. E. Tucker & J. Berthrong (Eds.), *Confucianism and ecology: The interrelation of heaven, earth, and humans* (pp. 187-207). Cambridge, MA: Harvard University Press.

Wang, H. (2004). *The call from the stranger on a journey home: Curriculum in a third space*. New York: Peter Lang

Wang, Y. (2007). Between science and art: Questionable international relations theories. *Japanese Journal of Political Science*, *8*(2), 191-208.

Zhang, Zai. (1978). *A collection of Zhang Ai* 《张载集》. Beijing: China Publishing House [中华书局].

CHAPTER 2

ISLAMIC SUFISM AND EDUCATION FOR PEACE

Michelle Ayazi

INTRODUCTION

"In education today, [the] soul is often ignored" (Peterson, 1999, p. 9). Education today focuses on parts, which causes many students to lose touch with the whole of themselves, humanity, the environment and the universe. There is a lack of holistic focus. Students in our educational system are being asked to compete against one another and academically specialize at younger and younger ages while spiritual and moral education—which are considered taboo—are being left out of the public school curriculum. This exclusion of heart and soul in education is manifest through the overrepresentation of medicated and drug-addicted youths, the prevalence of violence and suicide, the obsession with consumerism, and apathy toward reducing pollution and waste. The goal of education must change from emphasizing only intellectual development to the integrated development of mind, body, and soul, for it is the whole human being who is the best safeguard of any society (Moffett, 1994).

Education today teaches students to look for knowledge, answers, and fulfillment outside of themselves, which obscures students' true potential

Spirituality, Religion, and Peace Education, pp. 19–35
Copyright © 2010 by Information Age Publishing
All rights of reproduction in any form reserved.

and identity. On the other hand, Sufism—the mystical tradition of Islam—teaches that every one of us contains a precious mine of knowledge and ability that just needs to be excavated. It teaches that life's fulfillment should not and does not come from our material possessions or accomplishments, but from "living through this wondrous perfection within our own being" (Larsen, 2000, p. 2).

According to Sufism, education does not mean merely "acquired knowledge," but rather "innate, endowed knowledge" (Angha, 1996, p. 25). In other words, the student seeks answers and knowledge which cannot be found through reading or repeating the work of others, or through the traditional study of investigative and theoretical disciplines. Individuals are encouraged to seek this knowledge from within in order to become a balanced human being who knows their true identity, personality, values and purpose. Sufism believes that lives founded upon personal experience and absolute cognition—true knowledge and wisdom—result in peace and tranquility, and create a foundation on which to build a harmonious society (Angha, 1996). Those who practice Sufism seek true knowledge and wisdom, in addition to valuing intellectual learning traditionally taught in formal and informal educational institutions. It is in this respect that Sufism supports a holistic vision of education.

This chapter aims to emphasize that world peace cannot be achieved unless all individuals benefit from a state of spiritual well-being: A peaceful human society will be realized only through the inward harmony of each individual and each individual's harmonious existence in a unified system (Angha, 1996). In other words, each person needs to realize and embody peace within, first and foremost, before we can begin to experience peace on earth. The path to inner peace begins with a sincere desire on the part of the individual to truly know who they are and why they are here. By putting effort into discovering our unique and constant self—by embarking on this journey to discover true knowledge and wisdom—we can gradually begin to regain inner balance and harmony.

What are the basic beliefs and goals of Sufism and what is its relation to Islam? What is its conception of peace, and how does this conception relate to education? The purpose of this paper is to answer these questions and to summarize Sufism in a way that will attempt to elevate our understanding of peace and the role education can play in the pursuit of peace. It should be noted that this chapter will not attempt to define a Sufi curriculum or outline Sufi pedagogy. Rather, it will demonstrate how the goals of Sufism are compatible with the goals of a holistic, peace-oriented education. Ultimately, I hope that some readers will become inspired to further explore the application of these ideas in real-world educational settings.

WHAT IS SUFISM?

Sufism is a way, a discipline, a method that teaches the individual to explore and discover the reality of his or her true being. Sufism is the path to self-knowledge, and one who has reached this state of inner illumination and absolute cognition is called a Sufi, or *Arif*. The individual who is on the Sufi path to attain inner cognition is called a *salek*, or seeker. "The one who teaches this method of cognition is known as the *Pir*, or he who has attained the most exalted state of existence through annihilation and permanence in God" ("Sufism," 2009, para. 3).

Readers should know that there are several schools and orders of Sufism in the world.[1] The divine teachings of one particular school of Sufism, the Maktab Tarighat Oveyssi Shahmaghsoudi School of Islamic Sufism, will be highlighted in this chapter because its writings are prolific and accessible, and descriptive and practical. Moreover, the school has one of the largest memberships in the world, spans five continents and traces its origin back 1,400 years directly to the prophet Mohammad. According to Hazrat Salaheddin Nader Shah Angha[2] (1998), the present *Pir* of the Maktab Tarighat Oveyssi Shahmaghsoudi School of Islamic Sufism,[3] Sufism is the "reality of religion." This means that Sufism is the essence of religion: It is the way through which the holy prophets discovered their identity and purpose, attained knowledge of the ultimate truth, and attained cognition of the divine. Sufism is the heart and spirit of Islam.

Being a Sufi has nothing to do with the split in Islam between Sunnis and Shiites. Most Sufis believe that it is not enough to have faith in God, obey religious law (*Sharia*) and follow the examples set by the holy prophets (Chittick, 2000). They believe that Islamic devotional practices—including praying five times a day, giving alms, and fasting during the holy month of Ramadan—in addition to their outward form, all have an inner reality to them. Sufi practitioners not only partake in these outward practices, but they simultaneously strive to discover the truth and the reality behind them. Otherwise, they believe, spiritual progress is restricted. The ultimate aim in Sufism is to experience what the prophets experienced—to have direct cognition of the divine.

The word Islam, derived from the Arabic root *s-l-m*, means submission to the will of God. Submission in the context of Islam means to submit to the absolute knowledge which exists within each living being. This is submission based on certainty, which for each individual comes from direct experience and cognition—not submission based on one's imagination and blind faith. A true Muslim is one who has submitted based on absolute knowledge of God's existence. It is the priority of one on the Sufi path to discover this will—to discover who we are and what our purpose is, and to touch the source of infinite knowledge that is embedded within us.

Sharing the same root as the word *Islam* is the word *salam*, which means peace. Sufism teaches that to achieve harmony and peace within, one must uncover their true identity and personality. In Sufism, seekers aim to discover their true and stable self, their "I" (Angha, 2002). The prophet of Islam, Mohammad, has said, "He who cognized his true Self, has cognized his Creator" (Hadith Nabavi). In Sufism, God is synonymous with the true self, true knowledge, the absolute, the divine, existence and the universe.[4] Therefore, the pursuit of unveiling our true self, attaining true knowledge and wisdom, and experiencing peace and harmony within, all go hand in hand.

An Arabic/Persian word for Sufism, *Irfan*, captures its essence quite well. The word *Irfan* is derived from the Arabic word *ma'rifa*, which translates to "to cognize" or "to know" (Angha, 1996). Although the quest to "know thyself" is a timeless one, historians have traced Sufism's roots to the time of the prophet Mohammad.

The prophet Mohammad is considered by most Sufi orders as the first Sufi in an unbroken succession of Sufi Masters. However, since Sufism's basic teachings and goals are timeless ones, it is in a universal sense that we can say Sufism has existed since the time of Adam.

In 610 C.E. while the prophet was praying and meditating on Mount Hira during one of his periodic spiritual retreats, he received his first divine revelation. The Qur'an (Ali, 2002), Islam's holy book, is regarded as the word of God, spoken to the prophet Mohammad through the angel Gabriel over a 23-year period. All of Islam's devotional practices have a reality behind them that need to be discovered by the practitioner. Once discovered, these practices serve as a step towards self-knowledge. The Holy Qur'an states that its message is a continuation of previous divine scriptures (12:111), as Muslims believe that all the divine revelations of Judaism, Christianity, Buddhism, and all world faiths have come from one source—God.

It says in the *Hadiths*—the recorded words and deeds of the prophet Muhammad—that from time to time, the prophet would say, "The breath of the merciful comes to me from Yemen" ("History," para. 3, 2009). Hazrat Oveys Gharani,[5] who lived in Yemen at the time, and who had never met the prophet in person, had been receiving spiritual guidance and the essence and teachings of Islam from the prophet inwardly—from heart to heart. Before the prophet passed away, he had his cloak sent to Hazrat Oveys in Yemen and said, "Follow the way of Oveys … he is the preemptor of my genius." This cloak, symbolizing the highest level of inspired divine knowledge and the light of guidance, has been handed down through an unbroken succession of spiritual masters. All 42 Sufi Masters of the Oveyssi

School of Islamic Sufism have said that "spiritual learning and development is a matter of personal effort and discovery" (Angha, 2002, p. 167).

To the *salek*, truth and true reality are a mystery. The *salek* not only yearns to know, but actively works to discover this truth personally – to have direct experience in order to say with certainty that they know. Therefore, Sufism has been generally labeled the mystical dimension or mystical tradition of Islam (Schimmel, 1978). Christianity and Judaism similarly have mystical traditions within them.

It has become increasingly acknowledged that due to the limitations of our five senses, we cannot even begin to imagine what true reality is. For instance, our physical senses are unable to detect waves below or above a certain level, like certain sound frequencies or light waves. Furthermore, our senses are restricted to our physical body, which is just a temporal vessel. Our soul, on the other hand, is absolute: It is believed to have existed before the physical body came to be, and will continue to exist after our physical body no longer exists in its current form. What do we know about this soul—our true self? What is reality? Most cannot say with certainty. Therefore, according to contemporary Sufi literature, humanity's knowledge is incomplete (Angha, 1998). Sufism is a way that attempts to complete humanity's education so that one may cognize their true self and true existence—to transcend our physical limitations and social boundaries. It provides a path that can lead seekers to find within themselves the answers to ultimate questions about who they are, where they come from, why they are here, where they are going, and so on.

The answers to these questions exist within us, but they become buried and lost when we allow the physical world to consume us, and when we adopt social habits and behaviors to the point that our entire existence comes to be based on imitation and conformity. The aim of those on the Sufi path is to release all worldly habits and attachments that veil our true reality—"to cleanse the heart and transform the self" (Fadiman & Frager, 1997, p. 19). To transform the self means to move from our base state— the state of uncertainty and instability, in which we exist enough to satisfy our worldly needs and desires—to our divine state—the state in which we are free of the worldly attachments that distract us from our spiritual goals. Through this transformation, we experience balance and harmony, and have true knowledge of ourselves and of existence. This transformation is described by Angha (2002) as moving from the "i" to the "I":

> The "I" is the stable center [of the self] that brings all aspects of life into balance. When the I is discovered, cultivated and developed, it permeates the entire human being, and influences all aspects of one's life, be it the physical, mental, emotional, or spiritual.... [This concept] encompasses the whole universe, the unlimited wisdom of human existence, and all dimensions of life. (p. 109)

Sufi practices aim to liberate one from the limitations of the senses and society to "cognize the reality underlying all of existence and to learn how to use wisely the riches already bestowed on you by existence" (Angha, 1998, p. 47). What follows from this release is the discovery of our own identity, our origin, our essence and, ultimately, experience of the divine (Larsen, 2000).

It should be noted here that Islam does not place the spiritual in opposition to the material, just as it does not place true, inner knowledge in opposition to traditional, academic learning. Rather Islam "underscores the spiritual as the context of the material" (Said, Funk, & Kadayifci, 2001, p. 258). In other words, asceticism or self-chosen hardship is not involved in the process of reaching this state of cognition. We should all have the ability to live in this physical world and understand its workings, to experience joy and comfort, and work to have our basic needs met, while still pursuing the highest spiritual goals.

The Basic Beliefs of Sufism

Bayazid Bastami, the ninth century Sufi, described the history of Sufism by stating:

> Its seeds were set at the time of Adam, then sprouted under Noah and flowered under Abraham. Grapes formed at the time of Moses, and ripened at the time of Jesus. In the time of Mohammad, the grapes were made into pure wine. (Angha, 1996, p. 27)

The values of wisdom, peace, love, balance, oneness, self-discipline, nonviolence, self-discovery, and union with the absolute come from the heart of the human being, and so we see echoes of them in many spiritual traditions. "Just as a river that passes through many countries ... is claimed by each as its own is still only one river" (Fadiman & Frager, 1997, p. 2). The Muslim profession of faith is, "There is no god other than the one God." Sufis believe that although the messengers of the major faiths and traditions have been different people at different times, the source of their knowledge is one. Sufis seek to experience and know this "One." The basic beliefs and themes found in Sufism and Sufi literature that will be discussed in this section are: self-knowledge; unity and oneness; and perfection and harmony.

Sufism is primarily based on the goal of self-knowledge, which is believed to be synonymous with knowledge of the absolute, the divine, the universe, existence and God. This true identity which students of Sufism seek to discover existed long before the body or personality came into existence (Behbehani, 1991, p. 168). In other words, gender, race, ethnicity, religion, political affiliation, and sexual preference—labels which divide, consume and distract the human race—are irrelevant in this search because they are socially constructed and of this physical world. Moreover, our physical world, body, and emotions are constantly changing. But true knowledge or our true identity is that which is constant and unchangeable, according to Sufism. Sufis believe that it is in knowing yourself that you will be freed of your limitations and the false boundaries you have created between yourself, others, and existence (Angha, 1996). These boundaries prevent us from realizing peace.

Sufism is also based on the doctrine of unity and oneness. "There is only one law in the universe, and that is the law of Oneness. Knowledge, balance, and harmony are inherent in this law; that is why we see harmony and peace in the universe" (Angha, 1996, p. 24). The theme of oneness—with each other, with all life, with the entire universe—is repeatedly found in many disciplines, including religion, philosophy, and the sciences. In the language of those traditions we are told that we are all one, and that our separation from each other and from the totality of life is only one of appearance, and is an illusion (O'Riordan, 1999, p. 68). For instance, Taoism, Buddhism, and Hinduism recognize the universe as one whole, interrelated system. Qi (Taoism and Buddhism) and Prana (Hinduism) are the respective names of the life force and the energy which flows through all things and establishes their interconnectedness. In mathematics, all concepts are interconnected and interdependent, chemistry shows that everything in the material world is built from the same blocks, and quantum mechanics demonstrates that all particles in the universe are interconnected by a web of universal energy (Bohm, 1980). Unity and oneness is the essence of Islamic Sufism and is the foundation of education for peace.

Human beings, according to Sufism, are a complex masterpiece of creation—whatever exists in the universe also exists within each of us. As Imam Ali, the first Imam of the Shia, has said, "You presume you are a small entity, but within you is enfolded the entire universe" (Hadith Nahj al-Balagha). In other words, the perfection and order that exists in the universe, that keeps it in harmony, is the same perfection that each human is born with. Perfection and harmony, therefore, are other themes present in Sufi writings. Sufis believe that existence has bestowed every human with everything they need to reach an elevated spiritual state. It is in this state that inner peace is achieved.

The pursuit of self-knowledge, unity and oneness, and perfection and harmony is the essence of religion, which is why Sufism can be described as the "reality of religion." Moreover, Sufism's basic beliefs and goals are innately appealing to humanity's spiritual dimension: they are espoused, knowingly or unknowingly, by many sincere seekers of truth, knowledge, and peace who are not consciously students of Sufism.

The Sufi Conception of Peace

Since the end of World War II, the world has witnessed a swell of peace education programs, peace organizations and peace treaties (Harris, Fisk, & Rank, 1998). Yet we still do not have peace. What is peace? Have we experienced peace? Dreaming about peace, talking about peace and learning about peace is not the same as peace and will not lead to peace alone. Neither is peace merely an absence of violence and oppression. Then what is peace? How can we spread peace when we do not know what it is that we are spreading? How can we define peace when we are not sure if we have experienced it for ourselves (Angha, 1987)?

The root of these questions lies in knowledge and truth. In Sufism, the quest for knowledge and truth begins with the self: True knowledge exists within us. But we have to seek it. Put in the context of peace, Sufism teaches that through internal purification and realization of our true being, the "I", we can begin to experience inner tranquility and peace. Then we can say with certainty what peace is.

When we live in moderation and balance, free from material wants, desires, and attachments, free from ego, negative thoughts, emotions, and actions—all attributes of the base, or lower self—this is called "purity" in Sufism. To cleanse the heart means to achieve this state of internal purity. When we lead lives that lack purity, according to this definition, we prevent ourselves from experiencing peace and tranquility within.

The process of realizing the "I" can begin when we put effort into letting go of our attachment to our socially constructed self and strive to transcend our physical limitations to experience the interconnectedness of all life and existence. Becoming aware of our unity with each other and the interconnectedness of all of nature and the universe is transformative. In essence, Sufism is saying that the key to peace, stability and tranquility lies within the spiritual dimension of the human, and that "true peace is cognized through the inner freedom and spiritual elevation of each individual" (Angha, as cited in Wilcox, 1997, p. 75).

The attainment of inner peace, therefore, is required if we want to achieve outer peace—or world peace. This means the pursuit of peace ultimately is not a political or diplomatic endeavor, but an endeavor that should be directed by every human on earth, as we are naturally equipped with everything we need within us to achieve our inner peace and harmony. Sufis believe that when these empowering principles are embraced and acted upon by all, then sustainable world peace is achievable.

Most human activity is geared toward survival. But even when their basic needs are met, many people are not satisfied. Those who have more seem to want more. The ones who do not have enough are pushed further into mere survival mode. Both conditions are equally distracting in the quest for inner peace. Sufism teaches that earthly attachments and appetites prevent humans from recognizing their divinity and experiencing the more elevated states of their existence by distracting the individual from their spiritual path, thereby veiling their true identity and existence from them. Possessions and material pursuits do not fulfill them, because these things are not part of their true nature. The more people engage in worldly pursuits, the more disquieted they become, and the further they get from realizing "the light of knowledge" that is within them and their "inherent and infinite ocean of capacities and capabilities" (Angha, 1996, p. 27). As a result, without knowing it, they spend their days in darkness and ignorance, which Sufism teaches is the source of discontent, aggression, greed and oppression. Meanwhile, each individual dreams of living in a peaceful world.

The Sufi sage, Sheikh Abu Solaiman Davoud al-Ta'i taught that, "If you desire well being, renounce worldly attachments" (Wilcox, 1997, p. 8). When humans are able to truly realize there is more to existence than what their senses capture and that our material possessions and accomplishments are miniscule in the quest for truth and knowledge, they are better able to let go of their attachments. When humans realize through their spiritual quest that all life is equal and interconnected, they should begin to act accordingly. They should begin to detest privilege and monopoly and reasonably reject what cannot be shared by all, thereby paving the way to equity and peace (Gandhi, as cited in Kripalani, 2001).

From a Sufi perspective, we find dissatisfaction, dysfunction and conflict when there is no regard for the interconnectedness and oneness of life, no recognition of the perfection and divinity within each of us, and no use of our unlimited potential and boundless capacity. "People become misguided and wicked not because of their innermost nature" or disposition, but because their true identity has become veiled by their insatiable pursuit of material things and attachment to their socially constructed self (Said, Funk, & Kadayifci, 2001, p. 257). By putting effort towards cognizing the true self instead, Sufism teaches, we may begin to control ourselves from going astray in this sense.

"Wherever there is a ruin, there is hope for a treasure" (Rumi, as cited in Wilcox, 1997, p. 33). Man is the cause and motive for all demonstrations of war and peace. It is therefore necessary to endeavor to know man in order to truly understand the causes of his activities and behavior. "No one can know you the way you know yourself" (S. Angha, as cited in Wilcox, 1997, p. 67). How can I know you, or discover anything about human nature, if I do not know myself? Sufism teaches that first, we must work to know ourselves, discover our unity and interconnectedness with humanity and all life, and then we may begin to understand the universal nature of human beings. Once we understand the universal nature of human beings, then perhaps we can create laws and systems that are in harmony with this true nature. When we create and maintain laws and systems that impose structures disharmonious with the essential qualities of human beings, we see inequalities, disease, disorder, human rights violations, conflicts, discontent, and war. In other words, the perilous position humanity finds itself in is the result of a social order which is not in harmony with the true nature of human beings.

For instance, when we examine an ecosystem, every entity in that ecosystem serves an important purpose, which complements the function of all the other entities in the ecosystem, big and small. Each being contains true and stable knowledge which allows it to serve its special and important purpose—a purpose that is integral to the integrity of the ecosystem. If that being ceases to perform its innate function (by choice or by outside force), the balance of the ecosystem is thrown off and disorder ensues. Climate change and the extinction of some species while others proliferate are manifestations of overconsumption and exploitation—results of human interference in the natural existence of plant and animal life.

All people on earth have important and special talents and abilities that—if discovered, cultivated, and developed—bring order and harmony to our lives. Even every organ in the human body has absolute knowledge of its unique and vital purpose. When it fulfills this purpose in harmony with our other organs and bodily systems, we are physically healthy and balanced. When we deny the knowledge that is within us, when we do not perform what we are best at doing, then something begins to lack in our lives. When we are not following our natural path and doing what is natural to our being and to the universal nature of human beings, this incongruence of purpose and practice becomes manifest through discontent, disorder and imbalances. Similarly, if one of our organs, or even a single cell, does not perform its vital function to its fullest potential, our system becomes imbalanced and we can experience various kinds of disorders, illnesses, and death.

We can learn a lot from observing nature. When we look through a telescope into space, we see common patterns throughout the universe. Everything looks similar—the shapes of galaxies, the rotations of planets around stars, and more. If we observe plants, animals, humans, storms, and suns, we see that everything goes through the same process of being born, living, and dying. All of this activity happens in an infinitely intelligent, orderly, and harmonious way. Sufism asks: "What law prevails in the nearly infinite universe which governs all entities and their precise interrelationships, and prevents any disorder in their development and evolutionary motions as presented in the manifestations of nature?" (Angha, 1987, p. 28) What is the law that keeps the universe in perfect, complementary existence? Sufis believe this knowledge will be invaluable in our pursuit of a deeper understanding of peace, and that it can potentially lead to the fulfillment of peace for all individuals and societies, and to the rescue of our planet.

Sufis believe that love is the law of the universe. Love is unity and harmony. Love is the universe's deepest instinct—it is what connects all of existence. Atoms are pulled together because of love. Love is what "maintains the survival and balance of life" (Lin, 2006, p. 15). Without love, everything would cease to exist. Many faiths proclaim, "God is love" and in Sufism, the self is equated with the divine. Hence, Sufis believe that we are all by nature loving and kind beings—even those we label as misguided and wicked have the potential for goodness within them. When applying the beliefs of Sufism to education for global peace, therefore, the concepts of love and unity must remain central because "love is vital for spiritual growth" (Lin, 2006, p. 17).

EDUCATION FOR PEACE

Sufism presents the attainment of world peace as a process of transforming and knowing the self and fully realizing our unity with existence. At this point, though, one may ask, "How does Sufism and its conceptions of peace relate to education?" The following discussion attempts to provide an explanation of how Sufi principles could be applied to education for peace.

Students in American public schools spend much of their time preparing for standardized tests. When they are not preparing for standards-driven testing, they are preparing for college admissions tests. Once in college—just as in elementary, middle and high schools—students for the most part continue to memorize and repeat the findings of great people. Galileo Galilei is reputed to have said, "You cannot teach people anything, you can only help them to discover it within themselves" (as cited in Kerr, 1999, p. 24). It should be effectively communicated in schools that the findings and discoveries of other people are merely an introduction or stepping stone to students' own research and inquiry and that they should be urged to discover for themselves. If educators fail to emphasize this, then students will continue to carry in their minds the work of others, rather than drawing on all their innate gifts, talents, knowledge, and abilities. Students will continue to look for knowledge and answers from without, rather than from within. If educators neglect to instill in students the notion that they are perfect beings with more talent than they realize, students will consequently remain unaware of all their capabilities and potentialities. "Carrying other people's ideologies and revelations will cause a hindrance and impede them on their journey of self-cognition" (Angha, 1996, p. 19).

Educational systems and society encourage and reward students for competing against one another. Students compete on exams, during in-class discussions, and through class participation. There is competition in physical education and even in art and music classes. With more countries striving to compete in the global marketplace, many have adopted this competition-based model of education. Meanwhile, consumerism aimed at young people means that the social dimension of school is largely defined by possessions and outward appearances. The pursuit towards these material possessions, and the importance placed on them, causes selfishness, self-importance, discontentment, unfulfillment, jealousy, hatred, and conflict. Where are students' unique identity and personality in all this? Where are all their inherent talents, abilities, and goodness? They are accepting nonsense as the standard for their life, and this only gets worse as they enter adulthood.

The economic, materialistic, and competitive aims of most educational systems, policies and programs focus on just part of what education should provide its students and society. The goal of education must change from emphasizing only intellectual development to the integrated development of mind, body and soul, for it is the fully developed human being who is the best safeguard for any society (Moffett, 1994). Sufism's conception of building peace through encouraging and cultivating self-discovery in schools supports this notion wholeheartedly.

"Education is first and foremost the engine for creating new beings" (Lin, 2006, p. 9). Schools must provide an environment that fosters the fulfillment of students' highest potential—spiritual, emotional, physical and intellectual—and helps students see themselves as compassionate members of the same family and as part of nature, the world community and the universe. Each person must be permitted to naturally develop. They must be encouraged to know and be taught the importance of their true personality, identity, and creativity. Success should be redefined to embody the nonmaterial, and students should be guided to formulate goals that move beyond the surface. Schools should provide an environment where the talents and abilities of students are allowed to surface and to develop, so children can actually "realize their true self-worth and stand on their own strength" (Angha, 1996, pp. 19-20).

Through creativity, service, contemplative/meditative activities, cultivation of character, and constant remembrance of unity and divinity, spiritual guidance becomes increasingly accessible to the individual. The individual begins to realize and fulfill their innate abilities, which contributes to the work of peace because that individual is doing what is natural to their true being. As mentioned before, love is our natural propensity. It is love that will drive students to "follow the law of nonviolence deliberately and cease-lessly" (Gandhi, as cited in Kripalani, 2001, p. 78).

If children are taught and nurtured from this perspective—if they begin to recognize their true potential and realize their boundless capac-ity—then they can be of greatest benefit to themselves and to others, and they will not be sucked into the many destructive habits that plague the lives of adults and societies around the world (Angha, 1996, p. 44). In sum, educating students with these goals in mind and espousing these universal ethics of love, unity, and nonattachment in schools will be invaluable in our quest to understand and realize peace. Education for peace in the context of Sufism is the conviction that world peace cannot be achieved unless all individuals benefit from a state of spiritual well-being. However, it is up to the individual to decide how far they are will-ing to travel on the journey to self knowledge and inner peace.

HOW ARE THE GOALS OF SUFISM ACCOMPLISHED?

It should be noted that a basic Sufi principle is to "live in this physical world and still pursue the highest spiritual and mystical goals" (Fadiman & Frager, 1997, p. 17). Sufism does not advocate for separatism or isola-tionism. One must be able to live amidst abundance and luxury or war and famine and still stay on the path to cognizing their true self and true reality. Most would agree that staying on this path is a struggle. This inner struggle is what is meant in Islam by the word *jihad*. Therefore, not only does inner peace transcend politics, but class and economics are irrele-vant to it as well. With this in mind, how are the lofty goals of Sufism accomplished in one's personal quest (beyond the classroom) for knowl-edge and peace? According to Sufi teachings, the way to self-knowledge simply begins with an innate urge on the part of the seeker who genuinely wants to know the reason for their being (Angha, 1996).

"Definitions made by the senses do not speak of life's true essence" (Angha, as cited in Wilcox, 1997, p. 84). The two most prominent teach-ings in Sufism are that words cannot convey the meaning of experience and that true knowledge comes from direct experience. True knowledge, therefore, is derived from the seeker's own experience. Since spiritual answers cannot come from reason alone, the seeker must go through transformation to attain a state of true wisdom and knowledge.

In Sufism, transformation is guided by a spiritual teacher or guide, who has been inwardly revealed to the seeker. This spiritual teacher is called a Sufi master, or a *Pir*. The role of a *Pir* is essential in Sufism. A quote from the well-known Sufi poet, Rumi, illustrates this concept quite nicely, "Whoever travels without a guide needs two hundred years for a two day journey" (Wilcox, 1997, p. 36). Sheikh Safieddin Ardebili elaborates further: "The one who goes on this journey alone will drown in the mirage of the self" (Wilcox, 1997, p. 38). For instance, all humans are born with the potential ability to write. However, in order to write legibly and coherently, we need a teacher to gently support our hand and show us how to draw the characters, and so on. Without a teacher, our efforts would produce merely unguided scribbles. Each one of us contains this precious mine of knowledge and ability; we just need to excavate it. The purpose of the spiritual teacher in Sufism is to light our path—to guide our practices and teach us how to clear the dust which veils our reality so that we can discover truth.

Practical Sufism provides a set of instructions for the serious student, or *salek*, who wishes for freedom, stability, and knowledge in order to discover the reality of their being and attain inner peace and tranquility. Sufi practices include *tamarkoz* (Sufi meditation and concentration), *zikr* (remembrance of God) and prayer, in addition to the pillars of Islam, like fasting and giving alms. These different practices engage our mind, body and soul, and require self-discipline in order to purify our heart and bring into harmony the various levels of our being. Sufis believe that in order to have peace in the world, each person must realize peace within themselves. Through living a life of balance and moderation, and wholeheartedly performing Sufi practices under the guidance of the *Pir*, the practitioner may be able attain a state of true wisdom and knowledge, and be transformed from their base state to their spiritually elevated state.

CONCLUSION

Humanity is facing myriad problems: wars and conflicts, environmental destruction, social inequalities and injustices, and more. Those who are in positions of power and are responsible for the perpetuation of many of these injustices have been educated by a system that continues to lack a holistic perspective. This system is becoming increasingly impersonal and counterproductive as we continue to institute reforms which encourage standardization, testing and benchmarks. We are in desperate need of a paradigm change (Lin, 2006).

We need a new or revised, all-encompassing philosophy and practice of education which enables us to educate students holistically and turn education into a great endeavor for promoting peace, cross-cultural international understanding, and humility while cultivating love and compassion for all life. Making it a priority for students to experience and discover meaning, purpose, connection, creativity and joy are central to "constructively filling the spiritual void" in schools and for cultivating the next generation of peacebuilders (Kessler, 2000, p. xvii). I believe that by embracing the kinds of universal principles and aims that Sufism advocates, we can help fill this void.

Society as a whole needs to begin to teach children to love other humans as they would love their brothers and sisters, for we are all interconnected. We should teach students that because we are all born with a special purpose, everyone is unique and divine. We should also teach that everyone is perfect and has more ability than they know of. We should teach students that although we may have different terms or labels for things, most of humanity believes in the same essential truths and values—the same essential virtues—because the source of all these teachings is one. It should be noted that "a soulful education [can embrace] diverse ways to satisfy the spiritual hunger of today's youth" while still remaining disconnected from religious dogma (Kessler, 2000, p. xiv). Put differently, the separation between church and state does not have to mean divorcing students from the type of loving and contemplative education that might aid in their holistic development and build peace.

"Inner and outer worlds are not mutually exclusive, rather they mirror and reinforce one another. Therefore, [just as] inner violence correlates with outer violence; inner peace correlates with outer peace" (Brantmeier, 2007, p. 121). Imagine, would anyone having gone through the personal transformation written about in this chapter steal, rape, murder, hoard or abuse (Angha, 1996)? There is nobody in the world who would not wish to live in a peaceful, compassionate, and loving society. However, in order to fully transform society in a sustainable way, each person needs to transform individually. The pursuit of world peace is not an endeavor reserved for grown-ups, peace activists or diplomats. "It is man who is the architect of his own environment" (Angha, 1987, p. v). This philosophy is empowering and, at the same time, speaks to the urgency in which we should begin this process if we would like to experience peace in our lifetime. That is why a paradigm change is needed in education, since education is where we can begin to transform students (Lin, 2006). Constructing a loving, harmonious, and peaceful world needs to be our educational priority, as opposed to some of the more economic and political goals that drive and have driven education policy and practice. Therefore, we need to bring the soul back into education in order to help students develop in a holistic manner, because lives founded upon true knowledge and values result in stability and peace, and create a foundation on which to build a harmonious society (Angha, 1996).

NOTES

1. Other Sufi orders include the Naqshbandi, Qadiri, and Nimatullahi Orders. The teachings of these orders center more on Sufi philosophy, whereas the teachings of the Oveyssi School of Islamic Sufism center more on practical Sufism
2. Hazrat Salaheddin Nader Shah Angha is the 42nd Sufi Master of the Maktab Tarighat Oveyssi Shahmaghsoudi School of Islamic Sufism in an unbroken lineage of Sufi Masters dating back 1,400 years, to the time of the prophet Mohammad.
3. Maktab Tarighat Oveyssi translates literally to "School of the way of Oveys."
4. The Muslim profession of faith, that there is no god but God, means that there is no reality but God "and that all the so-called realities of our experiences are secondary and derivative" (Chittick, 2000, p. 12). Sufis witness God in everything—everything is a manifestation and reflection of the Divine. This is why Islam proclaims the oneness of existence.
5. The conventional Arabic transliteration is Uways al-Qarani

REFERENCES

Ali, Abdullah Yusuf. (2002). *The Qur'an: Text, translation and commentary.* New York: Tahrike Tarsile Qur'an.

Angha, N. (1987). *Peace.* Verdugo City, CA: M.T.O. Shahmaghsoudi.

Angha, N. (1996). *Sufism lecture series.* Washington, DC: M.T.O. Shahmaghsoudi.

Angha, N. (1998). *Sufism: The reality of religion.* Riverside, CA: M.T.O. Shahmaghsoudi.

Angha, N. (2002). *Theory "I".* Riverside, CA: M.T.O. Shahmaghsoudi.

Behbehani, S. S. (1991). *The messenger within: Discovering love and wholeness through meditation.* San Francisco: Mellen Research University Press.

Bohm, D. (1980). *Wholeness and the implicate order.* London: Routledge.

Brantmeier, E. J. (2007). Connecting inner and outer peace: Buddhist meditation-integrated with peace education. *Infactis Pax. (1)*2, 120-157.

Chittick, W. C. (2000). *Sufism: A short introduction.* Boston: Oneworld.

Fadiman, J., & Frager, R. (Eds.). (1997). *Essential Sufism.* San Francisco: Harper.

Harris, M. H., Fisk, L. J., & Rank, C. (1998). A portrait of university peace studies in North America and Western Europe at the end of the millennium. *International Journal of Peace Studies (3)*1, 91-112.

History of the M.T.O. Shahmaghsoudi School of Islamic Sufism. (2009). Retrieved September 1, 2009, from http://mto.org.website/en/history/htm

Kerr, R. (1999). *Self-discipline: Using portfolios to help students develop self-awareness.* Markham, Ontario Canada: Pembroke.

Kessler, R. (2000). *The soul of education: Helping students find connection, compassion,and character at school.* Alexandria, VA: Association for Supervision and-Curriculum Development.

Kripalani, K. (2001). *Gandhi: All men are brothers*. New York: Continuum.

Larsen, B. (2000). *The perfect moment: Therapeutic lessons from a Sufi master.* Riverside, CA: M.T.O. Shahmaghsoudi.

Lin, J. (2006). *Love, peace, and wisdom in education: a vision for education in the 21st century.* Lanham, MD: Rowman & Littlefield Education.

Moffett, J. (1994). *The universal schoolhouse: Spiritual awakening through education.* San Francisco: Jossey-Bass.

O'Riordan, L. (1999). *The art of Sufi healing*. Riverside, CA: M.T.O Shahmaghsoudi.

Peterson, T. (1999). Examining the loss of soul in education. *Education and Culture, (XV)*1/2, 9-15.

Said, A. A., Funk, A. C., & Kadayifci, A. S. (Eds.). (2001). *Peace and conflict resolution in Islam: Precept and practice.* New York: University Press of America.

Schimmel, A. (1978). *The mystical dimension of Islam*. Chapel Hill, NC: University of North Carolina Press.

Sufism—Introduction and Origin. (2009). Retrieved on September 1, 2009, from http://articles.sufism.info/en/sufism.htm

Wilcox, L. (Ed.). (1997). *Sayings of the Sufi sages.* Washington, DC: M.T.O. Shahmaghsoudi.

CHAPTER 3

A JEWISH PERSPECTIVE ON PEACE EDUCATION

Reuben Jacobson and Moishe Steigmann

INTRODUCTION

A person studying Hebrew almost always learns the word *shalom* first. A homonym, *shalom* is both a salutation, meaning "hello," and a valediction, meaning "goodbye." It is also used in the most frequent rendition of "How are you doing": *mah shlomkha?*[1] This same word, *shalom*, also means "peace." Indeed, even back in biblical times, the customary salutation was "*shalom aleikha*," or "May peace be upon you." In other words, every time that a Hebrew-speaker greets another or says goodbye, he or she is wishing the other person peaceful times. The Orthodox Jew walking to synagogue in Brooklyn and the secular Israeli leaving a night club in Tel Aviv both cry out, "*Shalom!*" to their friend on the other side of the street. In short, peace is an omnipresent concept in the Hebrew language.

Similarly, peace is an omnipresent concept in Jewish ideology and daily living. Etymologically, the root of *shalom* is "making whole." Judaism presents concepts of peace, of "wholeness," for the individual, among people, in the home, in the environment, and in the cosmic realm. For

Spirituality, Religion, and Peace Education, pp. 37–61
Copyright © 2010 by Information Age Publishing
All rights of reproduction in any form reserved.

example, *shalom bayit*, literally "peace in the house," is the concept that personal and religious compromises between husband and wife should be made in order to maintain marital harmony. The concept of peace in this example primarily extends to the relationships between people.

Another concept of *shalom* deals with the cosmic realm, the natural state of completeness that is inherent in God's world. On the physical and spiritual levels, all elements of a substance are at tension, and it is the principle of peace that balances the components and relaxes the tension (Ravitzky, 1987). Thus, in Judaism, it is peace that balances the forces of the world and brings completeness to the work of God's creation. In summary, *shalom*—peace—is more than a simple word of greeting or departure; "peace" is a societal aspiration. By creating a peaceful home and by creating a peaceful society, Jews are helping to make the world complete and whole.

Given these lofty notions and ideals of peace, it is surprising to note that peace receives little explicit attention in primary Jewish source material such as the Torah. Should the scarcity of the word "peace" lead us to believe that peace is not important to Judaism? Should we believe that God's many instructions to Noah about how to build an Ark or to Aaron about how to prepare a sacrifice are more important than the principle of peace? The answer is a resounding "no." The fundamental point of the Torah and its teachings is that, by acting like a holy people created in God's image, we are creating a "whole" and peaceful society. Jews learn that all the rules, stories, and laws in the Torah are written to facilitate peace. As the Talmud (the Oral Law, handed down by rabbinic sages) teaches, "All that is written in the Torah was written for the sake of peace" (Gittin 59b).

Thus, the paradox of the primacy of peace in Jewish life and its scarcity in primary Jewish sources is understood; *peace is a foundational principle which guides Jews in daily living, prayer, and conduct between person and person, between nations, and between human and God*. It is the precondition of the Torah; it is the basis of all Jewish life, laws, and teachings. That freedom is mentioned only in the opening line of the Constitution of the United States does not negate its centrality and pervasiveness throughout the entire document. Similarly, the relatively scant explicit references to peace in the Torah do not undermine its role as a foundational principle of Judaism. While it is clear that an entire book could be written about the many meanings of "*shalom*," we will focus on its meaning as it relates to peace and education.

In Judaism, education has served a number of purposes. First, Jewish education is predominantly a religious and moral enterprise (Graves, 1909). Historically, Jews were taught subjects related to living a Jewish life. Second, Jewish education has been used to *create solidarity* and therefore has *nationalistic* functions. According to Drazin (1940), education took on a "nationalistic ideal" when Jews returned to rebuild the Second

Temple (approximately 537 B.C.E.). Drazin writes that Jews returning from the Diaspora believed that the survival of the people rested upon a spiritual foundation rather than one of borders and governance alone. Thus, education was used to unite Jews wherever they lived and under any government. Third, Jewish education changes over time due to the flexibility of interpretation.[2] The first idea has been an essential component of Jewish education throughout history. The second idea has developed over time out of necessity due to outside influences. The final idea has sustained Jewish education and the Jewish people for thousands of years and will be explored in greater depth below.

So, what does Jewish education tell us about how peace has been taught *l'dor vador*, from generation to generation? In this chapter, we begin with a brief history and philosophy of Jewish education to contextualize the importance of the source material for the teaching of peace. Next, we present the source material upon which peace education is based. We then describe how peace is taught in contemporary Jewish settings.

UNDERSTANDING THE TEACHINGS OF JEWISH TEXT

As we described in the introduction, peace is a foundational principle of Judaism. Despite its primacy, peace is sparsely addressed in Jewish source text. Why does this matter for teaching peace in Jewish contexts? Historically, Jewish education tends to rely on the pedagogy of reading source material (text) and interpreting it. If there is little text on a subject, that suggests it may hold less relevance to Judaism. However, we argued in the introduction that peace is fundamental to Judaism and encompasses all of the text, though not always explicitly discussed. In this section, we present a brief history of Jewish pedagogy to establish how Jewish concepts, including peace, have traditionally been taught throughout the generations. Next, we present references to peace in Jewish text. We conclude with a discussion of how peace has been interpreted from the source material, interpretations which have provided additional information about Jewish perspectives on peace and that help explain how peace is taught in Jewish settings.

Traditional Jewish Education: Source and Interpretation

Torah as Primary Source

The Torah is the source for ultimate truth, guidance on conduct, and instructions on faith. Therefore, the first step towards a Jewish philosophy of education is the recognition of the Torah[3] as the primary source for all

Jewish conduct and a secure base for Jewish education throughout our history. The Torah tells the story of God's creation of the world, describes the history of the Israelite people up to their arrival in Canaan, and presents God's commandments. This Divinely-given source is believed to contain everything within it. "Everything" means that not a single event, word, or space was created haphazardly and that all instructions and lessons for life can be found within it.

There are two Jewish teachings that clarify this concept of the centrality of the Torah. The first comes from Pirkei Avot (one section of the Oral Tradition handed down with the Torah) and instructs one to turn the Torah over and over, to read and re-read it, because everything is contained in it. Only constant and persistent examination over a lifetime could begin to reveal all its truths. The second, a *midrash* (an interpretation of the primary source text to help clarify and understand it), compares the Torah to a hammer splitting a rock. Just as the rock will break into many splinters, so, too, will the Torah reveal many meanings from one source (Rosenak, 1995).

These teachings demonstrate that the *Torah is the central component to Jewish education*. The Torah plays a significant part in religious activity demonstrated by community readings every Sabbath, every holiday, and throughout the week. The Torah itself presents the principles upon which Jewish practice is based; it tells Jews how to conduct themselves in their daily living. Rosenak (1995) describes the Torah as "both the ideal subject matter of education, and its blueprint" (p. 49). Drazin (1940) writes that the centrality of the Torah to Jewish life makes it "a synonym for Jewish education" (p. 11). Thus, the first component of a philosophy of Jewish education is: *The Torah is the primary educational source for religious and moral conduct that all Jews must learn.*

Study and Interpretation

The metaphor of the splitting rock elucidates that the primary source, the Torah, requires study. Therefore, the second step to building an enduring philosophy of Jewish education is the importance of study, or interpretation, of the source. Pirkei Avot begins with a description of how the Torah started as a Divinely-given source and then was passed down through the generations. It states that the Torah was passed on from Moses to Joshua, from Joshua to the Elders, from the Elders to the Prophets, and from the Prophets to the Great Assembly. The Great Assembly was a governing body that created laws for the Jewish nation based on its interpretation of the Torah. The Great Assembly stated three principles relevant to this analysis: "Be deliberate in judgment, educate many disciples, and set protective bounds for the Torah" (Pirkei Avot 1:1). "Protective bounds" indicates a reliance on the source for conduct with the allowance to interpret it to a degree.

How should we understand the limits of interpretation? It is generally accepted that any legitimate interpretation and application of the Torah has the same legal weight and validity as a direct teaching. How have Jews historically defined what is a "legitimate" interpretation? A story in the Talmud (Sanhedrin 33a) helps us understand this question through a dramatic dialogue between two rabbis. Rabina asked his colleague, Rav Ashi, whether or not the great legal interpretations of previous generations were of equal weight to those of the Mishnah (part of the Oral Tradition) itself. Rav Ashi's response was in the affirmative. Ultimately, Rabina queried if even *their* legal interpretations were considered as valid as those of their predecessors and of the Mishnah itself, to which Rav Ashi replied, "What are we, reed-cutters in a swamp?" Colloquially, Rav Ashi's rhetorical response was, "What are we, chopped liver?" In other words, study of Jewish sources is paramount. Those who turn over Jewish sources and learn them throughout a lifetime are empowered to interpret the sources and apply their teachings. Moreover, these interpretations and applications are considered as authentic as the original source itself! Thus, Jewish education traditionally relies on the study and interpretation of the Torah, the source.

However, Jews also learn by practicing Judaism. Rituals are taught *l'dor vador*, from generation to generation. The following saying, also from Pirkei Avot, illustrates this point: "The world is based on three principles: on the Torah; on serving God; and on acts of loving-kindness." This saying is accompanied by a tune often sung in Hebrew by students at Jewish day schools and camps. What does this childhood song help explain about how Jewish education has been taught? The saying highlights the Torah as the first principle. Tradition says that God delivered this book to Moses and it is the essential source for all Jewish education. The second principle, service to God, alludes to the motivation for Jewish practice. Jews are a God-fearing people who believe that there is only one God and that God is responsible for all things. As stated in Proverbs, 7:1, "the fear of the Lord is the beginning of wisdom." This fear motivates Jews to serve God. "Service" means many different things, but how one follows God's commandments is essential to its definition. The third principle, "acts of loving-kindness," refers to how Jews are to act with compassion, understanding, and charity towards fellow human beings. We have already described the importance of the first principle to a philosophy of Jewish education. The second and third principles demonstrate that the Torah is also the source for how Jews should teach daily practice and conduct—principles that guide our argument later in this chapter that leading a peaceful life means living a life of Jewish practice and conduct.

History of Jewish Education

Now that we have established that traditional Jewish pedagogy includes reading the source and constant study, interpretation, and practice, we present a brief history of Jewish education in order to illustrate how this pedagogy has developed over time.

Biblical Period

Sources on the historiography of pre-modern Jewish education are scarce (Chazan, 2005). Therefore, we will rely solely on one text for this period, *A History of Education Before the Middle Ages*, by Frank Graves (1909), who explains that, during Biblical times, the content of Jewish education was dominated by theological law. The only exceptions to religious education were music, poetry, mathematics, and astronomy. However, these subjects were only learned to enhance religious devotion and to keep track of religious festivals. There was no public means of education yet; education in this ancient community took place in the home.

After the destruction of the First Temple (586 B.C.E.), Jews were exposed to the traditions of the nations around them. During the Second Temple period (516 B.C.E.-70 C.E.), synagogues were built throughout the land. At first, synagogues were places of religious instruction rather than places of worship as is traditional today. Instruction continued to be mostly religious, legal, and moral, but also expanded to other subjects such as Greek, mathematics, and geography. Jews developed pedagogical methods and made education compulsory.

Rabbinic/Talmudic Periods (219-600 C.E.)

The Talmudic period can be described as one of extensive interpretation of the Torah in order to codify ethics and conduct. During this period, the Jews were spread out in exile throughout the known world. Rabbis in Palestine and in Babylonia compiled two Talmuds as records of the interpretations and applications of the Torah. The Talmudic scholars applied great attention to the structure of education. In the Talmud, they described the different periods of childhood, what should be taught at each age, the responsibility of the parent to educate children, the importance of education to being a useful person, and more (Cahn, 1962). The deep commitment to education during this time is exemplified by the Talmudic saying that a town without schools and school-children should be destroyed (Shabbat 119a). Most importantly for this chapter, the two Talmuds are considered extensions of the Torah and are hereafter included when we talk about "source" text or the Torah. For example, it is very common in traditional education for Jews to continue their study of the Torah by reading the Talmud.

Education was typically religious and was taught to continue the tradition and strengthen the nation. Interpretation begins to make a significant impact on the character of Jewish education. While the Torah remains the primary source of Jewish education, scholars wrote interpretations of the Torah in order to codify Jewish ethics and conduct. In future periods, the study of the Torah, the source, in addition to study of the Talmud, the record of its interpretation and application, would characterize typical Jewish education.

The Diaspora—Ashkenazi and Sephardic Philosophers (600- 1770[4])

In the Diaspora, Jews were spread amongst non-Jews around the world and were subjects of other nations. Education systems developed in different ways depending on where the Jews were located, who their rulers were and their financial and political circumstances.

The Jewish commitment to education endured through the Diaspora during the High Middle Ages. Ashkenazi Jews[5] hired tutors (*m'lam'dim*) to teach young children rather than send them to an elementary school. To be sure, Jewish education does not stop at a certain age. Consequently, parents were not to be interrupted by the educational needs of their children because it would interfere with their own study and prayer.

In addition, Jews believed that education should begin as early as possible. The youngest children were taught in order to begin developing their practices and morals. Those families who could not afford to pay a tutor could receive community charity to secure their services. Once the tutors had taught children how to read and the basic strategies for interpretation, the children would move to an academy to learn with a particular scholar.

During this time, education also continued to gain importance for Sephardic Judaism, where it became almost universal and supported by the community. This was also the time of the most significant Jewish education philosopher, Moses Maimonides (1135-1204), considered to be the definitive source of interpretation and codification of Jewish law for Sephardi Jews. He served as a source of authority and hope for Jews around the world, he was the leader of the Jewish community in Egypt, and he was even physician to the Caliph (Cahn, 1962). Maimonides taught that Jews should study Torah, for it is the ultimate good. He also taught that learning should be out of intrinsic motivation as opposed to extrinsic reward, such as an expected benefit after death in the World-to-Come. Maimonides thus outlined concepts of the ideal person, a conception of an educational theory to cultivate such a person, and what a good teacher should resemble (Rosenak, 1995). Maimonides placed the responsibility of education squarely on the individual but also prescribed a system of education in each town and placed great shame on those towns that ignored this prescription (Baron, 1942).

The development of Jewish interpretation slowed down from approximately 1650 until the Haskalah (Jewish Enlightenment, 1770-1880; see below). According to Zvi Cahn (1962):

> Creative Jewish thought almost came to a standstill … rabbis and teachers of the Talmud did not bring forth new or original ideas … they were busily engaged in hair-splitting debates on fine points of Jewish Laws in rabbinical academies … or else they buried themselves in the Cabala and mysticism to which the Jews had always turned at times of stress and oppression from without. The Jewish people were too busy trying to keep alive to be able to devote attention to such creative intellectual pursuits as the study of Hebrew literature, the writing of Hebrew poetry or the formulation of new thoughts. (p. 429)

This time period demonstrates that, while new interpretations were not taking the lead, Jewish education still served its purposes of solidarity and religious instruction. New interpretation and growth would have to wait for new philosophers.

The Haskalah (1770-1880)[6]

The Haskalah (the "Enlightenment") can be characterized as a time of increased secularism due to both internal and external forces. The world was modernizing at dramatic rates during this period. Interactions across borders and with other religions were rising. European Jews who had previously remained insular could hardly resist the forces of modernization. Maskilim, the leaders of the Haskalah movement, attempted to change the focus of education from the traditional study of Talmud to secular studies that would integrate Jews into secular society. They continued to teach Jewish studies, but it received reduced emphasis (Schoenberg, 2007). The Haskalah opened the door to wider interpretation of the Torah. This type of interpretation was much different from earlier times when interpretation was viewed as extensions of the source text and was considered to be divinely given. These interpretations led to the creation of a number of Jewish denominations such as the Orthodox, Conservative and Reform movements. No longer was Jewish education used to unite all Jews. Rather, interpretation was used to unite similar-thinking Jews.

Jewish Education in the Twentieth and Twenty-First Centuries

Currently, Jewish education takes on as many forms as there are interpretations on what Judaism is and how it should be taught. Forces of modernization have proven powerful, and most Jews have embraced the study of the secular with varying degrees of continued religious education.

While there has always been diversity in interpretation, the number of differences has certainly grown. Different sects of Judaism have arisen and can be defined partly by their level of secularism and strictness of interpretation.

This diversity has led to myriad styles of teaching Jewish education. A number of Jewish Day Schools, synagogue schools, camps, books, and websites have arisen to meet the needs of each group. One perspective is that this diversity has led to greater assimilation and could lead to the ultimate destruction of the Jewish people (e.g., through intermarriage). However, another perspective argues that this diversity makes Judaism relevant to all types of people and therefore brings more Jews into the fold of the religion in a way that is meaningful to their lives. The debate continues as each group slightly modifies Jewish education to meet its needs.

In this section, we have argued that a traditional philosophy of Jewish education includes constant examination and interpretation of the Torah, the source, in the historical context of the time. But what do the source texts that Jews have read over time say about peace? In the next section we will show what specific Jewish sources have to say about the value of peace.

SOURCES OF PEACE

Finding evidence of an explicit Jewish philosophy of peace in the sources is a challenge. However, given that peace is a foundational principle of Judaism, the few sources that do mention peace take on heightened meaning. In this section we discuss how peace is presented in the Torah, the Bible, the Talmud, and other commentaries on the Torah and how interpretations of these texts exemplify our argument that peace is consistent with all of Jewish living and teaching.

Peace in the Torah[7]

A Blessing for All Time

The most commonly recognized mention of peace in the Torah is found in a blessing. What is particularly noteworthy about this blessing, however, is not only the fact that peace is mentioned directly but rather that this blessing is the *only* blessing in the Torah that is still used in contemporary Jewish rituals and/or liturgy. Among God's many instructions to Moses, God told him to inform his brother Aaron, the *kohen gadol* (High Priest), to bless the Children of Israel with these words:

May the Lord bless you and keep you.
May the Lord make God's face shine upon you and be gracious to you.
May the Lord lift up God's face upon you and give you *shalom*—peace.
(Numbers 6:24-26)

We see in this ancient blessing that human beings, with God's approval, had the ability to convey blessings upon other people. The power of blessing another was thus not limited to God alone! In contemporary times, this blessing is still recited publicly by *kohanim*, the priestly descendants, at important holidays throughout the year and is recited by all during daily prayers. In addition, it is a pivotal ceremonial component of major celebratory life-cycle events. The Rabbi will typically bless a child at his *bar mitzvah* or her *bat mitzvah* and will typically bless a bride and a groom under the wedding canopy with this blessing. Parents also customarily offer this blessing every week on the holy Sabbath to their children. In other words, the blessing of peace may (or, perhaps, should) be offered not only from God to human beings but from person to person. Moreover, such a blessing is not limited to a particular time and place: this universal blessing is timeless. By emphasizing that peace is a blessing—an ideal—and not a law, the Torah itself provides further evidence that it is a foundational principle to Jewish living.[8]

Peace is not only a blessing to be bestowed upon the individual in the Torah but also upon a nation. Prior to establishing the Israelite nation in the land of Canaan, God promised peace to the people of Israel in return for their devotion. The following passage is one reward in a list of rewards preceded by the conditional:

If you observe my laws ... I will provide peace in the land, and you will lie down with none to frighten you; I will cause wild beasts to withdraw from the land, and a sword will not cross your land. (Leviticus 26:6)

Here, too, peace is presented in idyllic terms. If the Israelite people obey God's commandments, then they will, in turn, live in the land in peace. Thus, the ultimate aspiration is living peacefully. How can the Israelites achieve such an elusive goal? By following God's instructions, the words of the Torah. This promise of peace is therefore a reminder of its foundational role in the Torah; it is the ultimate objective.

Peace in the Context of War

It is important here, given the aforementioned passage from Leviticus, to address the fact the peace, in Judaism, is not synonymous with the absence of war. War may serve multiple functions. In ancient times war was often viewed not as an evil perpetrated by people but rather as a punishment from a god upset with human subjects. According to Ravitsky

(1987), war is a given in an imperfect world where humankind is flawed. War is perceived as a manifestation of God's intervention into our world and human beings' own wickedness. Given this perspective of war, it is not incongruous to suggest that a peaceful people (i.e., the Israelite people in the Torah) might nonetheless engage in war; the notion of Divine punishment was (and, for some today, still is) quite real.

Alternatively, that peace is the ultimate objective also need not require the absolute absence of war. Indeed, sometimes war is a tragic necessity in order for there to be peace. While many philosophers have argued that good cannot exist without evil and, similarly, that peace cannot exist without war, the full extent of that argumentation is beyond the reach of this chapter. Suffice it to say that the vision of a utopian society in which there is only good is not universally accepted. Indeed, many people recognize the necessity for war.

Nonetheless, it is imperative that, even during a time of a just war, that peace remains the goal. It is easy for one caught in the midst of war to lose sight of humanity. Thus, in the Torah, God instructed that even during wartime peace must be pursued. For example, the Torah teaches:

> When you draw near to a city to wage war against it, you shall call out to it for peace. (Deuteronomy 20:10)

God's instructions are clear: seek peace first. This passage illustrates the value of peace as the ultimate goal even in the face of war.

Stories of Peace

In addition to these explicit references to peace in the Torah, other stories of the Torah serve to illustrate that peace is a core value. For example, Grob (1987) cites Abraham's role as mediator on behalf of the wicked inhabitants of Sodom (Gen. 18:23) as an example of the primacy of peace as a core value. To be sure, Abraham, in his story, argued directly with God! Normally, disobedience of God would be cause for punishment. In this case, however, it seems clear that God approved of and even desired Abraham's challenges. From this we learn that peace is such an important value that we may even debate with God in order to try to achieve it. Grob also points out as an example of the centrality of peace God's injunction to Moses to desist from building an altar of hewn stones so that tools of iron—the metal used in forging arms—would not make their mark upon a sacred site of worship (Exod. 20:22). Thus, stories in the Torah serve as additional examples in which God emphasized the value of peace to Israelite leaders and the Israelite people in the Torah.

For the Sake of Peace

An interesting passage in the Torah suggests that peace is such a central value that one may even withhold the truth in order to pursue it. As noted in the Introduction, a core concept in Judaism is *shalom bayit*, peace in the house. When God first told Sarah (Genesis 18) that she would conceive a child, she laughed with incredulity, noting to God her old age and the old age of her husband, Abraham. God wondered aloud to Abraham why it was that Sarah laughed. Did Sarah not believe that God could enable an old woman to conceive? In God's dialogue with Abraham, commentators note that God did not mention Sarah's reference to Abraham's old age. It seems as though God is not telling Abraham the full truth. From this, commentators learn that, to spare one's feelings—to create *shalom bayit*, peace in the home—one may (or even should) avoid painful truths. In fact, the Talmud states this point explicitly: "One may deviate from the truth for the sake of peace ... it is permissible to utter a falsehood for the purpose of making peace between one person and another (Yevamot 65b)."[9] To be sure, as Ravitsky (1987) writes, the

> majority of passages on the subject of peace are concerned with family or communal life, that is, with internal peace among the people, and only a minority are concerned with external relations between Israel and other peoples, between nations and states. (p. 686)

PEACE IN THE BIBLE

We find that peace is discussed more frequently in the remainder of the Bible than in the Torah (though references still remain scant compared to other values, stories, and laws). In most cases, peace is referred to in idyllic terms. A few quotes will suffice to establish this point:

> I will abolish the bow, and the sword, and war from the land. (Hosea 2:18)

> Woe to whomever that builds a town with blood. (Habakkuk 2:12)

> And they shall beat their swords into plowshares, and their spears into pruning hooks; nation shall not lift up sword against nation, neither shall they learn war anymore. (Isaiah 2:4; and Micah 4:3)

> The wolf shall dwell with the lamb, and the leopard shall lie down with the kid, and the calf and the lion ... together. (Isaiah 11:4)

Unique among the citations of peace in the Bible is a particular injunction from Psalms 34:14: "seek peace and pursue it." The texts quoted above present peace as a messianic ideal. This injunction from Psalms, however, reminds us of our indelible role in the pursuit of that ideal: we have an obligation—both legal and moral—to seek peace. From this, we learn of our individual accountability to act peacefully (i.e., follow God's laws) and to do our part to create a just (i.e., peaceful) society.

While these passages do not represent an exhaustive list of references to peace in the Bible, they exemplify the primacy of peace in Judaism. Proverbs 3:17 explicates the centrality of peace: "Its [the Torah's] ways are ways of pleasantness, and all its paths are peace." Thus, as we argue in this chapter, the Torah itself may not provide numerous references to peace. Nevertheless, it is the Torah as a whole and the ideal of peace mentioned in the Bible (along with the injunction to pursue it) that place the value of peace at the center of Jewish life.

PEACE IN THE TALMUD AND OTHER COMMENTARIES ON THE TORAH

In the previous section we argued that, while there are few direct references to peace in the Torah and Bible, peace is a dominant principle of the entire Torah. Still, it is from the sources above and a broader normative value of peace in the Torah as a whole that the Rabbis established the dominant Jewish perspectives on peace during a historical time where the Jews were subjects of other nations in the Diaspora. Central to their interpretation is the aforementioned saying, "seek peace and pursue it." Of the many *mitzvot*, or commandments, there are two kinds: those that one does as the situation arises and those that one must go out and seek to accomplish. The interpreters argue that seeking peace belongs to the latter category. Thus, interpretation also establishes peace as a fundamental value of Judaism that should be pursued.

The Talmud and other commentaries on the Torah provide the following interpretations on peace, among others. They are sufficient to demonstrate the importance of peace and that people must be active in its pursuit:

> The only reason that the Holy One, blessed be God, created the world was so that there would be peace among humankind. (Bamidbar Rabbah 12A)

> Peace is what will save the Jewish people: God announces to Jerusalem that they [Israel] will be redeemed only through peace. (Deuteronomy Rabah 5:15)

> Hillel says: "Be among the disciples of Aaron, loving peace and pursuing peace." (Ethics of the Fathers 1:12)

Great is peace since all other blessings are included in it.... "Seek peace, and pursue it": seek it in your own place, and pursue it even to another place as well. (Vayikrah Rabbah 9)

Whoever establishes peace between one person and another, between husband and wife, between two cities, two nations, two families or two governments ... no harm should come to that person. (Mekhilta Bahodesh 12)

It is a mark of piety if a person accepts insults quietly and does not respond. (Shabbat 88b)

A true scholar is humble and ignores the slights of others. (Eruvin 54a)

Thus, the Talmud and other Torah commentaries note not only the primacy of peace in Judaism but also further compel the individual to actively engage in its pursuit.

TEACHING PEACE

In the above sections we argue that a Jewish philosophy of education rests on constant re-examination and interpretation of a source, the Torah; that peace is one of the greatest values in Jewish ethics; and that living a Jewish life is living a peaceful life. We discussed the source material on peace and how it has been interpreted and taught over the course of Jewish history. But, how do Jews teach about peace in contemporary times? First, we claim that Jews continue to teach peace through the formal exploration of the source and interpretation in various settings. Second, we describe how Jews teach peace congruently with the teaching of Judaism and its traditions. Finally, we extend our previous argument that peace is a part of the rituals and traditions of Jewish life and discuss how Jews teach peace by applying the values of peace and by living a Jewish life.

Traditional Education: Source and Interpretation

Jews continue to teach peace by interpreting source material, as is the custom with other notable topics in Judaism. *Yeshivot* (traditional Jewish academies) continue to devote all their time to the study of the sources and their interpretation, including the aforementioned texts about peace. The methodology and pedagogy in these educational settings, however, has changed little over the centuries: Jews are taught text, interpretation, and their application. Peace education occurs when specific texts are taught as part of the larger educational model of text study. Thus, in and of itself, peace education is not purposefully a focus of Jewish learning in *yeshivot*, though living a peaceful life (i.e., following Jewish law) remains paramount.

In contemporary times, new models of Jewish education have accompanied philosophical shifts in Jewish approaches to both pedagogy and ideology. As a result, there are many new educational settings and approaches to traditional Jewish learning. For example, peace is taught formally in full-time Jewish day schools, in synagogue-based religious schools, in Hillel Houses (centers of Jewish life on college campuses), and on websites. In addition, a growing set of educational models focus on informal Jewish education and experiential learning, where role-modeling a Jewish life and lifestyle (and, thus, a peaceful life and lifestyle) is the focus of Jewish learning in place of a more typical educational setting. Many of these contemporary educational settings include a unique approach to Jewish teaching: the application of peace education and Jewish values to everyday life. Thus, the goal of Jewish learning grows from studying text and interpretation to applying that acquired knowledge to our actions and interactions in our lives. In our exploration of contemporary education models in Jewish settings, we first offer examples of Jewish learning in select formal educational settings. Then, we illustrate opportunities for Jewish learning in informal settings and through experiential education.

Formal Jewish Education

A Note on Tikkun Olam

Before we discuss how peace is taught in formal Jewish settings, we need to present a concept that has gained prominence in contemporary Jewish settings: social justice. In many such settings, it is important to note that peace education is taught through the topic of social justice. The driving question in such an educational model is, "How do we make the world a better place?" Undoubtedly, living peacefully is one way to help accomplish that goal. Yet, ethical living, in this context, becomes the ultimate value. This is especially manifested through teaching about the Jewish concept of *tikkun olam*, or "repairing the world." *Tikkun olam*, the idea that humankind has a responsibility to join in God's work through repairing the world, has taken on new meaning since the 1950s, when it was used to refer to social action. With roots in the Mishnah and Kabbalah and brought to the forefront of Jewish education through the Reform Movement, Jewish organizations, movements, and educators have used the phrase as an explanation of Jewish thought on social action work.[10] Perhaps because of the popularity of this important Jewish concept and its connection to tangible acts (e.g., volunteering), it is taught more explicitly in many contemporary Jewish education settings than the concept of peace. We argue that teaching *tikkun olam* is ultimately a reflection of peace education and provide some examples of its prevalence in contemporary educational settings below.

Synagogue Schools

Peace is taught formally and specifically from a Jewish perspective in the synagogue schools. Jewish children from the various sects (e.g., Reform, Conservative) attend classes at their synagogue as part of their Jewish studies. Attending synagogue religious school is more than simply a rite-of-passage; it provides the critical supplemental Jewish education that children require as the basis for their ongoing Jewish learning and lives. We found evidence of how these schools teach peace through examination of the text and interpretation in the Reform movement's curriculum. The Reform movement has designed a centralized curriculum for its synagogues to use in their religious schools called CHAI: Learning for Jewish Life (Union for Reform Judaism, 2005). According to Joanne Doades, the Director for Curriculum Development, approximately 500 U.S. Reform synagogues and about 75 Conservative synagogues with religious schools use the CHAI curriculum.[11]

In this curriculum, students are exposed to a lesson on peace around the sixth grade. The stated purpose of the lesson is to explore the tension that there is the reality of war and conflict with the ideal vision of peace in Judaism. The lesson includes four components: enduring understandings to be taught, essential questions to be asked, lesson vocabulary, and learning activities (e.g., making a peace-quilt). Accompanying the lesson, and consistent with the philosophy of Jewish education we described above, are Jewish texts on peace. In fact, teachers are prompted to ask their students, "What can I learn from Jewish texts about war and peace?" Discussing source material and interpreting it is a fundamental aspect of Jewish education as described above. Contemporary Jewish school settings continue to use this pedagogy to teach concepts of peace.

Although the focus of this section on synagogue education has been on children, it is significant to note that adult education has a central place in synagogue life. Learning opportunities vary in each institution, but common educational forums include adult text classes, Scholar-in-Residence weekends, topical classes on contemporary issues from a Jewish perspective, and daily and weekly sermons on Jewish life and law.

University Education

Campus Jewish Studies departments have become more widespread and prevalent in accredited universities over the past few decades. While a review of the many syllabi and course descriptions is beyond the scope of this chapter, it is sufficient to note that teaching about peace from a Jewish perspective is part of many university curricula.

Perhaps the most well-known impact of Jewish life on university campuses comes from Hillel, the largest Jewish college organization. Although a non-academic setting, Hillel nonetheless represents an excellent source for how peace education is taught to university students. Hillel claims to provide "opportunities for Jewish students at more than 500 colleges and universities to explore and celebrate their Jewish identity through its global network of regional centers, campus Foundations and Hillel student organizations."[12] Many Hillel Houses across the country have their own dedicated Jewish educators, from rabbis to professors to teachers, specifically trained to reach college students. Hillel also makes education about peace available on its "Jewish Resources" web page.[13] Within this site there is a resource called "To Emulate God's Ways: A Hillel Curriculum on Character," which presents source text and guiding questions on various values, including peace. Similar to the synagogue curriculum, this approach is wholly consistent with the philosophy of Jewish education we have described above.

Online Education Sources

Over the last decade, a number of online resources have been developed that provide limitless opportunities for engaging Jewish philosophies for all ages and all levels of education. One of the newest sites is called MyJewishLearning.com: The Gateway to Jewish Exploration. The site claims to be "a transdenominational website of Jewish information and education geared towards learners of all religious and educational backgrounds" and partners with major Jewish organizations, including Hillel, the B'nai B'rith Youth Organization (a youth group for high school students), the American Jewish World Services, and the Coalition for the Advancement of Jewish Education, among others.[14] Their funders include some of the largest foundations in contemporary Jewish life. Their potential audience is large, and they attempt to make their content comprehensive and accessible.

The website contains a number of articles and other resources on peace that rely on Jewish text and interpretation. What is unique to their site is that they engage users by customizing materials based on user proficiency with Jewish study. The four levels the user may select from include primer, topical overviews, deeper explorations, and analysis and interpretation. The site allows for the users to delve deeper into their understanding of Jewish philosophies on peace that is consistent with the approach to Jewish learning described in this chapter. This site offers a preview of what customized and differentiated education may look like for Jewish and secular education in the future.

Teaching by Example: Teaching Judaism is Teaching Peace

The section above focuses on formal education as the guidepost for learning about peace. We maintain, however, that informal education and role-modeling a Jewish lifestyle are new approaches to teaching about peace that both complement and reinforce traditional, formal education. Indeed, we argue that living a Jewish life is synonymous with living a peaceful life. In other words, the Jew who observes Jewish laws, traditions, and/or cultures is a peaceful human being. Given this assertion, informal Jewish education and role-modeling assume a significant role in Jewish education. In a diverse culture and community such as the United States, a Jew cannot learn about daily Jewish life simply by walking the streets. Exposure to other religions and cultures is considered by most to be valuable, but such exposure makes inculcating a particular religious observance and ideology more challenging. Thus, while Judaism still maintains the necessity and centrality of formal Jewish learning, new approaches to Jewish education have emerged to complement and reinforce formal education in a multicultural society. In some instances, informal educational learning and experiential Jewish living have become the *primary* methodology of teaching Jews about Jewish living and peaceful living.

It is beyond the scope of this chapter to evaluate the relative roles of formal and informal Jewish education and also to enumerate all the newer informal educational forums, their impact on Jewish life, and the degree to which they complement or replace more traditional forms of Jewish learning. Still, we offer here several examples of how Jewish learning has entered the realms of informal education and experiential learning.

Jewish Camping Movement

Perhaps the most notable example of informal Jewish education and experiential Jewish learning is evident in the Jewish camping movement. Jewish camps have unique and significant value. First, many offer formal classes within the camp on Judaism, Hebrew, and living as a Jew in a multi-cultural community. In many ways, these classes serve a similar function as courses taught in Jewish day schools and synagogue religious schools. The unique educational opportunities in Jewish camps, however, is that they allow for Jewish youth to learn not only about Jewish texts and values but also to experience living a Jewish lifestyle and culture. A minority culture in the United States, Judaism has its own unique traditions, laws, customs, and values. In the camp milieu, Jewish children can learn about their distinctive heritage, share their common knowledge and experience with others, watch how their peers and staff interact, and apply that knowledge to begin formulating their own Jewish identity. Thus, the informal educational setting at camp and its opportunities for experiential learning play a critical role for contemporary Jewish youth in the United States.

University Settings: Hillel Houses, Fraternities, and Sororities

As noted above, Hillel Houses offer formal Jewish education to many university students across the country and the world. Perhaps even more important than teaching about Judaism in contemporary America is learning to understand and live Jewish culture. Hillel Houses offer college students, many of whom are beginning to embark on their search for their identity as Jews and as human beings, the opportunity to experience Jewish living and traditions in a similar way that camps offer that opportunity for children. By having a forum to meet and interact with other Jews, university students, through Hillel Houses, gain a rich and varied exposure to different ways of Jewish living in the United States. The opportunity to learn from and question peers and adult Jewish role-models is paramount in the development of these Jewish students' personal identities.

Many college campuses also have Jewish fraternities and sororities. While it is unlikely that formal Jewish education takes place there and while their primary focus, unlike a Hillel House, is not the religious and cultural development of the Jewish student, Jewish fraternities and sororities offer the social and cultural Jewish atmosphere often necessary to help a young Jew find her or his place in modern society. By providing a safe and social outlet for Jewish daily life, they help reinforce the secure notion that a Jew can be a fully integrated and accepted member of the larger American community. For Jews who have grown up in a Jewish milieu their entire lives, this experience is both eye-opening and inspiring; for Jews who have grown up primarily assimilated and with limited Jewish exposure, this community can help them begin to have a personal relationship with their tradition and religion.

Organizations

A number of Jewish organizations are dedicated to the promotion of peace and social action. However, few of them actually use the sources of a Jewish philosophy on peace as the basis for their positions. Rather, they rely heavily on the Jewish concept of *tikkun olam*, described above. One such organization is the Jewish Peace Fellowship. The Fellowship was created in 1941 to provide conscientious objectors to the military with a Jewish perspective for their arguments against participating in the military. They claim a Jewish position on conscientious objection based on Torah and other text sources. The Jewish Peace Fellowship published a book called *The Challenge of Shalom: The Jewish Tradition of Peace and Justice*. In this text, the authors argue for a broad meaning of *shalom*, peace, and the primacy of the value of peace.[15]

Another organization is the Shalom Center, founded in 1983 and run by Rabbi Arthur Waskow. The organization was created to oppose the nuclear arms race of the Cold War and has continued in their advocacy of environmental concerns, *tikkun olam*, the Israeli-Palestinian peace process, and the U.S.-led invasion of Iraq. In 1988, the Shalom Center, in conjunction with the Coalition for the Advancement of Jewish Education (CAJE), released *A Curriculum for Peacemaking: Na'aseh Shalom: Let Us Make Peace*. The focus of the book is to teach about and respond to the nuclear threat of the Cold War. The book is consistent with the philosophy of Jewish education because its lesson plans rely on text as source material and the interpretation of that text in the context of a nuclear arms race.

Synagogues, Day Schools, Youth Groups, and Other Jewish Settings

Though discussed in greater detail above, it is important to note that environments whose primary mission might be formal education also serve the critical mission of role-modeling a Jewish life. Synagogues and Day Schools, for example, set up their daily and weekly calendars to accord to a Jewish lifestyle. Rabbis, cantors, and educators serve as irreplaceable role-models for living a Jewish life in modern society. They are people to whom both young and old can turn for advice and counsel on religious and personal matters and who help inspire Jews to examine their lives from religious as well as secular perspectives. While it is nearly impossible to cover the full range of informal education and experiential learning offered in settings such as synagogues and day schools, it is imperative to note their tremendous impact in these arenas. It is also imperative to note here the impact of Jewish youth groups. These groups create Jewish social outlets for children from elementary school through high school. While educational programming is a component of these youth groups, their primary functions are as a social venue and as a form of leadership development. Indeed, each major denomination boasts its own youth group, and many transdenominational and nondenominational Jewish groups exist, as well.

The Jewish Home

Suffice it to say that any text, value or practice learned in a Jewish educational setting—either formal or informal—must be encouraged and reinforced in the home in order to truly inculcate it into a Jewish lifestyle. Judaism is not a religion that is lived exclusively in text books, synagogues, camps, and college campuses; living a Jewish life in the home is central and paramount. It is the primary mission and aspiration of any Jewish organization to help individual Jews create a Jewish life for him- or herself not only within the walls of the institution but in the home and world, as well. While these institutions may serve as the primary mode of formal Jewish education, they are inherently supplemental; it is in the home where Jewish living is ultimately learned.

Thus, it is ultimately parents who are the primary role-models for Jewish children. Indeed, the Hebrew word for parents, *horim*, shares the same roots as the word for teaches, *morim*.[16] While Jewish children, like any children, might live a religious life that eventually differs from that of their parents, parents undoubtedly have the greatest impact on the Jewish lives of their children. This concept, perhaps more than any other, places the imperative upon Jews to learn about their religion and to live Jewish lives: without that foundation, they will experience a tremendous challenge in passing on Jewish traditions and culture to their children.

LIVING A JEWISH AND PEACEFUL LIFE

In the previous section we described how Jewish life and thus a peaceful life is taught in contemporary settings. As we attempted to demonstrate earlier, living a Jewish life is synonymous with living a peaceful life. We therefore examine some aspects of Jewish living to illustrate this indelible connection.

Shabbat

Shabbat (the Sabbath) is the central focus of the Jewish week. The rest of the week is nothing short of preparation for the holy Shabbat. Jews work during the week and rest, as God did, on Shabbat. They take advantage of this day of rest to reflect on the glory of creation, their history as a people, their connection to the natural world, and their relationships with their family and friends. Such is the gift of Shabbat.

Essentially, Shabbat is a day of peace. Jews greet each other on this holiest day of the week by saying "*shabbat shalom* (a Shabbat of peace)." Indeed, there is a Kabbalistic teaching that Shabbat is a taste of the

World-to-Come. The World-to-Come, according to Jewish tradition, is where our souls live after we die. Our deeds in this world determine our place in the World-to-Come. Described as a "slice of heaven," Shabbat affords Jews the privilege of experiencing the World-to-Come here in this world, if only for one day each week. It thus provides Jews with the inspiration and motivation to try to transform *every* day into a holy day like Shabbat. Thus, when Jews wish each other "*shabbat shalom*, may you have a peaceful Shabbat," they are wishing each other a taste of the World-to-Come, a place of peace. Consequently, Shabbat—a day of peace—represents the highest ideal in Judaism: a life of peace and a world of peace.

Prayer

Jews are commanded to pray three times every day. In the era of the Torah, however, the Israelites employed not prayer but rather sacrifice as the primary standardized method of communicating with God. To be sure, it is God who commanded the Israelites to present offerings at both regular and irregular intervals. It is therefore noteworthy that one of the few Divinely-ordained required offerings is the Peace Offering.[17] Rashi, the eleventh-century, preeminent Torah commentator, taught that these offerings help bring peace into the world. Thus, by bringing a Peace Offering to God, the Israelites were helping to foster a peaceful society.

Although prayer existed before the destruction of the Second Temple in Jerusalem in 70 C.E., when the Second Temple was destroyed, Jews began to substitute prayer for sacrifice. Even after the destruction of the Second Temple, Jewish liturgy and prayer have continued to incorporate the concept of peace. One example from the *amidah*, the central prayer in Jewish liturgy, will suffice to illustrate this point. At its core, the *amidah* is a prayer of petition where Jews ask God to help them with their individual, communal, and universal needs. While some of the intermediate paragraphs vary from weekdays to Shabbat to other holidays, it is noteworthy that *every* recitation of the *amidah* ends with a blessing for peace. Whether day or night, weekday or Shabbat, Jews ultimately hope for peace. Indeed, one can reasonably assert that the prayer for peace in the *amidah* is the culmination of the prayer's petitions: one first prays for help for betterment as an individual in order to create a better society so that the world can exist in peace. To be sure, the final line of the addendum to the *amidah* is itself a well-known petition for peace: "May the Maker of peace in the heavens bring peace to us and to all of the people of Israel, amen." Hence, the central prayer in Jewish liturgy is nothing more than a practical vision for the creation of a peaceful world. In essence, when a Jew prays, he or she ultimately prays for peace.

Jewish living, namely prayer and rituals, includes practices that are explicitly taught. Taking the lessons of the previous two sections together, we argue that teaching a Jewish life means teaching the prayers and rituals (i.e., Shabbat) that are essential to peaceful and Jewish living. Jews are taught about the peaceful nature of Shabbat at day schools, at camp, and at university settings, among others; Jews learn the prayer for peace in the *amidah* in these settings as well. Thus, peaceful living is taught to Jews through practice of Jewish prayer and rituals.

CONCLUSION

In this chapter we have demonstrated that *shalom*, peace, is a foundational principle of Judaism. The value of peace is found first in the Torah, both in specific passages and in examining the source as a whole. Interpretations of the source text have further solidified the prominence of peace in Jewish life. We also argued that living a Jewish life is synonymous with living a peaceful life. Thus, peace may be taught explicitly through examination of text or indirectly through instruction on Jewish living, rituals, and prayer.

The primacy of peace continues to be a central feature of the Jewish community in contemporary times. Delivering a speech on the occasion of the historic signing of the Israeli-Palestinian Declaration of Principles at Washington, DC, on September, 13, 1993, Israeli Prime Minister Yitzchak Rabin said the following:

President Clinton, Your Excellencies, Ladies and gentlemen,

We have come from Jerusalem, the ancient and eternal capital of the Jewish people. We have come from an anguished and grieving land.... We have come to try and put an end to the hostilities, so that our children and our children's children will no longer have to experience the painful cost of war, violence, and terror. We have come to secure their lives, and to ease the sorrow and the painful memories of the past—to hope and pray for peace....

We, like you, are people who want to build a home, to plant a tree, to love, live side by side with you—in dignity, in empathy, as human beings, as free men. We are today giving peace a chance and again saying to you: Let us pray that a day will come when we will say, enough, farewell to arms....

We say to you today in a loud and clear voice: Enough of blood and tears. Enough.... It is customary to conclude our prayers with the word "Amen."

With your permission, men of peace, I shall conclude with words taken from the prayer recited by Jews daily, and I ask the entire audience to join me in saying "Amen": "May He who makes peace in His high heavens grant peace to us and to all Israel. Amen."

Rabin's prayer for peace taught people around the world—both Jew and non-Jew—that peace is a fundamental value for not only for Judaism but also for all peaceful societies.

NOTES

1.   A brief note of Hebrew grammar is required here. Hebrew words are inter-connected based on root letters. Hebrew, however, does have vowels as letters, as does English. Rather, there are vocalized markings above and below Hebrew consonants. Thus, the word shalom (root letters "sh," "l" and "m") is interconnected with shlomkha (also with root letters "sh," "l" and "m").

2.   Different Jewish sects emphasize different levels of interpretation (e.g., more traditional Jews are strict in their limits of how far from the source interpretation is allowed to go). We describe this variation in more detail in the next section.

3.   In this Chapter, "Torah" includes both the Written Law (the Five Books of Moses, the Books of the Prophets, and the Books of Writings) and the Oral Law (the Talmud, compiled in the seventh Century) whose teachings, according to Jewish tradition, were also revealed to Moses at Mt. Sinai. Both the Torah and Talmud are considered authentic Jewish texts and are the basis of Jewish religious, spiritual, ideological, and legal studies.

4.   Some would argue that the Diaspora ended in 1948 with the establishment of the State of Israel. Others would say that Jews are still in a state of Diaspora. For the purposes of this paper, we talk about what happened in the Diaspora from its beginning through the Haskalah (beginning approximately in 1770).

5.   Different lands led to different traditions and different names. Jews who lived in Eastern Europe were called Ashkenazi. Jews from Spain, the Middle East, and North African countries were called Sephardi.

6.   The Haskalah took place during Diaspora but we have chosen to treat it is a distinct time period because of its significant impact on the purposes of Jewish education and what it means for present and future Jewry.

7.   In this section, the Torah refers to the Five Books of Moses.

8.   We should note here that there is a law placed upon the Priests and the Israelite people to bring a sacrifice called the "Peace Offering" to God. Thus, there is a legal obligation to pursue peace, as well. This legal obligation is discussed later in this section and this particular sacrifice is discussed in more detail in Section IV.

9. In fact, in the Talmud (Ketubot 16b-17a), it is also taught that one should even lie to preserve peace among people: one should tell every bride on her wedding day – regardless of her physical appearance—that she looks beautiful in order to spare her feelings.
10. http://www.myjewishlearning.com/daily_life/GemilutHasadim/ TO_TikkunOlam.htm, Retrieved June 1, 2009
11. Personal communication, September 23, 2008.
12. http://www.hillel.org/about/default, Retrieved June 1, 2009
13. http://www.hillel.org/jewish/default, Retrieved June 1, 2009
14. http://www.myjewishlearning.com/index.htm, Retrieved June 1, 2009
15. Clearly, this position is based on their interpretation of the text, but theirs is not the only interpretation that reaches this conclusion. Rabbi Michael Broyde, a law professor at Emory University, argues that pacifism is allowed by Judaism in the right circumstances and that minimizing violence has been a priority in Jewish philosophy but that complete pacifism is not a high Jewish value (http://www.myjewishlearning.com/ideas_belief/ warpeace/War_Peace_TO/War_Pacifism_Broyde.htm, Retrieved June 1, 2009).
16. See note 1.
17. The third chapter of the book of Leviticus outlines not only the requirement to bring a Peace Offering but also its laws.

REFERENCES

Baron, S. (1942). *The Jewish community: Its history and structure to the American Revolution* (Vol. 2). Westport, CT: Greenwood Press.

Cahn, Z. (1962). *The philosophy of Judaism*. New York: The Macmillan Company.

Chazan, R. (2005). The historiography of premodern Jewish education. *Journal of Jewish Education, 71*, 23-32.

Drazin, N. (1940). *History of Jewish education from 515 B.C.E. to 220 C.E.* New York: Arno Press.

Graves, F. (1909). *A history of education before the middle ages*. New York: The Macmillan Company.

Grob, L. (1987). Pursuing peace: Shalom in the Jewish Tradition. In H. Gordon & L. Grob (Eds.), *Education for peace: Testimonies from world religions* (pp. 30-44). Maryknoll, NY: Orbis Books.

Ravitzky, A. (1987). Peace. In Cohen, A., & Mendes-Flohr, P. (Eds.), *Contemporary Jewish religious thought* (pp. 685-702). New York: The Free Press.

Rosenak, M. (1995). *Roads to the palace: Jewish texts and teaching*. Providence, RI: Berghahn Books.

Schoenberg, S. (2007). *The Haskalah*. Retrieved December 11, 2007 from http:// www.jewishvirtuallibrary.org/jsource/Judaism/Haskalah.html

Union for Reform Judaism. (2005). *CHAI: Learning for Jewish Life: Level 6 curriculum core*. New York: URJ Press.

CHAPTER 4

HOW CHRISTIANITY ADDRESSES PEACE AND WHAT THIS MEANS FOR EDUCATION

Rebecca L. Oxford

INTRODUCTION

Our world is torn apart by wars, interethnic misunderstandings, religious strife, financial devastation, class and caste distinctions, human destruction of the rainforest and the ozone layer, sometimes racially tinged responses to natural disasters, the strange simultaneity of starvation and food wastage, and the contrast between globalization and excessive concern for self. All of these problems exist on a massive scale and all of them relate to peace and conflict. Peace cannot be built or maintained when situations such as these occur and reoccur.

By peace I refer to multilevel peace: inner peace; peace among family, friends, and coworkers; peace among ethnic, political, and religious groups; peace among countries; peace between humans and other species; and peace between humans and the environment (earth and

Spirituality, Religion, and Peace Education, pp. 63–79
Copyright © 2010 by Information Age Publishing
All rights of reproduction in any form reserved.

beyond). Peace does not mean the absence of all conflict, because conflict is part of nature and human development. Peace is not merely the absence of war but, in my view, is instead a positive, active force for social justice, equity, and compassion.

Every religion has something to say about matters as important as these. What is the Christian message regarding multilevel peace in this time of world turbulence? What do Christianity and the Bible[1] say about mutual understanding, compassion, social justice, and our relationship with the Earth?

BACKGROUND

One of the world's greatest peacemakers was Jesus, the Christ. The name Jesus means "Savior" and the appellation Christ or Messiah, which was used to portray Jesus even before he was born (Matthew 2:4), means "the anointed one." Christianity is mainly a historical religion, founded on real events and personalization, not abstract principles. Jesus is seen to be a historical figure by religions other than Christianity, not as the son of God; in Islam, he is called Isa. It is difficult to find much definitive information about the history of Jesus' life, since information about Jesus and his teachings was handed down through oral traditions and was not written until at least 40 years after he died. The New Testament books were the first writings that included his words. However, they were not written to be historical accounts of his life but rather theological documents, based on oral traditions and collections of sayings (Tyle, 2006).

Jewish Beliefs at the Time of Jesus

Jesus was a Jew, well versed in Jewish tradition (Cohen, 1998). That meant he would have studied the Torah, the ancient Jewish scriptures, and would have been very familiar with words like this from Proverbs:

> Reckless words pierce like a sword, but the tongue of the wise brings healing. Truthful lips endure forever but a lying tongue lasts only a moment. There is deceit in the hearts of those who plot evil, but joy for those who promote peace. (Proverbs 12:18-20)

> A heart at peace gives life to the body, but envy rots the bones. (Proverbs 13:30)

Jews' view of the Spirit would have influenced Jesus profoundly. Jews believed that the universe had an invisible order and that the world was created through primordial waters. Jews populated Spirit not only with God (YHWH, or Yahweh) but also angels, archangels, cherubim, seraphim, and many other levels of angelic beings. Yahweh was described in metaphorical terms as shepherd, king, lord, father, mother, and lover (Smith, 1991). Spirit was sometimes seen as being located "over" the world, but more often Spirit was viewed as repeatedly intervening in Jewish history, for instance, by delivering the tablets of the Ten Commandments to Moses on Mt. Sinai and by helping the Jews escape their captors in the great Exodus from Egypt. In addition to Spirit intervening in human affairs, people can contact Spirit through prayer, fasting, and solitude, according to ancient Jewish tradition.

In addition to those beliefs, which Jesus would have known well, he also would have understood the Old Testament belief that God created the humans, male and female, in God's own image.

> And God created man in His own image, in the image of God created He him; male and female created He them. And God blessed them; and God said unto them: "Be fruitful, and multiply, and replenish the earth, and subdue it; and have dominion over the fish of the sea, and over the fowl of the air, and over every living thing that creepeth upon the earth." (Genesis 1:27-28)

The last part of this passage is not actually peaceful, as it gives humans too much power (dominion) and allows them to "subdue" the earth, not just replenish it.

Historical Life of Jesus

Jesus of Nazareth was born in a stable in Bethlehem, Judea between 7 and 4 B.C.E. during reign of Herod the Great. He was the son of a carpenter, Joseph, and a teenage mother, Mary, whom Christianity describes as a virgin when giving birth to Jesus (the "Immaculate Conception" doctrine). This doctrine reflects the many virgin birth myths around the world (Campbell, 1968). Out of fear of Jesus, Herod killed all male children age 2 and under in Bethlehem, but fortunately Joseph had been warned in a dream to take Mary and the baby Jesus into Egypt to save the baby. They returned from Egypt when Herod died, but they went to live in a different place, Nazareth in the district of Galilee.

As a boy of 12, he went with his parents to Jerusalem for a festival, and when they started for home he stayed behind in the temple, where he conversed with highly learned teachers (Luke 2:41-52). His parents searched for him for 3 days. When they found him in the temple, they upbraided him for causing them anxiety, but Jesus responded, "How is it that you sought me? Did you not know that I must be in my father's house?" (Luke 2:49).

As an adult, Jesus was baptized by John, an electrifying prophet who had predicted the coming of the Messiah. When Jesus came out of the water, the heavens opened and a dove came out and rested on him. A voice announced, "This is my beloved Son, with whom I am well pleased" (Matthew 3:13-17). His spiritual cultivation included fasting in the wilderness, where he was tempted by Satan to display supernatural powers as proof of divinity. He rejected all temptations (Matthew 4:1-11, Luke 4:1-13). Shortly after John the Baptist was arrested by the authorities, Jesus began to preach, teach, and heal in Galilee and called his first disciples. He was not at first accepted in his own town of Nazareth, but elsewhere he was followed by enormous crowds. A charismatic leader, Jesus preached, taught, and worked miracles. He mediated between the everyday world and the Spirit and was part of an ancient tradition of healers (Smith, 1991), although he surpassed any of them by being named as the Son of God.

Some say that Jesus' healing, preaching, and teaching career lasted only one to three years. During that time, he defied four Jewish groups: the Pharisees, the Essenes, the Sadducees, and the Zealots (Smith, 1991). The Pharisees wanted to purify Jews using an uncompassionate holiness code, which judged people sharply and set up barriers between the clean and the unclean. In contrast, Jesus showed compassion toward all; and one of the reasons the Romans viewed him with suspicion was that he chastised the Pharisees. The Essenes viewed the world as too corrupt for Judaism and hence withdrew from the world into communes, but Jesus wanted his followers to maintain full engagement with the world. The Sadducees were overly accommodating to the Romans, but Jesus called for giving unto Caesar the things that are Caesar's and giving unto God the things that are God's. The Zealots launched resistance movements against the Romans, but Jesus was more concerned about inner transformation than outward resistance movements.

Jesus did not call himself God and did not reveal a human ego. He was humble in all things. When he was called good, he asked why people called him good and said that only God is good. He ignored social barriers and hated injustice and hypocrisy. He called God "Abba," or Daddy, and used many metaphors for God. His followers felt that in Jesus they saw God in human form.

Just before Passover in the final year of his life, Jesus purged the temple of the money-changers with a whip of cords, not a particularly peaceful tool. Some experts, such as Hyland (2002), state that the money-changers in the temple were part of a system supporting the ritual sacrifice of animals and that the temple was awash in the blood of innocent animals, such as sheep, cattle, and doves (John 2:13-16). Although the money-changers were players in the system, it was probably the entire culture of blood sacrifice that Jesus was aiming to overthrow by eliminating the money-changers who helped people buy animals to kill in the temple. Because of the money-changers and the animal sellers, the "house of prayer" was becoming a "den of robbers" (Matthew 21:12-13), said Jesus, recalling the same comment from the Old Testament prophet Jeremiah (7:11). These actions and statements by Jesus made the chief priests and law scholars fear him and start looking for a way to kill him (Mark 11:18).

At age 33, he was captured by Pontius Pilate and crucified next to two common thieves. Christians believe that he was resurrected on third day after his death and ascended into heaven. He appeared to certain disciples (eating, being touched, and walking through closed doors). For most, Jesus entered into another mode of being. Apostle Paul said, "If Christ was not raised, then all our preaching is useless, and your trust in God is useless" (1 Corinthians 15:12-20). This does not explain why Christians have so strongly emphasized Jesus' bloody death, which seems to hold, for many, far more fascination than the resurrection itself. Robins and Post (1997) noted that the central image of Christianity is an instrument of execution, the cross, and they pointed out the bloody imagery in Christian hymns, such as "Washed in the Blood of the Lamb," "The Old Rugged Cross," and "There Is a Fountain Flowing with Blood."

The profound impact Jesus had on his followers was so great his disciples continued his ministry, striving to demonstrate his love and teachings to others. They formed the Christian church of which Jesus is the central figure. They preached the "Good News" (gospel), which included not just what Jesus said, but also stated that Jesus was the Son of God and the Savior. There are about 2 billion practicing Christians in the world today (Weigel, 2002).

PEACE IN THE WORDS OF JESUS

Jesus said little or nothing beyond what was already in the Old Testament or its commentary, the Talmud (Klausner, 1925). However, what was very new was the way he said it: passionately, vividly, and invitationally (Smith, 1991). He invited people to see things differently. Instead of telling them what to do, thus causing them to work with their reason or will, he told parables or simple stories linked with people's daily lives, thus stimulating imagination and acceptance (Smith, 1991). He thus located authority for his teachings in the hearts of those who heard them.

In the Sermon on the Mount, Jesus explicitly addressed peace: "Blessed are the peacemakers for they will be called sons of God" (Matthew 5:9). To be a peacemaker, one must have mercy and purity of heart. "Blessed are the merciful, for they shall obtain mercy. Blessed are the pure in heart, for they shall see God.... Blessed are those who are persecuted for righteousness' sake, for theirs is the kingdom of heaven" (Matthew 5:7-8, 10). In the *Jerusalem Bible*, though not in all other versions, this verse was added in the Sermon on the Mount: "Happy the gentle: They shall have the earth for their heritage" (Matthew 5:4). In this sermon, Jesus urged people not to hide their light under a bushel but "let your light shine before men, that they might see your good works and give glory to your Father who is in heaven" (Matthew 5:14). In other words, peacemaking, mercy, purity, and gentleness, among other qualities, should be openly displayed.

Love Your Neighbor

Two of Jesus' greatest teachings about peace are found in this exhortation:

> The first [commandment] is, "Hear, O Israel: The Lord our God, the Lord is one; and you shall love the Lord your God your God with all your heart, and with all your soul, and with all your mind, and with all your strength." And the second is this, "You shall love your neighbor as yourself." (Mark 12:29-31; Luke 10:27)

Jesus' words synthesize two statements from the Old Testament: "Hear, O Israel: the Lord our God is one Lord, and you shall love the Lord your God with all your heart, and with all your soul and with all your might" (Deuteronomy 6:4-5); and "You shall love your neighbor as yourself" (Leviticus 19:18).

Who is one's neighbor, and what does loving one's neighbor mean? This is explained in Jesus' parable of the Good Samaritan:

> A man was going down from Jerusalem to Jericho, and he fell among robbers, who stripped him and beat him and departed, leaving him half dead. Now by chance a priest was going down that road; and when he saw him, he passed by on the other side. So likewise Levite, when he came to the place and saw him, passed by on the other side. But a Samaritan, as he journeyed, came to where he was; and when he saw him, he had compassion, and went to him and bound up his wounds, pouring on oil and wine; then he set him on his own beast and brought him to an inn, and took care of him. And the next day he took out two denarii and gave them to the innkeeper, saying, "Take care of him; and whatever more you spend, I will repay you when I come back." Which of these three, do you think, proved neighbor to the man who fell among the robbers?" he said, "The one who showed mercy on him." And Jesus said to him, "Go and do likewise." (Luke 10: 30-37)

Jesus' disciples in the early days of Christianity continued his message of love. For instance, John said, "God is love, and he who abides in love abides in God, and God abides in him," according to the first letter of John (I John 4:16). John's gospel stated, "For God so loved the world that he gave his only Son, that whoever believes in him should ... have eternal life" (John 3:16). These statements indicate that love is central to Christian life.

Do Not Judge Others Without Looking at Yourself

In the parable of the adulterous woman, Jesus told the legal teachers and the Pharisees to look inside themselves at their own mistakes before condemning the woman and stoning her:

> The scribes and the Pharisees brought a woman who had been caught in adultery, and placing her in the midst they said to [Jesus], "Teacher, this woman has been caught in the act of adultery. Now in the law Moses commanded us to stone such. What do you say about her?" This they said to test him, that they might have some charge to bring against him. Jesus bent down and wrote with his finger on the ground. And as they continued to ask him, he stood up and said to them, "Let him who is without sin among you be the first to throw a stone at her." And once more he bent down and wrote with his finger on the ground. But when they heard it, they went away, one by one, beginning with the eldest, and Jesus was left alone with the woman standing before him. Jesus looked up and said to her, "Woman, where are they? Has no one condemned you?" She said, "No one, Lord." And Jesus said, "Neither do I condemn you; go, and do not sin again." (John 8:3-11)

Many Christians believe in a Second Coming, in which the Messiah will come again. God, not humans, will do the judging, according to the New Testament.

Repent of Sins and Be Forgiven

Jesus called people to repent of their sins. This meant they had to do something different; being a Christian did not involve passivity. God offered full forgiveness of sins, even if a person had been an evil-doer throughout life. It did not matter how late in life repentance occurred nor how enormous the sins were. Acts 3:19 stated, "Repent therefore, and turn again [be converted], that your sins may be blotted out, that times of refreshing may come from the presence of the Lord."

Jesus' parable of the Prodigal Son in Luke 15:11-32 is an example of human repentance and God's forgiveness and love. A man had two sons. The younger son demanded his share of the inheritance while the father was alive. Receiving the inheritance, the son went to a foreign land, where he riotously wasted the money and had to become a swineherd. He came back to his father and apologized. His father greeted him with great love, clothed him in the best robe, and had a celebratory feast to celebrate his return. The older brother resented such unearned graciousness, but the father said that "It was fitting to make merry and be glad, for your brother was dead, and is alive; he was lost, and is found" (Luke 16:32). The parable about the lost sheep reflects the lesson of God's love and forgiveness: the shepherd risked 99 sheep for the one that had gone astray (Luke 15:3-4).

At first Jesus stated that the Kingdom of God would come gradually as the people of Israel repent, but later this message became much more urgent. "Now after John was arrested, Jesus came into Galilee, preaching the gospel of God, and saying, 'The time [*Kairos*] is fulfilled, and the Kingdom of God is at hand; repent, and believe in the gospel" (Mark 1:14-15).

Forgive Others, Just as God Forgives You

A related message is that just as God forgives the sinner, Christians are called upon to forgive those who sin against them. Jesus said,

> Do not resist one who is evil. But if any one strikes you on the right cheek, turn to him the other also.... Love your enemies and pray for those who persecute you, so that you may be sons of your Father who is in heaven; for he makes the sun rise on the evil and the good, and sends rain on the just and the unjust. (Matthew 6:39, 44-45)

It is not up to Christians to punish and persecute others; they will have their day of reckoning, and human retribution is not necessary. How many times should Christians forgive? Jesus said "seventy times seven" (Matthew 18:22).

Be Freed of Care

Like the Buddhists and others who abjure materialism, Jesus stated that we should not worry about food or other material things. God feeds the birds of the field (Matthew 4:4) and will hence feed humans. Jesus disparaged riches and stated that it will be more difficult for a rich man to enter heaven than for a camel to pass through a needle's eye (Matthew 19: 23-24; Mark 10:24-25; Luke 18:24-25). With less concern about material things, there is less likelihood of conflict and war. In fact, Jesus told people to sell everything they had and give it to the poor, then come follow him (Luke 18:22).

Find Spiritual Peace in Oneself

Jesus emphasized finding spiritual peace within oneself, through a relationship with God. The apostle Paul writes of this concept in a letter to the Philippians.

> Rejoice in the Lord always, again I will say, Rejoice. Let all men know your forbearance. The Lord is at hand. Have no anxiety about anything, but in everything by prayer and supplication with thanksgiving let your requests be known to God. And the peace of God, which passes all understanding, will keep your hearts and your minds in Christ Jesus.
>
> Finally, brethren, whatever is true, whatever is honorable, whatever is just, whatever is pure, whatever is lovely, whatever is gracious, if there is any excellence, if there is anything worthy of praise, think about these things. What you have learned and received and heard and seen in me, do; and the God of peace will be with you. (Philippians 4:4-9)

The Bible has a wealth of knowledge regarding how to live Christian lives at peace within ourselves, with others, and throughout the world. Spiritual disciplines that Jesus followed have been explained as inward, outward, and corporate disciplines (Foster, 1978). Inward disciplines of Christianity include meditation, prayer, fasting, and study. Outward disciplines include simplicity, solitude, submission, and service. Corporate disciplines include confession, worship, guidance, and celebration. Christian mystics experienced the "dark night of the soul," ecstasy, and rapture (Borg, 1988; Dupré & Wiseman, 1988; Underhill, 1954/1974).

In spite of the many peaceful and loving messages Jesus gave, he also talked about bringing violence. That is the strange subject of the next section.

AN IMMENSE PARADOX: JESUS BRINGS THE SWORD

Though Jesus repeatedly proclaimed peace, he also stated a great paradox: "I have not come to bring peace, but a sword" (Matthew 10:34). The full statement is:

Do not think that I have come to bring peace on the earth; I have not come to bring peace, but a sword. For I have come to set a man against his father, and a daughter against her mother, and a daughter-in-law against her mother-in-law; and a man's foes will be those of his own household. He who loves father or mother more than me is not worthy of me; and he who loves son or daughter more than me is not worthy of me; and he who does not take his cross and follow me is not worthy of me. He who finds his life will lose it, and he who loses his life for my sake will find it. (Matthew 10:34-39)

How do Jesus' many words about peace cohere with his statements about bringing a sword? Or do they? Conflicting interpretations exist. Some focus on actual physical violence and others on metaphorical violence.

Interpretations Referring to Actual Physical Violence

One interpretation is that Jesus called for violence, in which the sword would literally attack those family or household members who did not believe in him while sparing family or household members who were believers. If we consider the family or household to include all humanity, the argument could easily be extended to justify capital punishment, vigilante justice, the Crusades, the Inquisitions, and torture of detainees at Guantanamo Bay and Abu Gharaib Prison.

The Center for Church Music (2009) notes that military-style hymns were formerly a staple in the North American Christian musical diet, with titles such as "Stand Up for Jesus, Ye Soldiers of the Cross," "Soldiers of Christ Arise," "Fight the Good Fight," and, most famous of all, "Onward, Christian Soldiers." The militant verses of "Onward, Christian Soldiers" (Baring-Gould, 1865) describe the "mighty army" that is the Church "marching as to war," led by Christ and the cross. When the great day of victory comes, "Hell's foundations quiver." "Kingdoms, nations, and empires" are destroyed, but the mighty army is victorious, as sung "through countless ages" by "men and angels."

This hymn clearly evokes images of brothers, men, and a male army fighting on behalf of Christ. To my mind, this raises the historical link between violence and male-dominated cultures that was clearly identified by Eisler (1987) in *The Chalice and the Blade: Our History, Our Future*. Christian apostle Timothy stated, "Take your share of suffering as a good soldier of Christ Jesus. No soldier on service gets entangled in civilian pursuits, since his aim is to satisfy the one who enlisted him" (II Timothy 2:3-4). Timothy's verses do not seem turned inward toward individual moral struggle but instead seem to reflect an outward battle against evil or against those who do not believe in Christ.

On the other hand, although Jesus mentioned bringing a sword, he did not describe his followers as soldiers. In fact, Jesus said, "Put your sword back into its place; for all who take the sword will perish by the sword" (Matthew 26:52).

A different physical interpretation of "I have not come to bring peace, but a sword" is that Jesus predicted violence to occur *against* his own followers. The family members who did not believe or who were not willing to give up their worldly goods would be angry at the true believers and would therefore use violence against them.

Metaphorical Interpretations

We have seen the contradictions and complexities that arise in any concrete interpretation of Jesus' statement, "I have not come to bring peace, but a sword." Are there some metaphorical interpretations instead? Yes, in fact. For instance, Paul stated that the word of God is "the sword of the Spirit" (Ephesians 6:17), meaning that God's word is a weapon of spiritual rather than physical violence. In the same verse, Paul described salvation as a helmet. Just before that he mentioned the "breastplate of righteousness" (Ephesians 6:14) and taking "the whole armor of God, that you may withstand in the evil day, and having done all, to stand" (Ephesians 6:13). In this reference, the sword (the word of God) was one of the protections against evil.

New York Times columnist William Safire (2004) indicated that Jesus' statement about bringing the sword, not peace, meant that inner peace occurs only after the individual has undergone a personal, moral struggle. He said this in a negative review of the gratuitously bloody and violent film by Mel Gibson about the death of Jesus.

William Sloane Coffin (1992), former Yale University Chaplain, who later became the Senior Minister at the Riverside Church in New York and the head of the international peace organization, SANE/FREEZE, argued that Jesus' statement about bringing the sword referred to a "sword of truth," which paradoxically "heals the wound it inflicts." To Coffin, cutting through the delusional self-righteousness of the U.S. regarding foreign and domestic affairs requires the sword of Christ's truth. He condemned government decisions that were based on self-interest but were defended as moral.

It is our pride-swollen faces that have closed up our eyes here at home to an almost unimaginable neglect of the poor, the bloat of the military, the size of the deficit, the sorrow of the aged and infirm among us.

Thus, Jesus had to bring the sword of truth.

The metaphorical explanations of Jesus' statement, "I have not come to bring peace, but a sword" do not explain the rest of the statement, that is, about families being torn asunder by the sword. It seems that no one has developed a completely convincing argument about what Jesus meant by bringing the sword, not peace, as this message conflicts with so many other statements he made during his lifetime.

PEACE AND UNPEACEFUL EXAMPLES OF CHRISTIAN BEHAVIOR

Christianity has done great things in society. It manifested itself in amazing works of art, music, and literature. It emphasized monogamy and the sanctity of the family. It supported the great monasteries and universities and kept knowledge alive during the Dark Ages. It is still a powerful force for good behind many governments and cultures.

The positive teachings of Jesus and the spiritual disciplines of Christianity have been expressed in the lives of Christians, such as Martin Luther King, martyred leader of the U.S. civil rights movement (King, 1958, 2001); Peace Pilgrim, who walked 25,000 miles to promote peace (Pilgrim, 1994); and Kenya's Wangari Maathai, leader of the Green Belt Movement to plant trees and improve the status of women (Tippett, 2008). The lives of the saints have much to teach us about the meaning of peace in Christianity.

On the other hand, the Christian church has sometimes shown a barbaric side. For instance, the first Christian emperor, Constantine (272-337 C.E.), reversed the persecutions of the Christians that had occurred under Emperor Diocletian, gave power to the Christian Church, and to some extent increased religious tolerance—but Constantine also had his wife and son killed and continued to persecute certain sects. The Crusades killed millions from late eleventh century through the fifteenth century and, sporadically, even after that. The ostensible purpose of the Crusades was to recapture Jerusalem from the "infidels" (Muslims), which Jesus himself would never have encouraged because of his love of peace. The Crusades were also spurred by worldly and ecclesiastical politics, including the desire of popes to strengthen their power. Greed and cruelty besmirched any high ideals the Crusaders might have had (Runciman, 1951-1954). The Crusades established Christianity as an enemy of Islam. The ongoing hatred that the Crusades brought is incalculable. Samuel Huntington (1996), author of *The Clash of Civilizations and the Remaking of the World Order*, points out that both Christianity and Islam are (a) missionary religions, seeking to convert people; (b) teleological religions, meaning that they assert their values to be the goals and purpose of human existence; and (c) all-or-nothing religions whose followers assert their faith to be the only correct one. Whether or not we believe that the clash of civilizations is inevitable, the competition between Christianity and Islam—sometimes leading to violence—would at least be understandable.

Another unpeaceful demonstration of Christian power was the series of Inquisitions occurring in different countries starting in the twelfth and thirteenth century and continuing, in various forms, through the nineteenth century. Papal support encouraged the Inquisitions, which included torture and resulted in many deaths. The fact that inquisitorial techniques were also used in secular courts did not make them any more justifiable. Constantine's internecine murders, the Crusades, and the Inquisitions did not reflect Jesus' values about peace; they revealed some ugly aspects of the Christian Church in the world.

The brutal face, rather than the divine face, of the Christian Church is revealed when some denominations of the church say that only people who join their particular group will reap religious rewards, such as going to heaven. The brutal face is shown when certain Christians beat and kill gay people in the name of morality and when certain other Christians burn crosses on the lawns of African Americans or Hispanics. These steps reflect judgmentalism and intolerance that defy the words of Jesus.

The Church degraded women when patriarchalism took over Christianity in the second and third centuries C.E., at which time women were stripped of ecclesiastical authority and feminine images of God were banned. Joseph Campbell (1968) said that the all-male imagery of the Christian God radically unbalanced the symbolic/spiritual connotations of the sexes and of nature. Movements in the 1970s and 1980s tried to rebalance the symbolism by pointing not just to the masculine images of God in the Christian Bible but also to the Bible's feminine and nature-based images of God (Mollenkott, 1983; Oxford-Carpenter, 1984; Reuther, 1979). Unfortunately, these efforts at inclusiveness and symbolic balance did not have a major effect throughout the Christian Church.[2]

It is important to recognize both the positive, peaceful, and harmonious aspects of Christianity and the negative, discriminatory, and bellicose aspects. We need to understand the ideals of Christ and how far Christians and the institution of the Church have repeatedly strayed from those ideals.

CHRISTIANITY FOR PEACE EDUCATION

This section briefly provides some implications for peace education in formal settings in elementary and secondary schools. I am not suggesting that peace education should be Christian education. However, peace education in schools can be enriched by Christian ideals and principles.

Peace education can include the virtues Jesus taught: compassion, kindness, love, care, giving, mercy, purity of heart, acceptance of others, forgiveness, and inner peace. Christian love must be given to all people, even outcasts and harlots, not just some favored few. Christianity would say that peace education must talk about a personal relationship with Christ, but the values that Christ taught are meaningful regardless of whether one has such a relationship with Christ.

Jesus had great success in telling stories. He galvanized attention of all around him through his parables, the simple but amazingly revealing stories related to the life and times of his hearers. Christ's parables still have the ability to speak to many people today, but peace education cannot stop with old stories. Peace education must have contemporary stories as well, stories that reflect current life experiences: students trying to deal with the death of a friend, who drove a car off the road in a drunken stupor or was knifed while waiting for the bus; students being forced into gangs and dropping out of high school; teenagers sleeping in class after they have worked until midnight at two jobs; families trying to survive in a financial meltdown; children and adolescents facing bullying and scapegoating; and young girls being lured into online traps by sexual predators. Today's stories need not all be grim, of course. Peace education needs to face life as it is today and provide parables of hope, faith, and virtue for a new day. Only by appealing to the authority of the students' own lives can peace educators help peace develop and grow in those lives.

In addition to modern-day parables, biographical stories about Christians such as Martin Luther King, Peace Pilgrim, and Wangari Maathai can be used in peace education to show how some great people have lived their lives for peace and justice. Including true stories about younger people, such as Mattie Stepanek (2006), who was a young poet, philosopher, and peacebuilder before his early death from muscular dystrophy, would be very important. Children's books offer some deeply moving stories, fictional and nonfictional, that can be used in peace education. Some of these books show how children have reached inner peace even while devastation occurs, and other books reveal how children take steps to create peace in the world around them.

Peace education must create imagery and practice that are powerful, ethical, and fair. Peace education must help students learn not demonize or downgrade certain groups, such as women and girls or people of color. Gender equity is clearly not present when women, on average, still earn 78 cents to every dollar in the United States. In addition, some progress has been made toward racial equality, but such equality has not yet been attained as a daily reality for all. Peace education must develop an understanding of the equality of all humans, one of Jesus' major themes. Jesus' belief in equity should be a major plank in peace education. Compassion and generosity of the heart—rather than cruelty and intolerance—should be key messages in peace education.

Just as Jesus talked about rich people having a very difficult time attaining spiritual rewards, peace educators must help to reveal the ultimate futility of the emphasis on materialism that drives our societies today. Peace educators must find ways to show that friendship, compassion, and giving are more important than owning the latest Air Jordans, the finest leather jacket, or the fanciest car. Yet materialism seems to be such an integral part of most current societies that it cannot be denounced totally and immediately by peace educators. Students must themselves develop the understanding, through stories and experiences, that material goods and wealth are less important than other sources of wealth, those of the human heart and mind.

Ecological concerns are crucial to human survival and are a very important part of peace education. Caring about the world—about every animal, plant, and body of water in existence—can be a great way of focusing love and spreading peace. The focus of peace education can be on virtues and values taught by Jesus, as well as by other spiritual figures from other traditions.

NOTES

1. All Biblical quotations are from the Revised Standard Version (RSV, 1946/ 2002), except for one addition from the Jerusalem Bible (1966/1974).
2. They had an ongoing influence among some progressive Christian congregations, however, such as the Riverside Church in New York (Oxford-Carpenter, 1984).

REFERENCES

Baring-Gould, S. (1865). *Onward, Christian soldiers*. Grandhaven, MI: Center for Church Music. Retrieved from http://songsandhymns.org/hymns/detail/ onward-christian-soldiers

Borg, M. (1988). *Jesus: A new vision*. San Francisco: Harper & Row.

Campbell, J. (1968). *The masks of God: Creative mythology*. New York: Vintage.

Dupré, L., & Wiseman, J. (Eds.). (1988). *Light from light: An anthology of Christian mysticism*. New York: Paulist Press.

Foster, R. (1978). *Celebration of discipline: The path to spiritual growth*. San Francisco: Harper & Row.

Center for Church Music. (2009). *Devotional on "Onward Christian Soldiers."* Retrieved from http://songsandhymns.org/hymns/detail/onward -christian-soldiers

Coffin, W. S. (1992, Feb. 16). Not to bring peace, but a sword. Program #3519. *30 Good Minutes.* Chicago: The Chicago Sunday Evening Club. Retrieved from http://www.csec.org/csec/sermon/coffin_3519.htm

Cohen, S. I. D. (1998). *Jesus' many faces: What can we really know about Jesus?* Frontline Online. Public Broadcasting System. Retrieved from http://www.pbs.org/wgbh/pages/frontline/shows/religion/jesus/

Eisler, R. (1987). *The chalice and the blade: Our history, our future.* San Francisco: Harper & Row.

Hyland, J. R. (2002). Jesus and the money-changers. In K. Akers (Ed.), *Compassionate Spirit.* Colorado Springs, CO. Retrieved from http://www.compassionatespirit.com/JR-Hyland.htm

Huntington, S. (1996). *The clash of civilizations and the remaking of the world order.* New York: Simon and Schuster.

Jerusalem Version of the Holy Bible (1974). *The six version parallel New Testament: King James Version, Living Bible, Revised Standard Version, New English Bible, Phillips Modern Translation, Jerusalem Bible.* Wheaton, IL: Christian Life Magazine and New York: Iversen-Norman Associates. (Original work published 1966)

King, M. L., Jr. (2001). *The words of Martin Luther King, Jr.* (C.S. King, Ed.). New York: Newmarket.

King, M. L., Jr. (1958). *Stride toward freedom: The Montgomery story.* New York: Harper & Brothers.

Klausner, J. (1925). *Jesus of Nazareth: His life, time, and teaching.* New York: Macmillan.

Mollenkott, V. (1983). *The divine feminine: Biblical imagery of God as female.* New York: Crossroad.

Oxford-Carpenter, R. (1984). Gender and the trinity. *Theology Today, 41*(1), 7-25.

Pilgrim, P. (1994). *Peace Pilgrim, her life and work in her own words.* Hemet: Friends of Peace Pilgrim.

Reuther, M. (1979). *Mary, the feminine face of the church.* Philadelphia: Westminster.

Revised Standard Version of the Holy Bible (2002). Oxford, England: Oxford University Press. (Original work published 1946)

Robins, R. S., & Post, J. M. (1997). *Political paranoia: The psychopolitics of hatred.* New Haven, CT: Yale University Press.

Runciman, S. (1951-1954). *A history of the Crusades* (Vol. 1-3). Cambridge, England: Cambridge University Press.

Safire, W. (2004, Mar. 1). Not peace, but a sword. Op-Ed Section. *New York Times.* Retrieved from http://www.nytimes.com/2004/03/01/opinion/01SAFI.html?ex=1393477200&en=b9d26c6071938613&ei=5007&partner=USERLAND

Smith, H. (1991). *The world's religions.* San Francisco: Harper.

Stepanek, M. (2006). *Just peace: A message of hope.* Grand Rapids, MI: Andrews McMeel.

Tippett, K. (2008, Apr. 24). *Speaking on faith, interview with Wangari Maathai*. National Public Radio. Retrieved from http://speakingoffaith.publicradio.org/programs/plantingthefuture/>.

Tyle, L. B. (Ed.). (2006). Jesus of Nazareth. *UXL Encyclopedia of World Biography* (Vol. 6). Detroit, MI: Gale, Cengage Learning.

Underhill, E. (1974). *Mysticism*. New York: New American Library. (Original work published 1955)

Weigel, G. (2002). *World religions by the numbers*. Catholic Education Resource Bellevue, WA: Center. Retrieved from http://www.catholiceducation.org/articles/facts/fm0010.html

CHAPTER 5

PEACE EDUCATION AND THE RELIGIOUS SOCIETY OF FRIENDS (QUAKERS)

Mary Lee Morrison and Ian Harris

INTRODUCTION

Peace education, including its philosophical principles, values, skills (processes) and a life view turned toward service in the world, has been an integral part of the Religious Society of Friends since the early Quakers, under their fiery young leader, George Fox, who established the movement in the 1600s in England. Soon the faith spread to the American shores. Today there are Quakers around the world. Many Quaker meetings in Western Europe, the United States, Canada, and in other parts of the world worship in silence in what is known as the "unprogrammed" tradition. Members gather in prayer, "waiting upon the Lord" and, if felt called, a participant may rise and give a brief message to the gathered group. There are no ministers with a sermon to give, no prearranged textual readings, nor order of worship, as in most other Christian worship formats. In fact, Quakers are often known for what they *lack*, those things

Spirituality, Religion, and Peace Education, pp. 81–98
Copyright © 2010 by Information Age Publishing

that often distinguish other faith traditions, including creeds, systematic theological articulation of faith and hierarchical, administrative structure.

In the nineteenth century, as a result of shifting geographical, historical, and cultural factors, including United States westward expansion, a *pastoral tradition* developed among many Friends and Quaker missionaries began to evangelize throughout other areas of the world. Today this trend is evident in many Yearly Meetings, both in the United States, in Latin America, and in Africa, holding to a more Bible based, and, arguably, theologically more conservative approach to scripture and belief. There are now roughly three parts to the spectrum of Friends worldwide: on the "left" the liberal and unprogrammed Friends, in the "middle" Friends Meetings with pastors and belief in the authority of scripture, and those on the "right", with a more evangelical, fundamentalist approach. In spite of these liturgical differences Quakers in both the programmed and unprogrammed traditions have a strong commitment to nonviolence and peace education. This essay will focus, for the most part, on Quaker practice from the unprogrammed tradition.

The Religious Society of Friends is one of three pacifist Christian sects. The others are Mennonites who came from what is now Germany, and the Brethren who came from Central Europe, from what is now Slovakia. Early Friends espoused their particular form of Christianity that followed the nonviolent teachings of Jesus. They were seeking to recover what they considered to be the core of the gospel teachings: love for neighbor, equality between the sexes, turning the other cheek, and fostering reconciliation not rancor.

The concepts of peace education and Quaker worship are seamlessly one, and this is true both of the history and evolution of the Society of Friends and of its modern manifestations. Early forms of Quaker peace education were informal. Friends placed great importance on the family as educator. Family worship was an integral part of life. Feminist educator Sara Ruddick, though not identified as a Quaker, has summed up nicely the idea that the family's role in fostering growth is to nurture a child's developing spirit. She uses the metaphor of a flower unfolding from its bud. In the best practice of parenting, there is an intentionality, which, together with a culture of caring, leads to the nurturing of the values of peace and nonviolence (Ruddick, 1995). Families are where a child first encounters important *relationships* and, increasingly, psychologists are coming to understand the importance of models of healthy human development that are interactional. The latest brain research shows that children need consistent nurturing in order to develop positive, pro-social skills. Quaker sociologist Elise Boulding points to the family as the important incubator for the process of parents and children "co-creating" a life, mutually influencing the growth and development of the child. As the child matures, so do the parents and siblings (E. Boulding, 1989a). The Quakers and the other pacifist, Christian sects, the Mennonites and Brethren, set up their own schools in the colonies in order that the education of their young be removed from the temptations of the world. Provision was made for those children whose parents could not pay for school. This included non Quaker children. Quaker education influenced the slow and gradual ascension of the public school movement in the United States. Friends in the United States were active in the founding of grammar and high schools during the Colonial era and were supporters of apprenticeships and training programs, connecting real life experiences to educational processes (Lacey, 1988). Friends schools traditionally have stressed active nurturing, as opposed to punishment for transgressions. Children are assumed to be good, not depraved, an idea in contrast to early Colonial views on childrearing.

Each of us is given the birthright of the Inward Teacher, whether Quaker or not. An ethos of respect, nurturance, tolerance, and cooperation is nurtured in the Quaker home and in schools by a weaving of faith through self discipline and its outward manifestation that seeks to express love for one's fellow human beings through work in the wider world. Quakers see their role as developing the whole child and educating that child to follow an inner calling for service.

Education for early Friends was, as it is now, life centered, discerning God's will in the natural and social worlds as the aim, as opposed to memorizing scriptures. Importance was placed on the child's own experience of God. Home, Meeting and school were all considered educational agencies. School was, to early Friends, an outgrowth of the home. Early Quaker schools modeled cooperative learning and an emphasis on international understanding, which is still used in many classrooms. Quaker influence on U.S. public education extended beyond just the emphasis on the practical learning of skills to a strong belief in universal education. Since Quakers believe that all human beings have dignity, schooling was extended to Native Americans and to children from other faiths. In an early form of multicultural education, Quakers used humanistic principles to deconstruct enemy images, seeing all human beings worthy of respect and capable of learning, in contrast to Eurocentric images of Native Americans as barbarians or uncivilized savages.

Community service is an active component of most Quaker education. Such service helps students learn about other cultures so that they can understand the world as others see it. Such an education, based upon spiritual principles resting on the divinity within all human beings, helps pupils perceive global and local interconnectedness and the oneness of the human race.

Because of their testimony of peace, Quakers have thus been an instrumental part, from the beginning, of the growth and development of peace studies as an academic discipline. Most Quaker schools today have formal programs and curricula in educating for peace. At the elementary and secondary levels Quakers educators have produced curricula that promote the study of tolerance, international understanding, and nonviolence. At the university level Quakers in England in 1959 helped to establish the Richardson Institute for Peace and Conflict Research at Lancaster University. In the United States Quaker colleges, including Wilmington (Ohio), Earlham (Indiana), Guilford (North Carolina), and Bryn Mawr, Swarthmore, and Haverford (Pennsylvania) all have peace studies programs. In addition, some Quaker faculty at non-Quaker institutions, such as scholar Ted Herman at Colgate University, have been instrumental in establishing peace studies programs on their campuses. In 1903, in England, Woodbrooke was founded, a Quaker study center for adults that offers courses on peace and conflict, housed in the former family home of the famous British chocolate maker, George Cadbury.

CORE VALUES AND BELIEFS OF FRIENDS

Founded in the mid-seventeenth century in England, the Quaker movement represented a radical wing of the English Reformation. Early Friends took to heart the message preached by George Fox, the founder of the movement, that "Christ has come to teach his people himself" and that individuals have no need for an intermediary, such as a priest or minister, in order that he/she communicate with the Divine. This Inner Light, "Divine Seed," or Spirit of Christ, available to all, to men, women and children alike without regard to economic or social status, is also known as the Inward Teacher (Lacey, 1988). Quakers do not tell each other what to believe. Rather, they trust that each individual has the capacity and the obligation to discern the truth.

Within modern Quakerism the peace testimony of Friends is considered a central and informal "creed," though true creedal adherence was an abomination to early Friends, because they believed that Experience was the true teacher (Whitmore, 2007). The basis for the historic Friends Peace Testimony rests in early Friends' admonition to King Charles of England in 1660, addressing directly his concern about the restive, rebellious sect:

> We utterly deny all outward wars and strife and fightings with outward weapons, for any end or under any pretense whatsoever. And this is our testimony to the whole world. The spirit of Christ, by which we are guided, is

not changeable, so as once to command us from a thing as evil and again to move unto it; and we do certainly know, and so testify to the world, that the spirit of Christ, which leads us into all Truth, will never move us to fight any war against any man with outward weapons, neither for the kingdom of Christ, nor for the kingdoms of this world.

Elton Trueblood, a renowned mid-twentieth century Quaker scholar, has traced the roots of Quaker concern for the world to early Friends "quaking" before the Lord to learn what God was requiring of them. Haverford College Quaker scholar Rufus Jones, a contemporary of Trueblood's and who is often known as a spokesperson for Quaker mysticism, wrote that the mission of Quakers has been "to demonstrate and exhibit a type of religion which reveals the life of God in the lives of men [*sic*]" (Jones, 1941, p. 7) The fruit of the peace testimony is love manifested in many ways, including working on behalf of social justice and with those in need. The causes of war lie in the heart, as Fox and other early Friends knew. "Thus, the Friends' peace testimony was at root a witness to a kingdom already at hand, that is, a call to others to recognize the power of God working in their own lives" (Cronk, 1984).

Friends through the centuries have developed other *testimonies*, which are defined as lived experiences leading to the articulation of certain right orderings of one's life. These have included the testimonies of simplicity, harmony, equality and community, and recently, reverence for the environment. These testimonies are not *prescriptions* or how-to's for how to live one's life, but are considered guides to living, open to new interpretations in the light of the evolution of time and experience. Friends' views on simplicity have their roots in the idea that too much emphasis on the striving for worldly goods as a pursuit in and of itself is a detraction from a direct relationship between the individual and the Spirit, or Divine Seed.

A QUAKER PHILOSOPHY OF EDUCATION

Education has been integral to the development of the Society of Friends, at the same time being intentional and deeply woven into the fabric of Quaker life, from home to Meeting to school. Quaker education has historically stressed the values of a sense of belonging, joy in the world of nature, widening and deepening human relationships, and discovery of high spiritual aspirations through hearing the stories of individuals who have made a difference in the world and within Quakerism (Loukes, 1958).

Key to a Quaker philosophy of education is the belief that each individual has the capacity for discerning the truth. The truth does not solely come from the teacher or mentor. The community or classroom can become a touchstone in which an individual can test his or her individual leadings or insights into the truth. The process of getting clear about a particular discernment implies testing it out in a community of fellow seekers. In this way individuals are accountable to the communities in which they live and learn and the community can support the strengths and leadings of its members. Friends will often ask for "clearness committees" if they are not clear about their discernment. Such committees allow an individual to ascertain if his or her various leadings complement his or her gifts or strengths.

A document developed by Guilford College's Department of Educational Studies outlines the core objective themes for an ideal Quaker education. These include experience and scholarship that promote discovery of the truth, learning in community, wonder at the mystery of being and respect the sacredness of life. Education is continuous, people and cultures have value. There is deep and important ecology of humans and of the natural world, and these must be studied within their local and global contexts. These core values help shape the development of educators who respect individuals, support community, build in values of reflection and communication, respond to the spiritual dimensions of learning and living, value ambiguity and paradox, learn throughout life, seek insight into many cultures, and understand themselves as world citizens (Guilford, n.d.). Since Quakers have neither traditionally relied on "professors," the early Friends' term for priests of the church, nor upon theological hierarchy, an Inward Teacher is available equally to every individual, whether Quaker or not. According to scholar Paul Lacey (1988), scripture, silence and preaching only point the way to the true Teacher. To "mind the spirit" is to yield up to it and then to "answer" or to witness, that is, to help others turn toward their own Inward Teacher. This process of tapping into the Inward Teacher must be done in the context of a community. Early Friends communities were, by their nature, insular places where education in the home and in schools took place. Peace work was a natural outflow of education and worship. Quaker values pointed to a life of service and continue to do so today. Today there are far fewer insular Quaker communities, though service to the world as an ethos remains highly visible.

Early Friends were suspicious of higher education. They feared that *ideas* would be promoted at the expense of *experience and feelings* (Brinton, 1951). Since they had no clergy (this is not true today, as in many parts of the world there are Quaker pastors), early Friends had no use for colleges, which, in the Colonies, were set up originally to train for the ministry.

Pendle Hill, located on the outskirts of Philadelphia, started as a uniquely Quaker theological institution of higher learning in 1930, and today serves as a retreat center for Quakers and non Quakers alike. Pendle Hill to this day does not offer advanced degrees. The nineteenth century saw the development of several degree-granting Quaker institutions.

The ends and means of a spiritually based and practical education cannot be separated. For Quakers, the realm of *ethics* involves how we should follow the will of God in our roles as workers, citizens, partners, parents, lovers and friends. A community *ethos*, at whose root is the Greek word for "habit," and ethical behavior must reinforce one another (Lacey, 1988). "Education is the one peaceful technique for creating changes for the better." In a 1951 lecture at Guilford College, Brinton, the long time director of Pendle Hill and Quaker theologian, laid out the ideals of a Quaker education as the development of both mind and heart, training in the use of the intellect, and practice in the ways of virtue (Brinton, 1951).

Contemporary Quaker educator Parker Palmer, formerly Director of Education at Pendle Hill, has added to Brinton's words the idea of *knowledge based on compassion*. The teacher is a mediator between the subject and the student. The teacher's role is to evoke the truth the student holds within. As Palmer (1998) states, the human heart is the soul of good teaching. The teacher's role is inextricably dependent upon his or her self-knowledge, intellectually, emotionally and spiritually.

Quaker educators stress the importance of nonviolence and strategies for peace in the content of what they teach. What is taught about peace depends upon the developmental needs of the students. For example with elementary aged children Quaker educators might talk about the various aspects of love—caring, empathy, forgiveness, compassion, and friendship—and how they contribute to peace. In middle school, high school and with adults there is an emphasis on the concept of peace itself, together with what a call to peacemaking asks of us. Quaker educators emphasize the importance of peace pedagogy. The classroom becomes an important laboratory where individuals learn to live with each other without resorting to destructive conflict and violence. To do this teachers shape their learning programs with the help and participation of students. This means, on the one hand, building programs based on students' interests and experiences, and on the other, working with students to determine classroom limits and agreed upon accepted behaviors.

Peace educators encourage students to share their own experiences with violence so that students can practice empathy in their classes and learn that their own experiences aren't unique. Pupils may also learn from each other strategies for coping with fears and anxieties that come from living in a world where conflict is ubiquitous. Students with different perspectives may actively (and emotionally) disagree with each other, but the process of hearing (and respecting) each other's views and trying to incorporate the views of others while analyzing conflict and violence becomes an important part of building a democratic learning environment.

For older students the teacher serves as a facilitator who keeps the class moving. He or she asks questions and provides new resources which shed insight into problems. Often opinions need to be clarified and summarized. The teacher does this in a way that helps relate discussions to the goal of that particular lesson. The teacher also checks periodically to see if a discussion is moving in a way agreeable to the group.

Another important function of the teacher is to make sure everyone's point of view is heard in such a way that looking at different perspectives becomes a positive learning experience rather than contending to prove who is right. The peace educator shows a warm concern and interest in the participants, affirming each of them for their contributions. Thus, the teacher in a democratic classroom becomes a mediator, one who maintains the cohesiveness of the learning group, serving as a powerful role model for peaceful behavior. Each participant in the classroom helps construct the truth.

The following section, *People and Programs,* provides several examples of Quaker peace education in practice. There are Quakers mentioned who have worked as academics, teachers and community educators. The selection of programs describes community education and peace studies programs initiated and run by Quakers and includes school based programs.

PEOPLE AND PROGRAMS

People

Kathy Bickmore

Kathy Bickmore is currently Professor of education at the Ontario Institute for Studies in Education (OISE) at the University of Toronto in Canada. By the fall of 1979 at the height of the new anti-draft and anti-nuclear weapons period, she had moved to Cleveland to develop violence transformation programs. Dr. Bickmore subsequently taught at Cleveland State where she conducted collaborative research to support a peace education program in the Cleveland School district called WAVE (Winning against Violence Everywhere), one of the most successful conflict resolution programs in the United States. This program, now led by Carole Close, has established a Center for Conflict Resolution that runs a variety of conflict resolution programs in the urban Cleveland area. In Cleveland every school now has a designated conflict advisor and a peer mediation program.

Beginning with facilitating initial workshops with this curricula, she began training high school students and teachers in the promotion of the principles of nonviolence. In 1984 Dr. Bickmore authored, with John Looney and Prill Goldthwait, two colleagues associated with the American Friends Service Committee, *Alternatives to Violence: A Manual for Teaching Peacemaking to Youth and Adults* (Bickmore, 1984). She edited a special edition of *Theory and Practice,* "Teaching Conflict Resolution: Preparation for Pluralism" in 1997 (Bickmore, 1997). She has written numerous articles about teaching conflict resolution and does research on peace education in schools. In addition, she teaches an undergraduate teacher education course, "Managing Conflict in Classrooms and School Workplaces," and a graduate course, "Teaching Conflict and Conflict Resolution."

Dr. Bickmore's work has addressed a key issue in peace education, which is the risk that an undue focus on issues around international peace education, including global war, faces the problem of being irrelevant to youth facing conflicts that are occurring in their everyday lives. Kathy Bickmore recognizes that peace education must bridge the local to the global. She teaches peer mediation and peacemaking as a kind of service learning, engaging pupils in peacemaking in their communities and engaging processes of thinking about inclusive peacemaking as active democratic citizenship.

Elise and Kenneth Boulding

This dynamic couple and their 50 year partnership has had tremendous influence both on modern Quakerism and on the development of the field of peace studies. The life and work of Quaker sociologist Elise Boulding, a matriarch of the twentieth century peace research movement, has been a celebration of the unique contributions of women in visualizing, making, and building global peace and of the importance of families as laying the foundation for peace. Women's acculturation toward nurturing, networking and connections have afforded them opportunities for learning those skills most needed for building a better world, a theme Elise Boulding uses in many of her writings. The founder of numerous organizations and networks in peace research, peace studies, women's studies, futures, and activism, Elise Boulding has made major contributions to the contemporary fields of peace education, peace studies social reform.

Elise Boulding and her husband, Kenneth were cofounders in 1965 of the International Peace Research Association (IPRA) and in 1970 helped to found COPRED, the Consortium on Peace, Research, Education and Development, the North American branch of IPRA. The author of numerous publications, Boulding's books include *Building a Global Civic Culture: Educating for An Interdependent World* (E. Boulding, 1988) *One Small Plot of Heaven: Reflections on Quaker Family Life by a Quaker Sociologist* (E. Boulding, 1989b) and *Cultures of Peace: the Hidden Side of History* (E. Boulding, 2000). Elise and Kenneth helped found the peace studies program at the University of Colorado and Elise was a founder of the peace studies program at Dartmouth College. Both of them have used their platforms as academics to promote peace education through the academy and have both been peace activists.

Kenneth, an economist and Quaker poet, who died in 1993, was considered a major contributor to early thinking on systems theory. He wrote a peace study guide published by Friends World Committee for Consultation (K. Boulding, 1942).

George Lakey

George Lakey, the founder and executive director of Training for Change, has been a leader in the field of nonviolent social change since the 1960s and has published extensively for both activist and academic readers. Lakey has most distinguished himself as a community educator. He has worked in the United States with mineworkers, steelworkers, and civil rights leaders, and, internationally, with South African antiapartheid activists, Cambodian human rights organizers, and many others.

George Lakey has published numerous book chapters, pamphlets, and articles on social change, and his work has been translated into at least six languages. His books include *A Manual for Direct Action* (Lakey & Oppenheimer, 1964), *Powerful Peacemaking: a Strategy for a Living Revolution* (Lakey, 1987), and *Grassroots and Nonprofit Leadership: A Guide for Organizations in Changing Times* (Lakey, 1995). Although he has taught peace studies courses at the University of Pennsylvania, Haverford College, Temple University, and Swarthmore, George Lakey is best known for giving leadership to a number of social change movements. In late 1989 he led a team of Westerners in Sri Lanka who for 24 hours a day accompanied human-rights activists at risk of assassination. He has done neighborhood organizing, once successfully preventing tree-cutting and another time creating a neighborhood festival to celebrate ethnic diversity. He cofounded the Movement for a New Society, which for nearly 20 years specialized in organizational innovation. Lakey founded and directed the Philadelphia Jobs with Peace Campaign, a coalition of labor, civil rights, poverty and peace groups. He was a designer of and staffed the Campaign to Stop the B-1 Bomber and Promote Peace Conversion, which mobilized sufficiently to gain cancellation of the B-1 in 1977 and raise the visibility of the concept of economic conversion. He was director of A Quaker Action Group when it assisted Puerto Rican nationalists in stopping the U.S. Navy from using the inhabited island of Culebra for target practice. Lakey was also a founder of Men Against Patriarchy, which organized pioneering projects for the early men's antisexism movement of the mid-70s.

Parker Palmer

The ideas of contemporary Quaker educator Parker Palmer are the modern manifestations of the historical beliefs and teachings of early Friends, as they have evolved to the present, particularly Friends as educators. While not known as a peace educator per se, his ideas resonate with the idea of peace as being both a pedagogical process and as an inward state.

Palmer is the founder and Senior Partner of the Center for Courage Renewal. The center's mission, as stated on the website "is an educational non profit that strengthens individuals, professions and communities through retreats and programs that help people reconnect with who they are and with what they do" (http://www.couragerenewal.org/). A member of Madison, Wisconsin Friends Meeting, Parker Palmer is the former educational director of Pendle Hill, a Quaker retreat center in Wallingford, PA.

Palmer is best known for his workshops, speaking and writing on the role of the teacher and of the importance of self searching and knowledge, and of the process of spiritual seeking toward vocational calling. His seven books include *A Hidden Wholeness, Let Your Life Speak* (2004), *The Courage to Teach* (Palmer, 1998), *The Active Life* (Palmer, 1999), *To Know as We are Known* (Palmer, 1993), *The Company of Strangers* (Palmer, 1983) *and the Promise of Paradox* (Palmer, 2008). Parker Palmer eloquently points to the importance of *community,* as educators actively connect students to their own Truths within themselves. The role of the teacher is to draw out the truth each student holds within. To reach the human heart, both in the student and teacher, is the real goal of education (Palmer, 1998). A setting in which Truth is practiced, the ideal form of education is one in which intense listening and speaking occur.

Programs

Alternatives to Violence and Help Increase the Peace (AVP/HIPP)

The Alternatives to Violence Program (AVP) is a Quaker inspired and developed community-building experience that, in prison settings, engages "inside" trainers (inmates who have been trained in AVP) and "outside" trainers (volunteers from the community who have been trained), to address, in a 15 hour format for each workshop, the root causes of violence, oppression and injustice, seeking to transform oppressive structures, beginning with each individual's experience with violence. There are three levels of workshops, from basic through training for facilitators, each held over a week-end in a prison. AVP was begun several decades ago, and has proved successful to those whom it touches, both the inmates and the volunteer trainers and participants. AVP is now used internationally in peacebuilding efforts, including workshops in Bolivia, Burundi, Kenya, Rwanda, Uganda, and Colombia (for further information, visit http://www.avpusa.org/).

Help Increase the Peace (HIPP) is the youth version of AVP. Conceived in Syracuse, New York and modeled after AVP, the format of the workshops is essentially identical, although some activities used are different, based on HIPP's serving a younger population. HIPP is being used in schools, in community settings, mostly in the U.S. but there is growing international interest in HIPP. Since it began in 1991 it has expanded to nineteen states. Now based in Baltimore, HIPP teaches young people and adults communication skills for conflict resolution. It confronts prejudice and teaches positive social change skills. The training introduces alternatives to violence and anti-bullying techniques and allows participants to practice various options by modeling and role playing. Exercises include self-affirmation and discovery of how insensitivity can magnify problems (http://www.afsc.org/hipp/).

American Friends Service Committee

The American Friends Service Committee (AFSC) carries out service, development, social justice and peace programs throughout the world. Founded by Quakers in 1917 to provide conscientious objectors with an opportunity to aid civilian war victims, AFSC attracts the support and partnership of people of many races, religions, nations, and cultures. Its endeavors are based on the Quaker belief in the worth of every person and faith in the power of love to overcome violence and injustice. The organization's mission and achievements won worldwide recognition in 1947 when it accepted the Nobel Peace Prize with the British Friends Service Council on behalf of all Quakers.

The AFSC is directed by a Quaker board and staffed by Quakers and other people of faith who share Friends' desire for peace and social justice. Various branches and local chapters of AFSC conduct their own peace education programs. In Los Angeles since the 1970s, the American Friends Service Committee's Middle East Peace Program has brought together Jews, Muslims, Christians, and others in Southern California to work in common cause for peace and justice in the Middle East. Volunteers and staff organize speaking tours, public events, and other educational campaigns to work for peace and justice in the Middle East. The Southeast regional office in Atlanta has a similar program that began in 1976.

The Connecticut Program Office of AFSC in Hartford, Connecticut, is the founder and lead partner of the Connecticut Coalition for Peace and Justice (CCPJ), a greater Hartford coalition of peace activists that has spawned numerous local peace and justice groups in communities around Hartford. AFSC-CT works with Connecticut United for Peace, a state-wide coalition of peace and justice groups, in promoting grassroots education about the war in Iraq and the conflicts in the Middle East. Many of its educational efforts focus on local drug violence, poverty and unemployment, discrimination against immigrants, as well as racial disparities in housing, educational opportunity, and incarceration rates in Connecticut.

World-wide AFSC provides humanitarian relief to victims of natural disasters, war and oppression. The American Friends Service Committee is a practical expression of the faith of the Religious Society of Friends (Quakers). Committed to the principles of nonviolence and justice, it seeks in its work and witness to draw on the transforming power of love, human and divine. The AFSC community works to change conditions and relationships both in the world and in ourselves, which threaten to overwhelm what is precious in human beings (http://www.afsc.org/).

Creative Response to Conflict

Created in 1972 by the New York Quaker Project on Community Conflict, and initially known as Children's Creative Response to Conflict, the organization developed a practical and theoretical framework for teaching nonviolence through character and social skills development, using an innovative experiential approach incorporating multiple learning modalities. In 1994 it incorporated as Creative Response to Conflict, Inc. Besides the central office in Nyack, NY, CRC has affiliate branches throughout the United States, in Europe, and in South and Central America. CRC materials have been translated into nineteen languages including Serbian, Croatian, German, Russian, Spanish, and Welsh.

Under the guidance of director Priscilla Prutzman CRC designs and facilitates workshops and programs on social skills and conflict resolution for parents, young people, and those who work with young people from all racial, ethnic, class, ability, sexual orientation, and language backgrounds. CRC's organizational mission is to achieve a nonviolent and just world by helping youth and those who work with youth to learn to resolve conflict though cooperation, communication, affirmation, bias awareness, bullying prevention, mediation, and creative problem solving (for more info, see http://www.crc-ny.org/).

Friends Council on Education

FCE (Friends Council on Education) is an umbrella organization of K-12 Friends Schools, offering resources and programs to nurture and support the life of the schools. The FCE web site describes the following philosophical ideas for Quaker education are listed. Embedded in these concepts are the testimonies of Friends: simplicity, community, harmony, peace, equality and global stewardship (http://www.friendscouncil.org/).

> Friends believe that each person has the capacity for goodness and a responsibility to attain that goodness. Our schools create deliberate moral communities—communities that value the process of reflection and inquiry, and are rooted in the fundamental Quaker belief in truth as a process of continuing revelation. Quaker pedagogy is based on the principles of teachers as caring facilitators of the learning process, dialogue as the foundation of learning in the classroom, and curricula reflecting Friends testimonies and values. Friends schools support the development of persons who are creative thinkers, peacemakers, and confident humanitarians, contributing to responsive and responsible public leadership in the world. The Friends Council on Education supports the development of teachers and leaders who can make this possible.

> Friends schools teach students to:

> Resolve conflict with alternatives to violence through thoughtful listening and active engagement with different perspectives. Value and embrace the diversity of cultures and religions represented in their schools, and in the larger national and global communities. Search for truth through asking questions thoughtfully, respectfully, and responsibly.

> Develop the courage to take action in alignment with their core moral beliefs. Work for the good of society through active service learning activities in their communities and around the world—"letting one's life speak."

Peace education is embedded within these pedagogical processes. Each member Friends School carries out the activities of peace education in accordance with the institution's individual mission.

Following is a sample of a curriculum currently used by one Friends School, the Meeting School in Rindge, New Hampshire. The Meeting School (TMS), founded 50 years ago in rural New Hampshire, is a small co-educational boarding school which is also a working farm. Students live and work in community. TMS's peace education program is embedded within its mission and the Quaker testimonies are lived out both in the work students do in classes, but also in governing structures, which fully involve all members of the school and follow Quaker principles of unity in decision making.

All students are required to take a peacemaking class. This includes a leadership development and youth empowerment component. The format is experiential. Students study the role of violence and oppression in their own lives and how these relate both to school structures and those of the wider society. Students study nonviolent communication as well as contemporary peace and justice issues. Engagement in community-based projects is an important element of the curriculum. Topics are generated by student interest. Examples have included a school wide Hunger Banquet, a campaign to stop eating all meat not grown sustainably on the school grounds, and the development of a meditation group (Garrett, personnl communication, 2008).

Peace Studies

Many Quaker academics have been involved in setting up peace studies programs that address the effects of political and social violence, the causes of this violence, and what can be done to resolve conflicts peacefully and work toward a more just and sustainable world. The rapid growth in these programs in colleges and universities in North America and Western Europe reflects alarm about growing levels of violence (the nuclear threat, low intensity conflict, the cost of the arms race, environmental destruction, domestic violence, ethnic and regional conflicts) and the need for real and practical peacebuilding skills. Those concerned about global issues are turning to education as a means to heighten awareness, to stimulate research into alternative forms of dispute resolution, and to promote nonviolent alternatives and methods to create a more sustainable planet.

Students can now major in peace studies at over 350 universities and colleges (Harris & Shuster, 2006), although many may take a single course or choose a certificate program, which are growing in popularity. Multidisciplinary peace studies courses, often involving several academic departments including political science, sociology, history, women's studies and psychology, capture the dynamic ways that the problems of conflict and violence erupt in human communities and across the world and offer opportunities for analyses and solutions.

Traditional peace studies courses found in political science departments focus on the international political system, and its penchant for war. Sometimes this type of peace curricula has been called "security studies," with an emphasis on the study of traditional forms of security such as the military. More recently, because of a change in the nature of global warfare, the focus has moved to a more in-depth look at ethnic and religious rivalries within a nation, as opposed to wars between nations.

Since the beginning of the twenty-first century, there has been considerable growth in the field of peace studies in the areas of global sustainability and civic peace. Instructors in communications departments on university campuses often teach courses on media violence, mediation, and negotiation. Professors in psychology departments teach about aggression and human violence. Most recently schools of social work and criminal justice have been offering courses to explain domestic violence and civil crimes. Schools of education have also started to offer courses and degree programs on school violence and the teaching of classroom skills in conflict mediation. Quaker teachers found in these institutions of higher education have promoted curricula of conflict resolution, antibullying and violence prevention. Learning how to achieve peace is an extremely complicated undertaking that requires years of study and practice. It is hopeful that peace studies continues to grow as an academic discipline.

CONCLUSION

Quakers have been involved in peace education throughout their 400 year history. These examples of people and programs illustrate both the commitment that Quakers have to peace education and the diversity of approaches. Quaker efforts to create and preserve peace, in informal community settings as well as formal schools and colleges, suggest a different way of educating people than the traditional authoritarian approaches to education. Quaker educators believe in empowering their students to address issues of violence in their lives and to take action to build a more peaceful world. These educational efforts are not just to provide knowledge about the problems of violence and strategies for peace, but also to encourage students to seek solutions to bring about peaceful resolution of conflicts. Rather than relying on rules, standards and set curricula, Quaker approaches to education are child centered and depend upon building relations, where pupils are not the passive receptors of knowledge but rather the cocreators of knowledge.

Quaker educators have argued forcefully against wars and other forms of state sponsored terror. Through international Quaker organizations such as the American Friends Service Committee, Quakers have taught nonviolence skills to thousands of people. Quaker work within school and academic settings has provided peace curricula and content areas that address the many forms of violence and skills needed for peace. Spiritual belief in the divine spark that exists within all people have made Friends leaders in a multicultural approach to education that seeks to draw upon different social and religious traditions in the pursuit of truth.

Peace has never been separate from Quaker pedagogy. Quakers first educated in the home and were instrumental in promoting public education in America. Since Colonial times, Quakers have established schools and colleges which promote the values and spiritual beliefs of Friends. The teachings of Quakers have always had, at their core, the concept of love, love of one's fellow humans, love of the gift of life and love of the natural world. If love is at the heart of things, it naturally follows that when love becomes obscured or is out of site, in a suffering world, where darkness sometimes reigns, each of us must act, in a restorative way, to work toward a world where Goodness and Light may once again prevail. This work, within the context of community, is at the heart of Friends' work for peace in the world.

REFERENCES

Bickmore, K. (1984). *Alternatives to violence: A manual for teaching peacemaking to youth and adults*. Cleveland, OH: Cleveland Friends Meeting.

Bickmore, K. (1997, Winter). Teaching Conflict Resolution: Preparation for Pluralism. *Theory Into Practice, 36*(1), 2.

Boulding, E. (1988). *Building a global civic culture: Education for an interdependent world*. New York: Teachers College Press.

Boulding, E. (1989a). *One small plot of heaven*. Wallingford, PA: Pendle Hill Press.

Boulding, E. (1989b). *One small plot of heaven: Reflections on family life by a Quaker sociologist*. Wallingford, PA: Pendle Hill Press.

Boulding, E. (2000). *Cultures of peace: The hidden side of history*. Syracuse, NY: Syracuse University Press.

Boulding, K. (1942). *A peace study outline: The practice of the love of God*. Philadelphia: Philadelphia Yearly Meeting Book Committee.

Brinton, H. (1951). *The function of a Quaker College*. Greensboro, NC: Guilford College.

Cronk, S. (1984). *Peace be with you: A study of the spiritual basis of the friends peace testimony*. Philadelphia: Tract Association of Friends.

Guilford. (n.d.). *The process of developing program objectives for education studies at Guilford College*. Greensboro, NC: Guilford College.

Harris, I., & Shuster, A. (Eds.). (2006). *Global directory of peace studies and conflict resolution programs*. San Francisco: Peace Studies Association.

Jones, R. (1941). *The vital cell*. Philadelphia: Book Committee, Philadelphia Yearly Meeting of Friends.

Lacey, P. (1988). *Education and the Inward Teacher* (Vol. Pendle Hill Pamphlet 278). Wallingford, PA: Pendle Hill.

Lakey, G. (1987). *Powerful peacemaking: A strategy for a living revolution*. Philadelphia: New Society Press.

Lakey, G. (1995). *Grass-roots and non-profit leadership: A guide for organizations in changing times*. Philadelphia: New Society Press.

Lakey, G., & Oppenheimer, M. (1964). *A manual for direct action*. Chicago: Quadrangle Books.

Loukes, H. (1958). *Friends and their children: A study in Quaker education* (2nd ed.). London: Friends Home Service Committee.

Palmer, P. (1983). *The company of strangers*. New York: Crossroad.

Palmer, P. (1993). *To know as we are known: Education as a spiritual journey*. San Francisco: Harper San Francisco.

Palmer, P. (1998). *The courage to teach: Exploring the inner landscape of a teacher's life*. San Francisco: Jossey-Bass.

Palmer, P. (1999). *The active life*. San Francisco: Jossey-Bass.

Palmer, P. (2004). *A hidden wholeness: A journey toward an undivided life*. San Francisco: Libri.

Palmer, P. (2008). *The promise of paradox: A celebration of contradictions in the Christian life*. San Francisco: Jossey-Bass.

Prutzman, P., Stern, L., Leonard, B. M., & Bodenhamer, G. (1988). *The friendly classroom for a small planet*. Philadelphia: New Society.

Ruddick, S. (1995). *Maternal thinking: Toward A politics of peace*. Boston: Beacon Press.

Whitmore, C. (2007). *Practicing peace: A devotional walk through the Quaker tradition*. Notre Dame, IN: Catherine Sorin Books.

CHAPTER 6

HINDUISM AND PEACE EDUCATION

Priyankar Upadhyaya

INTRODUCTION

Hinduism, one the oldest and most varied of our great religions, is universally acknowledged as an outstanding resource of values of peace and tolerance.[1] Often credited as a showcase of ethnic pluralism and multireligious synergy, the Hindu way of life is endowed with such transformative dictums as: *"Ahimsa Paramo Dharma"* (nonviolence is the ultimate religion) (Upadhyaya, 2007. p. 98), and *"Vasudhaiv Kutumbkam"* (the whole world is our family) (*Maha Upanishad,* Chapter 6, Verse 72). This image of peacefulness has surmounted the streaks of violence that often coincides with the Hindu discourse on peace (Gandhi, 1999; Upadhyaya, 2009). Seemingly Hinduism holds a rich promise to unfurl edifying pedagogies to explore religion and spirituality as potent sites for peacebuilding—a concern that has lately assumed salience in peace studies (Appleby & Hesburgh, 1999; Johnston & Sampson, 1994; Kazanjian & Laurence, 2000; Sponge, 2006).

Spirituality, Religion, and Peace Education, pp. 99–113
Copyright © 2010 by Information Age Publishing
All rights of reproduction in any form reserved.

However the long and prolix lineage of Hinduism with myriad transferences defies a precise representation of its peacefulness. One has to reckon with far too many texts, contexts, and contrary interpretations. It might however be possible to conjure up a composite template exemplifying major visions of peacebuilding in Hinduism through its long tracks from its foundational cannons to the modern times. Hence this chapter attempts a broad-brush view of how peace was envisaged and disseminated in diverse epochs of Hinduism. It tries to bring into a continuum the impartation of spiritual peace through ancient Hindu scriptures[2] and how it was reconnected through mass based spiritual movements like *Bhakti* during the medieval era, then transmitted down to the twentieth century when it infused the pedagogy of tolerance and nonviolence as enunciated by Gandhi and many others. It also explores the history of the "lived religion" of Hindus and their contemporary beliefs and practices to unravel the elements of social and multicultural peace which might serve as an instructive educational trajectory to harness peace in societies marked with social diversities and economic disparities.

HOLISTIC VISIONS OF PEACE

Notwithstanding the acceptance of vastly disparate viewpoints, Hinduism contains a distinct stream of spiritual values which has continuously engaged the attention of seers, sages, and common masses. Most outstanding of these values is the quest of an inclusive peacefulness that transfer norms for the individual and the community. The *Vedas* and the *Upanishads* for instance offer one of the earliest references of a global family. The central concern in these highly revered treatises is the realization of the essential unity of the entire humanity in the spirit of "Live and Let Live." There are countless visions of holistic peace. *Yajurveda* for instance declares, "One who sees all creatures as if they were his own selves and himself in others—his mind rests in peace" (*Yajurveda* 40-46). The search for the truth of unity transcends the barrier between human lives and the larger universe. A celebrated prayer of peace from *Atharvaveda* thus invokes: "Peace be to earth and to airy spaces! Peace to the heaven, peace to the waters, peace to the plants and peace to the trees!" (*Atharvaveda* 19.9.14). Such unison with nature prompted Nobel laureate Rabindranath Tagore to call Hinduism as the religion of forests.3

The other recurring theme in Hindu discourse is *Ahimsa* or nonviolence. *Mahabharata*, despite being a war treatise, also accords the highest premium to nonviolence: "Nonviolence towards all beings is the highest duty. Nonviolence, speaking truth, and forgiveness are definitely more important than adherence to Vedas" (*Mahabharata* 11.12-14). The ancient sage *Patanjali* thus equates peace with mental bliss (*Chitta Prasadam*) which can be brought by practicing a sense of nonenmity kindness, forgiveness and avoidance in order to maintain a vibrant peace.[4] There are also instructive narratives in the *Mahabharata* when Lord Krishna highlights the search for common ground in order to negotiate peace between the two warring Pandwas and *Kurus* (Appadorai, 1981, p. 31).

Leading Hindu texts have mostly favored peaceful means to resolve a dispute. The use of coercion has been seen as the last resort and often counterproductive. There are frequent calls to eradicate the sources of enmity rather than achieving peace through victory. The *Mahabharata*, the grand treatise of warfare, declared, "Victory through a war is deplorable if it could be achieved without a war. Nothing is greater than a victory gained through dharma." And further declared, "Victory creates enmity. The defeated is engrossed in suffering. Having kept himself aloof from victory and defeat, the peaceable person sleeps undisturbed" (Upadhyaya, 2007, p. 178). The *Mahabharata* also brings out the negative ramifications of warfare, 'No war is better than waging war. A person of knowledge may have no truck with war" (*Mahabharata* 26.1). Or else the logic continues, "War is thorough and thorough distress. Who remains unhurt while hurting others" (*Mahabharata* 70.53). It is no wonder Gandhi finds the futility of violence as the core message of the *Mahabharata*.[5]

Commitment to peaceful means and nonviolence infused the core of Jainism and Buddhism—the two concurrent Indian religions founded by *Mahavira* and Buddha.[6] Both streams decry violence as a sin and emphasize nonviolence as an article of faith in their respective system. While *Mahavira* included nonviolence (Ahimsa) as one of the five intrinsic virtues to attain inner peace and happiness (Basham, 1958), the Buddha sought conquest through and by the power of true faith, compassion and love. He was emphatic that: "Enmity is never extinguished by enmity. It is effaced by friendliness. This is the eternal moral principle" (cited in Upadhyaya, 2007, p. 276).

The early Vedic schools (*Ashrams*) imparted the spiritual knowledge to young *Brahmans* to cultivate them as future priests. In course of time, pupils of the other two higher castes *Kshatriyas* and *Vaishyas* were also admitted to the privilege of education.[7] The post-*Vedic* system saw the emergence and proliferation of varied centers of spiritual learning including Buddhist Monasteries and *Vedantic Mathas* led by *Shankaracharyas*.[8] The traditional Hindu mode of learning in Sanskrit (the elite language) however became less and less popular among Hindus during the Mughal and British rule.[9] New cults of popular religious learning such as in the *Bhakti* tradition, in course, articulated the spiritual message of love in regional languages and local dialects involving people of all castes and status.

PLURALISM AND DIALOGUE

The liberal and plural character of Hinduism and its capacity to assimilate reforms and exogenous ideas reveals an instructive model of intercultural and interreligious peace. Often described as a river, constantly refreshed by fresh streams, the Hindu civilization has shown a lively propensity to respect and absorb traditions and rituals from other cultures. Tribal religious traditions in India and "village Hinduism" are examples of "little traditions" within Hinduism.[10]

Admittedly Hinduism lacks a cohesive character which typically defines other major religions of the world. It has admitted the fusion of the divergent and often contrary viewpoints since the very beginning (Radhakrishnan, 1993).[11] There is neither a single founder, nor a holy book that represents Hinduism quintessentially and it does not ordain its adherents to accept any one singular path of worship. No aspect of Hinduism claims monopoly of truth either in its vision of God or in the paths to self realization, salvation. Seemingly Hinduism comes out as a mosaic with no singular vision claiming the centerpiece. Often defined as a way of life or a culture, Hinduism embodies a range of creeds and cultural norms and "little traditions" which imbue the quotidian life of its followers.

The intrinsic countenance of plurality relates perhaps to the fact that Hinduism did not exist like a single uniform religion in ancient India. Many doubt if Hinduism is a religion indeed; they construe it as a collection of many forms of belief and practice loosely linked together (Knipe, 1991, p. 2). Some influential opinions hold that the term "Hinduism" was floated by the British colonialists as an ethnographic expression to connote the religious traditions of the non-Muslim majority who lived beyond the Indus River. Hinduism thus accorded structure and coherence to the European experience of the Indian culture and served the administrative needs of British rulers to classify the Indian population into large aggregate categories such as "Hindus," "Buddhists," "Jains," and so forth (Dalmia & H von Stietencron, 1995, pp. 20-21).[12] There are of course opinions to the contrary which discerns a continuing lineage of Hinduism since early Harappan-Vedic period to the modern phase (Malkani, 1993; Savarkar, 1938).

Amid these contestations, the description of "Hinduism" has been endorsed by the Indian modernizers as an overarching religious identity—a position which has been accepted in course by the majority of Hindus as a self description.[13] But ascription to Hinduism as a singular identity has not diluted the lineage of tolerance and the impulse of multicultural living. There is a general endorsement of the diverse and accommodative character of Hinduism notwithstanding the political mobilization by the so called forces of *Hindutava* in recent past.[14]

The respect for plurality has been equally matched by the spirit of dialogue as the best course of learning and education (Sen, 2005).[15] Traditional Hindu texts are replete with such dictum as: "*Vade Vade Jayate Tatva Bodho*" (through continuous dialogue alone does one arrive at the core truth) (Panda, 2004, p. 2). The reconciliation of diverse viewpoints has been intrinsic to Hindu quest for truth. Even the nature of divinity has been subjected to intellectual debates through the *Upanishads* and by Sufi and *Bhakti* mystics of medieval times to religious leaders in the modern era. The *Rig-Veda* thus pronounced "*Ekah va idam vi babhuv sarvam*" (That which is one has multiplied unto all) (*Rig-Veda* 8.59.2). And further "*Ekam Sad Vipra bahudha vadanti*" (the truth is one, the sages express it variously) (*Rig-Veda* 1.164.46).

The willingness to receive worthy ideas from all quarters has been a constant feature of Hinduism. The *Rig-Veda* thus says: "*A no bhadrah Krtavo yantu Vishvatah*" (May noble and auspicious thoughts come to us from all over the Universe) (*Rig-Veda* 1.89.1). In the similar vein, Lord Krishna declares in the *Bhagvat Gita*: "Whosoever comes to me, through whatsoever form, I reach him; all men are struggling through paths that in the end lead to Me" (Gita Ch. IV, verse 11). Romila Thapar, an eminent historian notices "the striking absence of fanaticism in the Hindu tradition" and how even dissidence was accommodated by allowing it a separate identity, "both independent within its own terms and yet a part of society" (Thapar, 1978, pp. 33, 36). Such a dialogical tradition and a nondualistic understanding tends to create a public space for negotiation and conflict resolution (Gandhi, 1995, p. 3).

The unique display of cultural pluralism seemingly attracted religious and cultural communities from outside India to find a preferred home in India. The inventory includes Syrian Christians Jews, *Parsi* and *Bhais* who arrived in different phases of migrations. The plural ethos of Hinduism enriched through its interface with Buddhism and Jainism and its creative encounter with Islam inspired a range of multireligious rituals and practices.[16] Hindus accepted the Buddha as the ninth incarnation of God, and even today Buddha figures in *Dashavatara Strotra* are recited daily by devout Hindus. Similarly the Indo-Islamic cultural confluence is manifest all over the country in thousands of intercommunity shrines, *dargahs*, and pilgrimages, which are revered by all communities.[17]

The dynamic evolution of Hinduism saw the emergence of many iconoclasts and the religious reformers who transcended the religious boundaries to enhance their cultural experience. For instance, *Dara Shikoh*, the Mughal Emperor *Shah Jahan's* beloved son translated the *Upanishads* (Hindu religious scriptures) into Persian with the aid of Hindu pundits. The holiest Hindu, the city of Varanasi, is a quintessential example of such syncretism. This oldest city of India is often hailed as a gathering place of all religions and cultures wherein devotees of all religions including both Hindus and Muslims actively participate in each other's festivals (Upadhyaya, 2010). Such interreligious synergy has encouraged voluntary cultural assimilation of groups, without either compulsion or conversion becoming an issue. The shared religious and cultural practices in the public space have facilitated a peaceful transaction of intercommunity demotic superstitious and local practices (Ahmad, 1984). An instructive instance is the practice of Hindu and Muslim soldiers offering respective religious prayers side-by-side which often leading to syncretistic modes of worship (Bayly, 1985).

BHAKTI: DEVOTIONAL RELIGION

Although the Vedic mode of education contained edifying norms and values about peacefulness, yet its scope remained confined only to a limited section of the community. Only the high caste pupil was entitled to receive the education in Sanskrit which was not the language of common people. However, the emergence of popular strands of Hinduism during post the *Vedic* era liberated it from the shackles of elitism and made it a people's movement. Nothing is as significant as is the *Bhakti* movement of devotional religion which was led by saint-poets both men and women from all regions and castes. The word *Bhakti* draws from the verb *Bhaj* which literally means adoration. Most of the *Bhakti* songs are in regional languages like Tamil, Kannada, Marathi, Gujarati, and Hindi, rather than in Sanskrit. Poets composed their devotional songs and prayers in regional languages and local dialects. Driven by the pain and suffering in their material surrounding, the *Bhakti* protagonists expressed the love for the deity whom they worshiped and from whom they received the joy of personal communion. Instead of expressing anger and hate they found solace in expressing love and devotion to God and to fellow beings. This revolutionary transference opened up gates for scores of downtrodden masses from lower castes into the mainstream of Hinduism through such secular sects as *Chaitanya, Warkari and Kabir Panth*. By devotion to one's Lord that renounced all other loyalties, one could inwardly defy many of the conventions of caste, class, and gender, while outwardly conforming to them. It also made it possible for the devotee to accept the insights of other traditions. Hinduism being a "lived religion" of people readily adopted the proliferation of the *Bhakti* tradition within its folds.

The spiritual traditions *Bhakti* also intersects theologically with the Sufi tradition of Islam; both emphasize love, tolerance, and accommodation as the essence of enlightenment. There are many poets who influenced both *Bhakti* and Sufi traditions and demonstrated ways in which they could be brought together. This confluence paved the way for Hindus and Muslims to transcend their religious insularity and enrich each other's cultural practices (Alam, 1999; Burman, 1996; Sikand, 2003). The popular songs of Sufi poet-saints like *al-Hallaj, Baba Farid, Kabir Das, Sheikh Mohammad, Latib Saheb, Lalla, Shah Muni,* and *Shishunal Sharif Sahib* created a composite ethos of amity and understanding between the two faiths. Kabir Das, the fifteenth century poet-saint rejected ramparts of religious and caste divide and espoused for the essential unity of mankind. He is equally revered in both as a follower of Bhakti and also as a Sufi and again, the legend is that both Hindu and Muslim sparred bitterly over his remains.[18]

PEACE AS SOCIAL REFORM

The evocation of religious values of peace and social harmony intrinsic to Hindu ancient scriptures and in the lived tradition of *Bhakti* were carried forward in course by various religious movements. These movements were led by a chain of social reformers and leaders who reinterpreted various tenets of ancient Hindu texts in a progressive way thus opening doors for the common masses. Using religious resources, these leading voices raised questions related to structural and cultural violence. Interestingly most of these reforms looked at education as a transformative tool and set up new educational institutions to carry out their societal reforms.

Raja Rammohan Roy (1774-1833) was one of the early religious reformers to raise awareness against idol worship and such superstitious cultural practices like widow burning, polygamy and child marriage. His work drew from such Hindu scriptures like the *Upanishads* and the *Gita* to undo the scourge of the caste system, untouchability and oppression of women. In similar vein, Swami Dayanand Saraswati (1824-1883) used indigenous Hindu discourses to oppose such oppressive cultural practices as untouchability and prohibition of widow remarriage. To this end he established Arya Samaj which, in time, inspired the foundation of several hundred schools and colleges throughout India to spread the spiritual values of social equality and development in the Hindu community.[19] Most outstanding of these reformers was Vivekanand (1863-1902) who introduced teaching of *Vedanta* and Yoga to the West and accorded Hinduism a status as a world religion. In his interpretation of *Advaita* philosophy, he found everyone as being a representative of divinity, and thus, worthy of dignity and equal treatment. He opposed caste discrimination and emphasized the task of ending poverty and illiteracy as critical religious work. No spiritual and religious attainments according to him were possible amid such endemic poverty.[20] Vivekananda founded the

Ramakrishna Mission which continues to remain an active site of peace education and spiritual learning in India and around the world today. There are several hundred educational institutions inspired and supported by the Ramkrishna Mission.

Rabindranath Tagore (1861-1941) was yet another face of Hinduism whose life and work is a great source of peace education. Tagore's writings, including the much celebrated *Gitanjali,* drew inspiration both from the Hindu spiritual scripture and India's diverse religious traditions. He looked at education as the transformative agent and felt that "the imposing tower of misery which today rests on the heart of India has its sole foundation in the absence of education. Caste divisions, religious conflicts, aversion to work, precarious economic conditions—all centre on this single factor" (Sen, 2001). Tagore set up an innovative system of education at small township of Santiniketan (Abode of Peace) which draws on India's spiritual tradition as well as cultural influences from abroad. Nothing, perhaps, expresses his values as clearly as a poem in *Gitanjali,*

> Where the mind is without fear, and the head is held high; Where knowledge is free; Where the world has not been broken up into fragments by narrow domestic walls;... Where the clear stream of reason has not lost its way into the dreary desert sand of dead habit;... Into that heaven of freedom, my Father, let my country awake. (Sen, 2001)[21]

GANDHI: ETHICS FOR PEACE

Mahatma Gandhi is definitely the tallest apostle of peace education who was from within the spiritual tradition of Hinduism. While he respected the spiritual values of all faiths and religions and derived inspiration for selfless service as much from Hinduism as from Christianity and Islam, his basic concepts of nonviolence (*Ahimsa*) and power of truth (*Satyagraha*) and sacrifice is permeated by Hindu philosophy. He also successfully employed the religious terminology to lace his commitment for intercommunal harmony and elimination of structural violence in all its insidious forms— untouchability, exploitation, and inequality. He popularized the term *Daridra Narayan* given by Vivekananda in his appeal to offer care, dignity and love for the poor from all religions. Drawing from various Hindu perspectives as also from other religions, Gandhi envisaged a holistic and sustainable vision of sustainable peace (Bondurant, 1958; Galtung, 1985; Gandhi, 1948; Horsburg, 1968). His vision of a nonviolent civilization is essentially a critique of the modern state and its paradigm of violence. He had no doubts that the modern state, based on force, was incapable of dealing with the forces of disorder, whether external or internal. He firmly believed that positive peace could be brought only by peaceful means and never by nonpeaceful means. The Gandhian-based vision of *Satyagrah* (struggle for truth) has inspired millions of African Americans to raise their voice for equality and freedom from oppression decades even before Martin Luther King Jr. brought them to the forefront of the civil rights movement (Kapur, 1992). So intense was his influence that there were calls for a "Black Gandhi" who would lead oppressed African Americans to liberation.

Mahatma Gandhi was quite emphatic about the role of education in promoting a culture of peace. Speaking as far back in 1931 he said "If we are to teach real peace in this world, and if we are to carry on a real war against war, we shall have to begin with the children" (Gandhi, 1931). He looked at education as an opportunity for spiritual growth and to realize the absolute ideals of nonviolence and truth. Gandhi wanted to include religious studies in education to teach values of forbearance, tolerance, and a value of nonviolence. Such curriculum of religious instructions, according to Gandhi, should include a study of the tenets of faiths other than one's own. (Gandhi, 1923). Gandhi's generic contribution to peace education reflects in innumerable institutions throughout the world which swear by Gandhi and his ideals.

MODERN SAGES AND GURUS

Some more recent sages and gurus have distinguished themselves by disseminating the Hindu spiritual learning of peace. Jiddu Krishnamurti (1895-1986), for instance, gave a spiritual dimension to religiosity and felt that what is sacred or truly religious could not be conditional, culture-bound or time-bound.[22] He wanted children to be so educated that they become religious human beings and develop an understanding of correct action, the depth and beauty of relationship, and the sacredness of a religious life (Forbes, 1997). His innovative mode of education meant to address the problems like the ecological crisis, poverty, hunger, and violence.[23] He founded several schools around the world to promote a global and holistic outlook to promote religious spirit in a scientific temper (Narayan, 1999). The institutions emphasize human freedom, self-inquiry, honest search for truth, compassion, and on building personal relationships that transcend conflict (Krishnamurti, 1974).

Seen as an incarnation of God, Sri Sathya Sai Baba (1926-) also stands out for his commitment to the spiritual values of *Satya* (truth), *Dharma* (righteousness), *Shanti* (peace) and *Prema* (love). He commands the following of several million people in different parts of the world and from all religions and faiths. The life and work of Sai Baba is a notable example of someone who promoted the message of love across communities through dissemination of over a thousand spiritual centers of learning all over the world. These include education centers for young children known as *Bal Ashrams* which celebrate festivals of all major religions and teach through *Bhajans* (prayers) which are nonsectarian and universal in appeal. Sai baba also set up an institute of higher learning with an emphasis on a liberal and diversity based approaches to the quest of ultimate reality as manifest in *Vedas, Upanishads* and *Bhakti traditions*.[24]

Other notable personalities who harnessed peacefulness from Hindu sources include Maharishi Mahesh Yogi who promises to transform the negative attitudes and bring in the ethos of peace through the technique of transcendental meditation. Mahesh Yogi offered a Vedic technology through which a community of peace-creating experts would dissolve social stress and political, religious, and ethnic tensions that fuel crime, terrorism, and war. To disseminate his message of peace, Mahesh Yogi created a chain of disciples as well as educational institutions to radiate harmony and peacefulness through an underlying field of consciousness.[25] Sri Sri Ravi Shankar, (1956-), a disciple of Maharishi Mahesh Yogi, and an exponent of *Advaita Vedanta* has also worked through the Art of Living Foundation to relieve both individual stress and societal violence. By employing *jñāna-yoga* as a practical tool, he has encouraged peaceful dialogue in various violence torn regions including Iraq, Sri Lanka, and several places in India.

TOWARD CLOSURE

Evidently the above discussion, based as it is on randomly selected texts and glimpses of the lived religion of Hindus, may not be truly representative of the veritable ethos of Hinduism. Nonetheless it reveals rather vividly the cardinal salience of peace in the Hindu worldview as manifest through its varied spiritual and multiple visions of peacefulness. It also brings out the interminable processes through which values of peace were continually disseminated and received. It shows that despite frequent dislocations and deviations, the streak of humanism and tolerance mostly found an upper hand in the Hindu way of life. This is evident in the way even the war treatise like the *Mahabharata* highlights the virtues of peacefulness, tolerance and even forgiveness.

Collective Hindu wisdom offers a holistic vision of peace in which the human community, ecology, and planetary concerns are tied in a mutually enriching manner. Such a comprehensive vision of peace corresponds closely to the current notion of "positive peace" and should justifiably claim a *niche* in the burgeoning curricula on peace education. In addition to its innate quest of inner peace, the annals of Hinduism also resonate with the norms of pluralism, dialogue, human dignity and equality. These community values were always at a premium as Hinduism traversed for over three millennia from *Vedic* times through the devotional tracks of *Bhakti* in medieval age to Gandhi's visions of nonviolence in twentieth century. As a *"lived religion"* Hinduism has unraveled the edifying norms of multicultural peace, augmenting its image as an instructive site of peace education—especially its human and psychosocial dispositions as unity promoting attitudes (Danesh, 2006).[26] The vibrant fusion between *Bhakti* and the Sufi tradition of Islam also suggests the possibility of dialogue between religious groups with strong, differing beliefs.[27]

There are obviously excellent resources within Hindu traditions of religious pluralism which may help us build bridges of understanding, loyalty, and trust across the frontiers of our religious diversity (Rambachan, 2000). Bringing religion back to the center stage of peacebuilding is indeed the call of the day. There are of course worthy initiatives all around the world in this direction, ranging from the education of young children for interreligious understanding to the induction of interfaith centers in higher education institutions. Though still in a fledgling state, these initiatives are our best hope to surmount the challenges of interreligious disaffection and violence.

NOTES

1. For an outstanding account of Hinduism, see S. Radhakrishnan, *Eastern Religions and Western Thought*, Oxford University Press, 1959. Karan Singh, *The Sterling Book Of Hinduism*, New Dawn Press: Berkshire Paperback—2005)

2. Vedas (knowledge) contain a large body of texts originating in Ancient India during 1500-500 B.C. The Four Veda include: Rig-veda, Yajurveda, Samaveda, and Atharvaveda. The essence of Vedas (Vedanta) is explicated in 11 main Upanishads. Other leading texts in Hinduism are: Bhagavad-Gita, and epics like the Mahabharata, the Ramayana.

3. Rabindranath Tagore, "Excerpts from The Religion of the Forest" Retrieved from http://www.online-literature.com/tagore-rabindranath/creative-unity/3/

4. See Patanjal Yog Darshan, Samadhi Paad, 1/33

5. Gandhi cites many texts from Mahabharata to substantiate this position.

6. The Indian Constitution considers Buddhism and Jainism as a part of Hinduism.

7. Only Bhahmans had the priviledges of imparting instructions. For an interesting account of Bhahmanic education see F. E. Keay, *Ancient Indian Education: An inquiry into its origin, development and ideas*. Oxford University Press: 1990, pp 11-57.

8. There are archeological evidences of such Centres of Hindu learning in Taxila (now in Pakistan), Nalanda, Benares, and Nadia which were operating as early as in fifth century B.C. See Radhakumud Mookerji, *Ancient Indian Education—Brahmanical & Buddhist*, Motilal Banarasidass Varanasi: 1989

9. The Mughals ruled most of South Asia from the mid-sixteenth to mid-nineteenth, followed by the British rule which continued till the mid-twentieth century.

10. The whole of the *Atharva Veda* is an example of assimilation of tribal traditions into the mainstream of Hinduism.

11. The nondual tradition in Hinduism reflects in Advaita or a, not; dvaita, dual (nondualism) and Suddhaadvata (pure nondualism). See S. Radhakrishnan, *The Bhagvadgita*, HarperCollins Publishers New Delhi: 1993, pp. 14-16.

12. See among others Vasudha Dalmia and H von Stietencron, *Representing Hinduism: The construction of religious traditions and national identity*. SAGE: New Delhi. 1995, pp. 20-21.

13. The word "Hindu" is derived from the name of River Indus, which flows through northern India. In ancient times the river as called the "Sindhu," but the Persians who migrated to India called the river "Hindu," the land "Hindustan" and its inhabitants "Hindus."

14. The so called "Hindutva" approach seeks to create a non-inclusive and insular collective identity for Hindus. See among others, Sandria B. Freitag,Collective Action and Community : Public Arenas And The Emergence of Communalism in North India -Delhi: OUP, 1990 and Jose Kuruvachira, *Politicisation of Hindu Religion in Postmodern India: An Anatomy of the Worldwide, Identities and Strategies of Hindu Nationalist in Bhartiya Janata Party* (Rawat Publications : 2008)

15. Amartya Sen has given an outstanding account of dialogical tradition and heterodoxy in Hindu tradition. See Amartya Sen, *The argumentative Indian: Writings on Indian history, culture and identity*, Penguine: London: 2005. pp. ix-xiv and also pp. 3-33

16. In addition to Islam, the Din-i Ilahi also contained aspects of Jainism, Zoroastrianism, and Hinduism. The Sikh religion too blends elements of Islam and Hindus.

17. The dargah of Moin-ud-din Chisti in Ajmer, Bahadur Shahid shrine, dargah of Saiyid Abd al-Qadir Shahul Hamid Nagoori in Nagore attract both Hindu and Muslim pilgrims. According to recent estimates, around 90% of Muslims in India and Pakistan visit dargahs of Sufi saints. See Markandey Katju, Take on this intellectual challenges" *The Hindu*, Nov. 25, 2008, 40.

18. He is revered as a Vaishnavite Bhakta by Hindus while the Muslims revere him as a peer, the Sikhs call him a Bhagat and the Kabir Panthis worship him as God incarnation.

19. The Dayanand Anglo-Vedic Schools System, also familiarly known as the D.A.V. Public Schools System is the single largest nongovernmental education society in India

20. "God the poor, is the only God that exits ... the poor God of all races, G. S Banhatti, *Life and Philosophy of Swami Vivekananda*, Atlantic: Delhi, 1995, p. 212

21. See note 20

22. See http://www.infed.org/thinkers/et-krish.htm

23. See http://www.jkrishnamurti.org/krishnamurti-teachings/ view-text.php?tid=43&chid=297&w=

24. It has three campuses, respectively at Prashanthi, Nilayam Brindavan, and Anantpur.

25. See http://www.permanentpeace.org/evidence/index.html

26. H. B. Danesh defines peace education as a means to transform the conflict based worldviews through a more integrative, unity-based worldview which opens up possibilities of unity amid diversity. See Danesh, H.B. (2006). Towards an integrative theory of peace education, *Journal of Peace Education, 3*(1), 55-78.

27. Bhakti–Sufi intersection is seen by many as an effective path to authentic dialogue on the conflict in Kashmir. See for instance, Ainslie Embree, *Has Religion a Role in Making Peace in Kashmir, in Douglas Johnston* (Ed.), *Faith Based Diplomacy: Trumping Realpolitik*, Oxford: 2003, pp 33-75.

REFERENCES

Ahmad, I. (Ed.) (1984). *Ritual and religion among Muslims in India*. Delhi, India: Manohar.

Alam, J. (1999). The composite culture and its historiography. *South Asia, 22*(Special Issue), 29-37.

Appadorai, A. (1981). *Domestic roots of India's foreign policy.* Oxford, England: New Delhi.

Appleby, R. S., & Hesburgh, T. M. (1999). *Ambivalence of the sacred: Religion, violence and reconciliation.* Lanham, MD: Rowman & Littlefield.

Bayly, C. (1985). The prehistory of "Communalism?": Religious conflict in India, 1700-1860. *Modern Asian Studies, 19*(2), 81-84.

Bondurant, J. (1958). *Conquest of violence: The Gandhian philosophy of conflict.* Princeton, NJ: Princeton University Press.

Burman, J. J. R. (1996). Hindu-Muslim Syncretism in India. *Economic and Political Weekly, 18*, 1211-1215.

Basham, A. L. (Translation) (1958). *Acaranga* Sutra, Jainism. From abridged version In T. de Bary (Ed.), *Sources of Indian tradition* (pp. 62-63). New York: Columbia University Press.

Dalmia, V., & von Stietencron, H. (1995). *Representing Hinduism: The construction of religious traditions and national identity.* New Delhi, India: SAGE.

Danesh, H.B. (2006). Towards an integrative theory of peace education. *Journal of Peace Education, 3*(1), 55-78.

Forbes, S. H. (1997). *Jiddu krishnamurti and his insights into education.* Presentation at the first Holistic Education Conference, Toronto, Canada. Retrieved from http://www.infed.org/thinkers/et-krish.htm

Gandhi, M. K. (1923, December 8). *Young India*. Ahmedabad, Nav Jeeran Press.

Gandhi, M. K. (1931, October 28). Speech At Montessori Training College, London. Retrieved from http://www.peace.ca/montessoriandgandhi.htm

Gandhi, M. K. (1948). *Nonviolence in peace and war* (3rd ed.). Ahmedaba, India: Navajivan.

Gandhi, R. (1995). *Peace and identity: Some reflections on the South Asian experience.* Institute of Conflict Analysis, George Mason University, Occasional. Paper 10 p. 3.

Gandhi, R. (1999). *Revenge & reconciliation: Understanding South Asian history.* Westminster, London: Penguin Books.

Galtung, J. (1985). A Gandhian theory of conflict. In D. Selbourne (Ed.), *In Theory and practice: Essays on the politics of Jayaprakash Narayan* (pp. 95-104). New Delhi, India: OUP.

Gita, B. (2002). Ch. IV, verse 11. Mitchells, NY: Three Rivers.

Horsburg, H. J. N. (1968) *Nonviolence and aggression: A study of Gandhi's moral equivalent of war.* London: OUP.

Johnston, D., & Sampson, C. (Eds.). (1994). *Religion the missing dimension of statecraft.* New York: Oxford University Press.

Kapur, S. (1992). *Raising up a prophet: The African-American encounter with Gandhi.* Boston: Beacon Press.

Kazanjian, V. H., Jr., & Laurence, P. L. (Eds.). (2000). *Education as transformation: Religious pluralism, spirituality & a new vision of higher education in America.* New York: Peter Lang.

Knipe, D. S. (1991). *Hinduism: Experiences in the sacred.* New York: HarperCollins.

Krishnamurti, J. (1974). *On education.* Chennai, India: Krishnamurti Foundation India.

Maha Upanishad. (1989). Translslated by Warrie. Auk. Chennai: Chapter 6, Verse 72, p. 89.

Malkani, K. R. (1993). *The politics of Ayodhya and Hindu-Muslim relations.* Delhi, India: Har-Anand.

Narayan, G. (1999). *As The river joins the ocean: Reflections about J. Krishnamurti.* Creekside Way, Canada: Edwin House.

Panda, G. (Ed.). (2004). *Rambhashuk Samvad.* Varanasi, India: Sahaiv Bharati.

Radhakrishnan, S. (1993). *The Bhagvadgita*, New Delhi, India: HarperCollins.

Rambachan, A. (2000). A Hindu perspective on moving from religious diversity to religious pluralism. In V. H. Kazanjian & P. L. Laurence (Ed.), *Education as transformation: Religious pluralism, spirituality & a new vision of higher education in America* (pp. 175-180). New York: Peter Lang.

The Rig-Veda. (2009). Translated by Ralph T. H. Griffith. Santa Cruz, CA: Evinity.

Savarkar, V. D. (1938). *Hindu Pad Padashahi.* New Delhi, India: Bharatiya Sahitya Sadan.

Sen, A. (2005). *The argumentative Indian: Writings on Indian history, culture and identity.* London: Penguine.

Sen, A. (2001). *Tagore and His India.* Retrieved from at http://nobelprize.org/nobel_prizes/literature/articles/sen/#11

Sikand, Y. (2003). *Sacred spaces: Exploring traditions of shared faith in India.* Delhi, India: Penguin Books.

Sponge, B. (Ed.). (2006). *Religion and reconciliation in South Africa: Voices of religious leaders*. Radnor, PA: Templeton Foundation Press.

Thapar, R. (1978). *Ancient Indian Social History: Some Interpretations*. New Delhi, India: Orient Longman.

Upadhyaya, R. (2007). *Arsh Subhashit Saahasri*. , Varanasi, India: Bharatiya Sanskriti Sansthan.

Upadhyaya, P. (2009). Peace and conflict: Reflections on Indian thinking. *Strategic Analysis, 33*(1), 71–83.

Upadhyaya, P. (2010). Communal peace in India: Lessons from multicultural Banaras. In K. Warikoo (Ed.), *Religion and Security In South and Central Asia*. London: Routledge.

Yajurveda. (1987). The texts of White Yajurveda (Ralph T. H. Griffith, Trans.). Varanasi, India: Munshiram Manoharlal.

CHAPTER 7

A TIBETAN PEACE PERSPECTIVE

Jia Luo

Peace is born out of
equanimity and balance.
Balance is flexibility,
an ability to adjust graciously to change.
Equanimity arises when we
accept the things that are.

—If you expect your life to be up and down, your mind will be much more peaceful.

Lama Yeshe (Kornfield, J. 2008, p.144)

INTRODUCTION

Peace education is an interdisciplinary academic field that is related to many subjects such as philosophy (Page, 2008; Woodhouse, 1991), sociology (Bolton, 1972), religion (Dalai Lama, 1989; Coward & Smith, 2004; Lehman, 2007), epistemology (Fleckenstein, 1991), anthropology (Tuzin, 2006), ecology (Rüdig, 1988; Wolfgang, 1988), political science (Aron, 1981; McSweeney, 1999; Vanhanen, 2003), psychology (Bar-Tal, 2000; MacNair, 2003) and holistic education (Miller, 1996; Sloan, 2005).

Spirituality, Religion, and Peace Education, pp. 115–131
Copyright © 2010 by Information Age Publishing
All rights of reproduction in any form reserved.

This chapter focuses on conceptualizing peace education from a Tibetan perspective. Tibetan Buddhism and the culture of Tibet offer a unique perspective on peace and peace education. This chapter includes the following components: (1) the need for peace education in today's world; (2) a theory of peace education based on the Tibetan ethos; (3) the relation of peace education, natural ecology, and the Tibetan ethos of the interconnectedness of all life; (4) a critique of modern education that focuses on competition and individual achievement in contrast with a Tibetan approach to learning that focuses on developing compassion and wisdom in students.

The teachings of The Dalai Lama around the world have already provided a foundation for much of this work, whose principles can be applied to the development of a peace curriculum for schools. Although the approach presented is based on the Tibetan ethos, the theory should be developed in the broader context of holistic and transformational education. In this chapter, I define the Tibetan cultural ethos through the six perfections of giving, morality, patience, diligence, meditative concentration, and wisdom. Thus, the relevance of each of the six components of the Tibetan ethos to peace education will be discussed in this chapter.

PEACE THEORY

Cultural Research Based on Conceptualizing Peace Theory

Buddhism entered Tibet at various times and in forms from India, China, and Central Asia. Tibetan Buddhism has thus been influenced by Hinayana, Mahayana, and Tantric Buddhist traditions and practices as well as by the native Tibetan animistic religion, Bŏn. Differing combinations of these various traditions have led to four schools of Tibetan Buddhism: the Nying-ma; the Sa-gya; Ka-gyü and Ge-luk (Dreyfus, 2003; Erricker, 2008). In the eleventh century, the great Indian scholar, Atisha, harmonized various traditions, reconciling *sutras* from the Hinayana, Mahayana, and Tantric traditions, and came to Tibet to teach Tibetan Buddhists this system. Later, Milarepa developed further approaches to meditation that allowed a practitioner to achieve enlightenment within one lifetime. Finally, Lama Tsong-Khapa refined the philosophical concept of *interdependent co-arising* and systematized a comprehensive programme of Buddhist education and practice (Dreyfus, 2003; Erricker, 2008; Thurman, 1984). Tibetan Buddhism is composed of a blend of several traditions, Hinayana Buddhism, Mahayana Buddhism, Tantric Buddhism, Tibetan developments of Buddhist philosophy, and Tibetan folk traditions of animism that reflect respect for nature and all life. This chapter draws upon the several of these streams of Tibetan philosophical tradition to present a framework for elementary school peace education curriculum that is informed by the Tibetan Buddhist ethos, but is not specifically Tibetan, or religious. Rather, it places ethics and morality at the centre of the curriculum.

The primary basis for the conception of peace used in this approach is the Buddhist concept of compassion for all sentient beings, which provides a basis for combining respect for humans, like most peace education approaches, with respect for all living beings that is the basis for environmental education. Furthermore, while the original conception derives from Buddhism, there are concepts in other cultural and religious traditions that can contribute to a theory of peace within the Christian, Islamic, and other traditions that are compatible with this Tibetan ethos (Batchelor, 1992; Gross, 1997; Lehman, 2007; Mullin, 2002; Paige, Satha-Anand, & Gilliatt, 2001; Thurman, 1997).

Peace Theory and the Tibetan Ethos

Galtung (1985) states that over the last 25 years peace research has faced a series of major dilemmas in carrying out its work, which includes the definition of the field and the conception of peace in various civilizations. Clearly, peace is a complex concept, related to many other fields such as psychology, sociology, philology, education, political science, and spirituality. There are five different definitions of peace in the current Merriam-Webster, most of which are based on absence of the negative. Moreover, several scholars have equated peace with absence of war (Galtung, 1985; Hall, 1993).

Peace clearly is holistically related to many other areas, and not just about war itself. Now, the key issue from a Tibetan Buddhist perspective is how the curriculum can be a vehicle to reduce greed, hatred, and ignorance. Thus, effective peace education needs to be based on an adequate understanding of what peace is. This notion of peace education, understood as involving nondominant relations between different cultures, requires major academic research work towards the construction of a concept of peace that takes into account and synthesizes peace knowledge from different cultural perspectives in order to develop a critical peace theory that truly does not privilege the perspectives of any one culture, thereby establishing an effective theoretical foundation for peace education.

There are contributions that Tibetan perspectives can bring for extending peace theory. First, the Tibetan understanding of peace focuses on greed as a cause of lack of peace. Thus, within Tibetan thinking, war is caused by cultural, political, and national greed. In the past, reconciliation had been made by the greater force of one side. However, a Tibetan proverb says: one enemy is too many, a hundred friends are not enough. Tibetan philosophy says, rather, let us see the opponent as a teacher of tolerance. Yet today's competitive society and education system teaches young people to satisfy individual and collective greed, encouraging this negative mind over the positive mind of compassion and wisdom.

Second, within the Tibetan ethos, the quality of human relationships is primary; all other concerns are secondary. Seeing peace education as *good relationships* is an example of developing peace within very practical contexts. *Good relationships* do not simply mean absence of conflict. Peace is also internal to the body and is present when there is a balanced interrelationship between the systems in the body; peace is also internal to the family and is present when all family members' interrelationships are based on mutual love and care for each other; peace is also internal to communities and is present when social interrelationships are based on trust, sharing and mutual assistance; peace is also internal to international affairs and is present when interrelationships among countries are based on sharing and supporting each other, not on domination and control. This conception of peace from the interpersonal to the international is based on presence of positive characteristics and not simply on absence of negative characteristics. It seems easy to understand, but how can it be practiced and taught in the classroom?

Clearly, it is very important to nurture the young generation through holistic education with soulful compassion based on developing wisdom. Trying to build peace theory as a new ground for all children from around the world is a first step to develop peace in their lives

What and how should we teach peace as form of embodied holistic knowledge in the classroom? First, we need to build the peace curriculum from multiple sources that are based on how wisdom and compassion are practiced within diverse contexts. Second, we need to understand the relationships that exist in society and the different perspectives on peace (Bahry, Darkhor, & Luo, 2009).

Peace education attempts to balance the physical, emotional, intellectual and spiritual learning through making connections with our own self and others in our environment. It is more than just about stopping war and violence. Its is about developing self-awareness and making meaningful connections with the community, the global society, and the universe.

Peace Knowledge From Various Civilizations and From Research

There are a variety of concepts of peace that are based upon different cultural perspectives and as a result many researchers are not taking a holistic approach to peace education that can apply to all beings. It is crucial that researchers integrate the multiple notions of peace concept into an international peace curriculum and start to practice it in school classrooms; teaching peace lessons based on one cultural perspective is limiting. The Tibetan holistic peace approach attempts to provide a more inclusive and integrative perspective to peace education that is based on care and respect for all beings. Thus, the two major challenges that the researchers and practitioners are: (1) an inadequate theoretical framework for peace education; (2) an inadequate understanding of the mutual interaction of body, emotion and mind, which affect teaching and learning.

From the Tibetan perspective on peace, we cannot understand peace without understanding the factors that affect our mind (Murge bsam dan, 1997, pp. 23-39). In fact the Tibetan analysis of the mind is extremely detailed and includes several categories of factors that influence mental states. The first major category is the five omnipresent factors (perception, recognition, touch, attention, and emotion,); the second major category consists of five determining factors (aspiration, belief, mindfulness, concentration, wisdom); the third major category includes six fundamental delusions (attachment, hatred, pride, ignorance, indecision, false view). Additional categories include near-delusions,[1] virtues,[2] and, the four changeable mental factors[3] (Rigzin, 2008. p. 286). All of these psychological factors may act upon the mind and interact with each other providing an extremely subtle framework to see how the human mind functions at different moments. From a Tibetan Buddhist perspective, peace requires harmonious interaction of all these mental factors. At the same time, according to Tibetan understanding, the lack of peace has complex origins in the mental states of persons. In order to establish a peaceful relationship between people, we must have a detailed understanding of the complex mental states that lead to conflict; if we can identify these psychological causes of conflict, then there are measures that can be taken to restore harmony.

Although a complete Tibetan psychological analysis is complex and can only be applied by experienced practitioners, there are some possible applications of this perspective to peace education. The main application is the insight that comes from the realization that our mind is in constant flux, changing from moment to moment. This has several consequences for peace. The first consequence is that while positive states may at any time change to negative states, it is also true that there is no permanent negative state and any key state can also change to a positive one, and moreover, can be consciously changed. Thus, the Tibetan perspective is a realistic, yet simultaneously optimistic orientation. Second, if a teacher is aware of the above factors and endeavours to develop her own positive mind, this can positively influence the attitudes of the classmates towards each other.

Buddhists refer to harmful mental states such as greed, ignorance and hatred as "delusions." As the Dalai Lama explained, "delusions are states of mind which, when they arise within our mental continuum, leave us disturbed, confused, and unhappy. Therefore, those states of mind which delude or afflict us are called 'delusions' or 'afflictive emotions' "[4]

Tibetan philosophy has a strong tradition of logical reasoning[5] and thus a major portion of the curriculum in monastery schools is practice in analyzing how various states of minds interact with each other with the effect of reducing compassion and wisdom.[6]

Research on Modern Education

The modern educational system pays too much attention to acquiring knowledge and does not give enough attention to spiritual and moral development. However, there is an increasing interest worldwide in the relationship of education and conflict. According to a recent study by the World Bank (2005), the three major educational factors that are implicated in the development of conflict are:

1. Curricula that exclude certain languages as subjects and medium of instruction
2. Curricula that present false images of cultural homogeneity
3. Curricula that are biased or exclude the perspectives of sociocultural groups. (p. 10)

Furthermore, curricula that embody a philosophy of national or cultural identity and frequently can lead to conflict between different cultural groups within a jurisdiction that do not agree with the representations of identities within the curriculum and the textbooks. A recent study of education in countries where there had been significant degrees of conflict found that in many countries' textbooks had taken an extremist approach to identity: either a separatist approach, where two parallel education systems virtually ignored one another and ascribed negative characteristics to members of the other group, or an assimilationist approach, where the dominant group attempted to use the education system to eliminate the cultural and linguistic basis for the identity of children of a subordinate group (World Bank, 2005, pp. 52-53).

In postconflict situations, inclusive approaches to education such as peace education are typically promoted as a means to reduce intergroup tensions that led to the original conflict. However, peace education is understood in many ways and implemented variously with a resulting wide variation in effectiveness. Programs dependent on external agencies and their funding have little internal support and are not sustainable once external funding disappears. Moves to force communities in conflict to send their children to study in common schools also frequently fail. Where initiatives to introduce peace education and common schooling of communities in conflict originate within the communities themselves, there is a greater chance of sustainability (Feuerverger, 2001; World Bank, 2005, p. 60). However, most of these approaches to peace education, even the relatively successful ones, are based on an incomplete understanding of peace. These misunderstandings of *peace* fail to foster among students a truly embodied understanding of peace.

Positive Peace From a Tibetan Perspective

This section explores a reconceptualization of peace education that depends on a *positive* understanding of peace from a Tibetan perspective. There is a great need for peace in today's world, and therefore *effective* peace education. A theory of peace education based on the Tibetan ethos would also take into account current theories and approaches to peace education from other cultures and perspectives. Peace education based on a Tibetan ethos synthesizes natural ecology theory and Buddhist teachings on the importance of an awareness of the deep interconnectedness of all life and the need to overcome delusions such as greed and hatred in order to establish true peace in the world. The modern focus on educational competition and individual achievement, conflicts with a natural ecology that understands the interdependence of all life.

However, to remedy this shortcoming, insights from traditional Tibetan perspectives can be combined with a critical analysis of the role of modern education in creating human conflict and threats to the environment. Many Western scholars have provided criticism of modernity and technology and their distorting effects on human life (Grant, 1969; Heidegger, 1977). Both of these philosophers ground many problems of modern technology in the modern conception that there are no recognized limits to human desires and capabilities. This relates to the Tibetan concept of desire and attachment, whereby each desire is satisfied temporarily, but incompletely, therefore, driving individuals, corporations and nations to never be satisfied and to always seek more (Thurman, 1997).

Modern education is constantly becoming more a preparation for the workplace than a place where children learn about ultimate, universal values and a healthy understanding of human life. Education has been infiltrated by marketplace values. Indeed, Grant (1969) criticized the university curriculum as just a site for technical training, rather than for deeper learning about universal values. In his view, even philosophy had ceased to be a pursuit of knowledge and understanding and had become another technical skill.

Thus, current curricula from primary school to university embody anti-human values, in the sense that they promote knowledge as a tool to satisfy desires and to compete with others rather than understand and feel compassion for others. Education does not serve as a preparation to live a good life, but prepares us for one narrow segment of our life, the workplace.

A proper peace education approach needs to educate children about respecting limits to human desire, cultivating knowledge of life as a whole, understanding the proper relationship of work, and respecting the natural environment and human beings' place in the universe. Within such a holistic conception of education, peace permeates the entire curriculum, touching everything teachers, children, and parents do within and without the school.

TOWARD ACTION:
THEORIZING PEACE AND EDUCATIONAL RESEARCH

It is important to understand that peace must come from our heart, not somewhere else. The Buddha said:

> The human mind can create conflict.
> It can also create peace.
> To find peace in the world
> We must find peace in ourselves.
> There is no higher happiness
> than peace. (Kornfeld, 2008, p. 139)

Currently, there is much talk within schools about respect for children, for diversity of religions and cultures, for the environment, and for global cooperation and peace. Unfortunately, this talk often is not reflected in actual practice in schools. The hidden curriculum (Kelly, 2004), even in peace education and environmental education, can teach children that modern society ultimately values personal competition and gratification more than building a just society based on human values. This author argues that grounding the curriculum in concepts derived from the Tibetan ethos that promote both reduction of greed and anger, as well as an increase of knowledge and understanding is one means of developing a truly effective peace education, and indeed, education as a whole, will move us toward a more just world.

A critical question, not only for peace educators, but also for all educators throughout the world, is how can education cultivate the qualities of the heart. Our children should become both knowledgeable and compassionate.

Holistic Learning and Peace Education

Perhaps this section should be titled "Learning Peace for a Whole Life." Clearly, children need to develop qualities of the heart for them to grow as truly peace-minded citizens. However, how can they learn these qualities; where can they learn them? In modern secular education, these qualities are seen as not the school's business and should be taught in the family, the community and religious institutions. But in recent years, the family structure is looser, community bonds are weaker, and fewer in urban society participate in organized religious life. Perhaps the schools, which are one of the sources of conflict, can become a site for reducing conflict.

So what is the key lesson for children? The mind and the heart are constantly changing often in negative ways. School instead of a place of knowledge and contentment, for many is a place where children's mental states and emotions are in constant flux. What is peer pressure, if not irrational fear of the minds of others that can cause children to harm himself for fear of ridicule of others. What children need to learn is emotional intelligence (Brecke & William, 2003; Goleman, 1995).

Like the universe itself, human emotion never stops changing, under the constant bombardment of our senses by external phenomena that are arising at every moment. Learrning peace at one time is insufficient, because our emotions are themselves changing in different situations. Even the ordinary mind, which perceives some parts of external reality, while ignoring other phenomena, is not even the same from morning until afternoon on the same day (Sogyal Rinpoche, 1994, p. 47).

According to Tibetan thinking, we can cleanse our mind every day, as if taking a morning bath. There are specific techniques for doing so that are not specific to any particular culture or religion that are suitable for adaptation in modern secular classrooms. These techniques, in the short term, have benefits for the interrelations of teachers and classmates, and for academic achievement. But more importantly, they establish an emotional and moral grounding for learning and human relationships that can last throughout the students' lives.

Children's Curriculum and the Tibetan Ethos

Each of the world's diverse societies has its own cultural ethos based on a variety of epistemological approaches and the meaning of knowledge. The Tibetan ethos has its own views on what knowledge is and how it justified, but more importantly, it does not take a neutral stand on how knowledge is used. Within the Tibetan ethos knowledge must be used to contribute to the six perfections of Giving, Morality, Patience, Diligence, Meditative, Concentration, and Wisdom. Thus, peace education depends on learning appropriate uses of the knowledge we obtain in school and from other sources. As the title of Fulghum's book (2003) clearly expresses the importance of basic education, "Everything I know, I learned in Kindergarten." Thus, primary school sets the tone for all children's subsequent learning, their attitude towards knowledge, and its uses. It is crucial to identify a plan for developing a holistic curriculum that embodies real peace concepts. Although a peace education curriculum cannot teach all these Perfections, if the curriculum touches children even a little, it is enough to establish a foundation for true peace.

In general, Buddhists believe that all life is suffering, but with *Compassion and Wisdom* we can reduce the suffering that arises from interpersonal conflict and unsatisfied desires. Therefore, curriculum should have the objectives of effective learning of problem-solving through intelligence applied to understanding of the self and others. However, a rigid curriculum that transmissively teaches children inert information about morals and peace only helps them reproduce facts about peace on tests and does not necessarily help them to enact peace in their lives. We need to not transmit mere facts; we need to transform their understanding.

Tibetan villagers participate twice a year in traditional dramas that embody the six perfections. All teenagers in a Tibetan village select a character to perform in the drama. This provides an opportunity for young people to mentally experience perspectives of the characters they play. These characters represent a broad range of personality and behavior types that can be found in their own village, some of whom act in negative ways. By experiencing the inner life of a character and the effect their behavior has on themselves and others, they can reflect on the characters, their motivations, their actions. This process helps the young person move toward greater compassion and wisdom without any direct instruction.

Drama as a Means for Peace

Inspired by the content and method of these traditional dramas, Tibetan stories were made an integral part of a recent experimental Tibetan primary textbook in China. The stories are given for pleasure and instruction, and the students were not assessed on their understanding of the language of the story. Instead, the pedagogical process is inspired by village dramas. First, each student is assigned a different story to read and discuss orally at home with their parents. Later in class, each student tells the story to the class in their own words. Then, students in small groups prepare their own drama through oral discussion that combines elements of each student's story into a harmonious whole. Students then practice together and each group performs their drama for the whole class. Afterwards, students divide into new groups to discuss their reactions to the plays. Students are constantly engaged in creative thinking, reflection on motives, actions and consequences, and also are immersed in a rich mental experience. The students gain insight into the Perfections and how they are manifested in peoples' behavior. No external rewards are used.

In 2000, I did an investigation as follow-up action research in several schools where I distributed this local curriculum and the accompanying textbook. Surprisingly, many parents were borrowing and reading the book with their children at home. In the school the teachers and principals were seeing that children were learning the stories but also nourishing the children in the moral sense and qualities of the heart. Children are highly interested and learn best through stories (Egan, 1986) and role play, and there are many more traditional Tibetan stories that illustrate the six Perfections,[7] which can be used by teachers to develop the peace curriculum further.

This approach of combining stories and role playing has great potential for effective learning of peace in other contexts. Primary school textbooks in every country are full of stories that contain morals and values. What is the difference between these stories and those that really teach morality? Tibetan stories may contain a moral, but they do not state what the moral is. The moral is learned by experiencing the story. Certainly, excellent teachers worldwide take this approach to literature and stories (Furman, 1990). However, textbooks often do not trust children to make the correct conclusions and they teach directly exactly what should be believed. This type of story leaves little to children's intelligence and does not stimulate their thinking. Further, by using such texts as the basis of reading and vocabulary lessons and testing children on appropriate conclusions, children are led to think morals are what we say in front of authorities, not what we live when they are not watching. The village cultural environment is the nest in which children grow and it deeply affects their consciousnesses. Thus primary school education should continuously build an environment where children absorb the surrounding culture, and then gradually develop their own perspective. The primary curriculum should be based on integrating a holistic village life perspective with the school perspective.

From Grades 1-3, it may be enough for children to develop wisdom and compassion through role playing; in later grades, or when children are sufficiently mature, they can also participate in group discussions, taking turns asking each other how they felt while playing the roles.

Qualities for Teachers of Peace Curriculum

What kind of qualities does an effective peace education teacher in primary school require? How can they develop the necessary knowledge, skills and attitudes and understanding? Ideally, a peace curriculum teacher requires a rich spiritual experience, deep understanding of nature and a holistic worldview. Furthermore, a peace education teacher should be someone who embodies the Tibetan ethos of peace, and is able to reduce the three delusions through meditation and practice of the six perfections within their daily life. From this point of view, peace curriculum teachers also need to be able to skillfully guide the combination of role play pedagogy and compassionate wisdom content within drama activities in the classroom.

Primary teachers should have the qualities of selflessness, attention, compassion and wisdom, the same qualities that children are developing the peace curriculum. Our minds tend to be scattered and our attention is divided, like water running in every direction at once. If we can channel our attention, this can have a powerful effect on teachers' teaching and students' learning. Thus, it is crucial for a primary school teacher to be able to restrain self-centerdness, practice patience, treat the self and others equally, take pride not only in one's own accomplishments, but also those of others, and demonstrate focused concentration. Within the Tibetan tradition, these abilities can be cultivated through two types of meditation that contribute to teachers practice and pedagogical skill: stabilizing meditation and analytical meditation. Both methods are beneficial, and the choice of method depends on the situation. Of course, the above mentioned spiritual qualities can be cultivated through other traditional spiritual practices.

Clearly, present models of teacher education as are not suitable to develop teachers of peace education curriculum. Peace education within a Tibetan ethos considers individuals as part of a unbroken network of relationship, with others in their community, with other communities and nationalities and with all of nature. Yet modern schools as part of a modern society, take a narrow view of education as having a specific competitive purpose in order to accomplish goals of individual persons, companies and countries. Clearly, human beings have ignored that we are a part of nature and universe and all existence. The Dalai Lama (2000) gives us advice for this:

When we have a deeper understanding of the Buddhism teachings of inter-dependernce—that even a single event has multiple causes and conditions that contribute to that event—then we will really have a deep philosophical basis for the ecological perspective—espect for the natural laws of the environment. The concept of interdependence helps to widen our perspective. It automatically makes us aware of the importance of causality-relations, which in turn brings forth a more holistic view. (p. 135)

A TIBETAN CRITIQUE AND OFFERING TO WESTERN EDUCATION

There are many commonalities of aims between Western peace education, citizenship education, global education and environmental education, and a Tibetan approach to peace education. However, there is also a key distinction: the aims of each of the above Western approaches overlap with Tibetan peace education, but only partially. Peace education, as enacted in some contexts, sees absence of interpersonal conflict as the aim; citizenship education takes preparation to participate in one society as an aim; global education takes international relationships as its main basis, while environmental education focuses on the relation between humans and their physical surroundings as its focus. From a Tibetan point of view, these aims should not be divided and are in fact one. Thus, the Western tendency to divide wholes into segments emerges again. A further difference is the continued emphasis on individualism and competition—environmental activists in competition with peace activists, and so forth. The Tibetan approach understands these oppositions as illusory, and therefore treats them holistically, as do some Western approaches (Miller, 2006; Wilber, 2005).

Essential Research to Establish Peace Theory

Within Tibetan philosophy, all nature is conceived as interconnected (Thurman, 1997), a very old view, which is comparable to modern ecology theory and related concepts such as the *Gaia* hypothesis (Lovelock, 2000). When all earth and all sentient beings are viewed as a community, then peace between humans and respect towards the earth and its ecology are both aspects of the same worldview. However, within a community, conflict often arises. Within Tibetan Buddhism, *all* human conflict is understood as arising from three sources within the human mind: desire, ignorance and hatred (Thurman, 1997). Thus, desire for material goods and wealth beyond what is needed to sustain our life is a cause of both interpersonal and international conflict as well as excessive environmental exploitation.

At this stage, work on peace education embodying the Tibetan ethos is at a preliminary stage. There is a need for work among Tibetan scholars to connect their traditions with the modern world. There is similarly a need for international researchers on peace and environmental education to familiarize themselves with Tibetan approaches to these questions. There is a further need to research concepts of peace from diverse traditions and integrate them in a broad conception of global peace education.

Desire for material comfort and convenience drives individuals and societies to use and seek resources excessively. The overuse of private automobiles for reasons of convenience and comfort drives individuals to pollute the atmosphere, corporations to compete for sources of petroleum, and nations to compete for markets and control of resources. It is not completely unreasonable to see a connection between global warming and human conflicts, such as the recent war in Iraq. Under the Tibetan ethos, such connections are expected. They are created by a combination of desire and hatred when others possess what a person desires and ignorance about the interconnectedness of all life. Therefore, conflict reduction requires including basic concepts in peace education such as the role of desire, hatred, and ignorance in human life

The time is now right to radically rethink the aims and methods of modern education. The global warming crisis, the increasing wars and smaller scale conflicts around the world all lead us to the same conclusion; something has to change before it is too late. Clearly, one part of a global change is a change in approaches to education. We urgently need to remake children's education from primary schooling through to the postsecondary level as a way to establish a peaceful global society in which every individual—strong or weak, every nation—rich or poor, has equal value and can make an equal contribution to the whole earth.

NOTES

1. There are 21 near delusions: anger, malice, concealment, outrage, jealousy, miserliness, conceit, dishonesty, haughtiness, harmful intent, nonembarrassment, nonconsideration, lack of faith, laziness, nonconscientiousness, forgetfulness, nonintrospection, dullness, agitation, mental wandering.

2. There are 11 virtues: faith, sense of shame, sense of dread of blame, lack of desire, lack of hatred, lack of foolishness, diligence, conscientiousness, mental flexibility, equanimity, not harming others.

3. There are four changeable mental factors: inconstancy of attention, regret, gross investigation, subtle investigation.

4. Retrieved from http://www.viewonbuddhism
.org/delusion_introduction.html

5. For more on Tibetan philosophy, see Tillemans (1999) and Patrik (2004).

6. Tsepak Rigzin (2008, pp. 97-98) explains mental delusions' causes: (a) nonelimination of latent delusions; (b) close association with the object prone to generate delusion; (c) entertaining wrong thoughts with a discussion of how to reduce these delusive minds.

7. The story about four animals who become friends despite their differences illustrates the role of compassion; the story about Milarepa displays the perfection of diligence; the story about Lama Tsongkhapa is an example of the perfection of wisdom.

REFERENCES

Aron, R. (1981). *Peace and war: A theory of international relations.* Garden City, NJ: Doubleday.

Bahry, S., Darkhor, P., & Luo, J. (2009). Educational diversity in China: Responding to globalizing and localizing forces. In G. A. Wiggan & C. B. Hutchison (Eds.), *Global issues in education: Pedagogy, policy, practices, and the minority experience* (pp. 103-130). Lanham, MD: Rowman & Littlefield.

Bar-Tal, D. (2000). *Shared beliefs in a society: Social psychological analysis.* Thousand Oaks, CA: SAGE.

Batchelor, M. (1992). Even the stones smile: Selections from the scriptures. In M. Batchelor & K. Brown (Eds.), *Buddism and ecology* (pp, 2-17). London: Cassell.

Bolton, C. D. (1972). Alienation and action: A study of peace-group members. *The American Journal o Sociology, 78*(3), 537-561.

Brecke, P., & Long, J. L. (2003). *War and reconciliation: Reason and emotions in conflict resolution.* Cambridge: MIT Press.

Coward, H. G., & Smith, G. S. (2004). *Religion and peacebuilding.* New York: SUNY Press.

Dalai Lama. (1989, December 10). *Acceptance speech, on the occasion of the award of the award of the Nobel Peace Prize in Oslo.* Retrieved from http://nobelprize.org/ nobel_prizes/peace/laureates/1989/lama-acceptance.html

Dalai Lama. (2000). *The transformed mind: Reflections on truth, love and happiness.* London: Hodder & Stoughton.

Dalai Lama. (2002). *The heart of compassion: A practical approach to a meaningful life.* Twin Lakes, WI: Lotus Press.

De Brito, A. B., Gonzalez-Enriquez, C., & Aguilar, P. (Eds.). (2001). *The politics of memory: Transitional justice in democratizing societies.* Oxford, England: Oxford University Press.

Dreyfus, G. B. J. (2003). *The sound of two hands clapping: The education of a Tibetan Buddhist monk.* London: University of California Press.

Egan, K. (1986). *Teaching as story telling: An alternative approach to teaching and curriculum in the elementary school.* Chicago: Chicago University Press.

Erricker, C. (2008). *Teach yourself Buddhiüsm.* London: Hodder Education.

Feuerverger, G. (2001). *Oasis of dreams: Teaching and learning peace in a Jewish-Palestinian village in Israel.* New York: RoutledgeFalmer.

Fleckenstein, K. S. (1991, March). *Planes of existence: Toward epistemological peace.* Paper presented at the annual meeting of the Conference on College Composition and Communication, Boston, MA. (ERIC Document ED 332 226)

Fulghum, R. (2003). *All I really need to know I learned in kindergarten* (15th Anniversary Ed.). New York: Ballantine Books.

Furman, L. (1990). *Creative drama handbook.* Denver, CO: Pioneer Drama Service.

Galtung, J. (1985). Twenty-five years of peace research: Ten challenges and some responses. *Journal of Peace Research, 22*(2), 141-158.

Goleman, D. (1995). *Emotional intelligence.* New York: Bantam Books.

Grant, G. P. (1969). *Technology and Empire: Perspectives on North America.* Toronto: Anansi Press.

Gross, R. (1997). Toward a Buddhist environmental ethic. *Journal of the American Academy of Religion, 65*(2), 333-353.

Hall, R. (May, 1993). How children think and feel about war and peace: An Australian study. *Journal of Peace Research, 30*(2), 181-196.

Heidegger, M. (1977). *The question concerning technology and other essays.* New York: Harper & Row.

Kelly, A. V. (2004). *The curriculum.* Thousand Oaks, CA: SAGE.

Kornfield, J. (2008). *The art of forgiveness, loving-kindness, and peace.* New York: Bantam Dell.

Lehman, J. (2007). Integrating creation care into the life of faith. *Columbia Theological Seminary's Vantage, 2*(2).

Lovelock, J. (2000). *Gaia: A new look at life on earth.* Oxford, England: Oxford University.

MacNair, R. (2003). *The psychology of peace: An introduction.* Westport, CT: Greenwood Publishing Group.

Miller, J. (1996). *The Holistic curriculum.* University of Toronto press.

Miller, J. (2006). *Educating for wisdom and compassion: creating conditions for timeless learning.* Corwin Press.

Mullin, G. H. (2002). *War and peace in Tibetan Buddhism.* Portland, OR: Mandala.

Murge bsam dan. (1997). *Collected works of Murge bsam dan* (Vol. 6). Xiningm China. Qinghai Nationalities Publishing House.

Page, J. S. (2008). *Philosophy of peace education.* New York: Columbia University, Teachers College.

Paige, G. D., Satha-Anand, C., & Gilliatt, S. (Eds.). (2001). *Islam and nonviolence.* Honolulu, Hawaii: Center for Global Nonviolence.

Rigzin, T. (2008). *Tibetan-English dictionary of Buddhist terminology.* Dharamsala, India: Indraprastha Press.

Rinpoche, S. (1994). *The Tibetan book of living and dying.* New York: HarperCollins.

Rüdig, W. (1988). Peace and ecology movements in Western Europe. *West European Politics, 11*(1), 26-39.

Sloan, D. (2005). Education and the modern assault on being human: nurturing body, soul, and spirit. In J. Miller (Ed.), *Holistic learning* (pp. 27-45). New York: Random House.

Thurman, R. (1984). *The central philosophy of Tibet: A study and translation of Jey Tsong Khapa's "Essence of True Eloquence."* Princeton, NJ: Princeton University Press.

Thurman, R. (1997). *Essential Tibetan Buddhism.* Edison, NJ: BookSales.

Tillemans, T. J. F. (1999). *Scripture, logic, language: Essays on Dharmakirti and his Tibetan successors.* Boston: Widsom.

Tuzin, D. (1996). The spectre of peace in unlikely places: Concepts and paradox in the anthropology of peace. In T. Gregor (Ed.), *A natural history of peace* (pp. 3-33). Nashville, TN: Vanderbilt University Press.

Vanhanen, T. (2003). *Democratization: A comparative analysis of 170 countries.* London: Routledge.

Woodhouse, T. (1991). *Peacemaking in a troubled world.* Flint, MI: University of Michigan.

World Bank (2005). *Reshaping the future: Education and postconflict reconstruction.* Washington, DC: Author.

Wolfgang, R. D. (1988). Peace and ecology movements in Western Europe. *West European Politics, 11*(1), 6-39.

CHAPTER 8

INDIGENOUS SPIRITUALITY AS A SOURCE FOR PEACEFUL RELATIONS

By Four Arrows, aka Don Trent Jacobs

In their text, *Native American Religions,* Denise and John Carmody (1993) explain that for traditional American Indians "spiritual" tends to mean "significant, inviting reflection, possessing power" (p. 233). When considering their reference to "power" it is important to note that for American Indians, as well as for most Indigenous Peoples around the world, spiritual power is a benevolent phenomenon. The "Great Mysterious," whether manifested in Grandmother Earth, Father Sky, the cardinal directions, a mountain or an elk, is a creative, beautiful and generous force. Humans, of course, are also manifestations of this Spirit and thus similarly embody these positive traits. In order not to be misled away from this healthy path, we require right learning to assure that our innately positive dispositions, those that contribute to peaceful relationships throughout life, are respected and nurtured. According to this understanding, Nature, in all of its forms, provides opportunities for such learning.

In using the term reat Mysterious to describe that which other spiritual traditions call "God," I am translating the meaning of most names that

Spirituality, Religion, and Peace Education, pp. 133–146

First Nations Peoples have given to the Creative Source of Life. Thus, spiritual power, however creative, beautiful and generous, is also incomprehensible. As such, Indigenous Peoples generally believe it is wrongheaded for someone to claim absolute knowledge about the details of such a great and mysterious concept. Ed McGaa (1990) explains this in his book, *Mother Earth Spirituality*:

> North American Indians believe there is a limit to the human brain, at least while a person lives upon this planet. Traditional Indians believe that attempts to describe to another two-legged an overly definite concept of the mysterious vastness of the Great Provider of All are crude and unmannerly and lack humility. (p. 44)

This honoring of the Mysterious is a fundamentally important idea to explore in any study that attempts to look at the possible influence of religion and spirituality on the promotion or suppression of human violence in the world. Unfortunately, Indigenous spirituality is often dismissed in discussions of world religions. For example, the famous comparative religions professor, Huston Smith, spent the majority of academic career ignoring primal cultures. In his 1991 revision of his famous 1958 book, *World Religions*, he finally apologized for it and changed his ways in his later publications (p. xi). Such dismissal of the importance of Indigenous spirituality goes hand and glove with the common rejection of the idea that primitive societies were largely peaceful societies. Consider briefly just a few of the "academic" publications that have attempted to give scholarship to this claim:

- Hugh Trevor-Roper's 1965 academic text, *The Rise of Christian Europe*, in which he says, "How unrewarding is any serious study of the gyrations of barbarous tribes in picturesque but irrelevant corners of the blog: tribes whose chief function in history, in my opinion, is to show to the present an image of the past from which, by history, it has escaped" (p. 9).
- Shepard Krech's book, *The Ecological Indian: Myth and History*, published by Norton in 2000, claiming that the demise of the buffalo was the fault of the Indians.
- Robert Whelan's 1999 book, *Wild in the Woods: The Myth of the Peaceful Eco-Savage* that asserts "conservation would not have occurred to the Indian, lacking the necessary understanding of the physical world" (p. 28).
- Christy Turner's University of Utah Press 1999 release, *Man Corn: Cannibalism and Violence in the Prehistoric American Southwest* that describes unrestrained cannibalism among the Hopi and Zuni.

- Michael L. Cooper's elementary school text, *Indian School: Teaching the White Man's Way* (1999) which explains how Indian names, like "Plenty Kill," reflect the savage past.
- Steven A. Leblanc's 2003 book, *Constant Battles: The Myth of the Peaceful, Noble Savage*, another University of Utah Press product, that concludes that technology and Western science have finally put mankind on the right trajectory for world peace in comparison to the barbaric behaviors of aboriginal people.

There are more examples of such "anti-Indianism" listed in my University of Texas Press text, *Unlearning the Language of Conquest: Scholars Expose Anti-Indianism in America* (2008), but these few make my point. Aside from racism, which is likely behind some of this shoddy research, I speculate that much of it stems from the authors' experiencing a worldview that is contrary to the Indigenous way of understanding the world. To grasp and embrace the Indigenous way of understanding the world is a risk to the deeply held convictions of dominant cultures and religions. For example, it might be difficult to support the dominant economic system, especially as it relates to the use of natural resources and distribution of wealth, if we embrace Indigenous spiritual beliefs that emphasize place and the sacred nature of all creatures, rivers, rocks, and trees. Similarly, the dominant civilizations' general support of its war machinery might crumble if most people believed that human nature is more inclined to peaceful co-existence than it is to violence. The spiritual emphasis on a balance between the sun and the moon and the male and the female that is common in Indigenous cultures might also be a challenge to the warlike tendencies that relate to the patriarchal cultures that now dominant the world (DeMeo, 2008, p. 135).

What might happen if educational curriculum and policy encouraged or even required teachers to teach about the peaceful Indigenous past? I suggest that it would create the same potential problem for the state that might occur if teachers taught, for instance, that Helen Keller was an antiwar activist or that Martin Luther King, Jr. wrote more about ending the war in Vietnam than he did about civil rights. In other words, the dismissal of Indigenous spirituality is a part of cultural and educational hegemony, whereas there is no need to suppress the teaching of Western religions because they tend to allow for confirming the notion that hierarchical structures, violence, and war are a part of the history of God and human societies.

Thus, historical facts that contradict the cultural and educational hegemony that ignores or dismisses Indigenous spirituality get little attention. There is a large body of research that disproves claims that war and belligerence were prevalent in most Indigenous cultures. For example, Yale's

Human Resource Area Files, an internationally recognized organization in the field of cultural anthropology founded in 1949 to facilitate worldwide comparative studies of human behavior, has a large data base revealing that warfare, religious conflict, genocide, and massive civilian morbidity and morality from social wars were rare in most Indigenous societies (Four Arrows, 2008, p. 135.) The remarkable research of Johan M. G. van der Dennen, published in her doctoral thesis and subsequent book, *The Origin of War: The Evolution of a Male-Coalitional Reproductive Strategy* (1995) also supports the idea that Indigenous Wisdom can help remember ways of living in harmony that can lead to peaceful coexistence:

> Peaceable preindustrial (preliterate, primitive, etc.) societies constitute a nuisance to most theories of warfare and they are, with few exceptions, either denied or "explained away." In this contribution I shall argue that the claim of universal human belligerence is grossly exaggerated; and that those students who have been developing theories of war, proceeding from the premise that peace is the "normal" situation, have not been starry-eyed utopians. (p. 595)

She goes on to offer evidence that shows all war is a deliberate and seemingly rational political strategy, based on perceived cost/benefit considerations and ethical judgments by those in power. She describes the complexities that may have led Indigenous people to develop social mores that actually limit rather than promote violence. For example, she refers to Plains Indians' emphasis on individual feats of bravery such as a counting coup or stealing horses were far more important objectives than killing an enemy. She offers a comprehensive literature review of both biological and cultural theories of war, including many references that establish that primitive societies placed a great emphasis on healthy reciprocity as opposed to competition. For example, Leavitt's (1977) research found war absent or rare in 73% of hunting and gathering societies and it nearly half of those employing agriculture of some form (pp. 49-58).

If we accept that Indigenous ways of being in the world have leaned more toward peacefulness than the ways of being common to the dominant cultures of the western world, then we might assume that these ways, which we also know were grounded in the spiritual understandings of the Peoples, played a role in such peacefulness. In fact, if we look at the eight sacred concepts practiced by the Lakota that can be found in many other Indigenous societies, we can begin to see the relationship between peaceful relations and Indigenous spirituality.

Wowaunsila—compassion and pity. This is about giving ourselves to the People, which include the two legged, four legged, crawling, flying and swimming creatures, and giving our time, our energy and our prayers. It is about community and helping one another. It is about remembering that we are all related.

Wowascintanka—thoughtful reflection. This is about respecting intuition, reason and experience in ways that assure that our own sense of right outweighs external authority.

Wolokokiciapi—peacefulness within oneself and with all others. This recognizes that the natural state of all life emphasizes peacefulness but that we must constantly work to develop the virtues to assure that we cannot be misled from the peaceful path.

Woksape—wisdom. Wisdom comes from respectful listening and close observation of the natural worked, including animals, birds, fish, insects, plants, rocks, and bodies of water. Such entities are the creators of all the virtues that are gifts to help us with peace.

Wohetike—courage. Courage is the strength of character that prepares us to meet danger, to live our values, and to tell the truth in the face of ignorance.

Wowahwala—humility. This relates to a genuine belief that no one is above another, no superior to the rest of creation. When one embraces this, it is difficult to practice enmity or prejudice to rationalize violence.

Wacante Ognake—generosity. Generosity and appreciation are primary concepts for the spiritual practices of most Indigenous cultures. It enabled us to survive generations of economic and personal hardships. When we can remember to concern ourselves with helping others, we can mend the circles that have been broken by our escape from reality to materialism and selfishness, ideas that serve war not peace.

Wowayuonihan—to have respect and give significance to all creations. How can war and violence against others occur when we have such respect?!

Such primary concepts in Indigenous spirituality are not mandates from on high nor are they goals for salvation. Rather, they are inherent in daily life on all levels and in all manner of education. I have said that the failure to teach about Indigenous worldview as a way to convince people that we are a peaceful species is a part of educational and cultural hegemony. This implies a degree of intentionality at the curriculum and policy levels. I believe such hegemony is also sanctioned by many of the world's dominant religions that seem to support violence in spite of the calls for "peace on earth" that most of them also promote, because these eight concepts are too often ignored or are inconsistently applied in the scriptures of orthodox, written religions Such an allegation deserves a hearing if our goal is to move toward world peace. It would not be about placing one religion or spiritual tradition over another, but to the contrary. In believing that God is a Great Mysterious force, it is not surprising that Indigenous Peoples believe that there are many paths to walk as a way and

many ways to live a life that recognizes that everything is related, the ultimate spiritual recognition for Indigenous Peoples. Moreover, a serious
study of most religions, as is being done in this book, shows that all the
world's great religions have, at one time or another, teachings that coincide with the peaceful directions found in the Indigenous worldview.
However, the phenomenon of religious fundamentalism says the opposite
in claiming exclusive salvation. It should not be surprising that it has been
politically used throughout Western civilization to rationalize state sponsored violence or prowar hegemony. Such approaches to spiritual understanding are the opposite of seeing God as The Great Mysterious because
they require an authoritarian claim to knowing God and His instructions.
I and others claim, in spite of the many Native Peoples around the world
who are exchanging traditional Indigenous spirituality for orthodox
Christian fundamentalism, I propose that Indigenous spirituality is not
compatible with Christian fundamentalism, and my arguments can generally apply to any form of such orthodoxy. Spiritual life is analogous with a
life of learning for Indigenous Peoples. In his article, "Canaanites, Cowboys and Indians," published in *Christianity and Crisis,* Robert Allen Warrior (1989), a member of the Osage Nation, agrees that the Bible and any
literal translations will always be incompatible with authentic Indigenous
ways of seeing the world. He says that the Bible:

> Is part of the heritage and thus the consciousness of people in the United
> States. Whatever dangers we identity in the text and the god represented
> there will remain as long as the text remains. These dangers only grow as
> the emphasis upon catechetical (Lindbeck), narrative (Hauerwas), canonical
> (Childs) and Bible-centered Christian base communities (Gutierrez) grows.
> The peasants of Solentiname bring a wisdom and experience previously
> unknown to Christian theology, but I do not see what mechanism guaran-
> tees that they—or any other people who seek to be shaped and molded by
> reading the text—will differentiate between the liberating god and the god
> of conquest. But we, the wretched of the earth, may be well advised this time
> not to listen to outsiders with their promises of liberation and deliverance.
> We will perhaps do better to look elsewhere for our vision of justice, peace,
> and political sanity- a vision through which we escape not only our oppres-
> sors but our oppression as well. Maybe for once, we will just have to listen to
> ourselves, leaving the gods of this continent's real strangers to do battle
> among themselves. (p. 263)

Spirit is something that has amazingly rich meaning, but is too great to
be explained assuredly by people. It can only be discovered, and then
used to increase the richness of experience. To be spiritual is to learn
about the significance of things, seeking deeper and deeper levels of
meaningfulness in all that we do, see, and create. Finding meaning in

such things as childbirth, the spawning of salmon, the sound of thunder, the joy of love, or the pain of injury calls for a very personal approach to learning. It requires contemplation, alertness, skills of observation, intuitive and reasoned reflection on experience, respect for the many great teachers of all sorts that one comes across, creative involvement, and courageous participation in life. All of this is possible in light of an authentic humility and a deep courage that come knowing that the incredible gift of life, its source and its finality cannot be defined, nor bottled into books written by humans and controlled by human institutions.

The influence of Christian fundamentalism and a criticism of it is not a rejection of the great teachings embodied in the Bible that are repeated by the founders of other dominant religions, but rather a rejection of the political dogma that arises from it. Today's "religious right" in politics and its 8-year history under the Bush administration should be an example if we consider the connections between it and the various forms of violence it tends to nurture. The resurgent requirement for exclusive salvation the religious right has brought to bear on American politics (and spirituality?) has involved a fraudulent call to patriotism alongside a revisionist view of America's founding that continues to ignore the influence of the Iroquois Confederacy on our constitution and hence its spiritual contribution to democracy (Johansen, 2008). There seems to be an effort to convince people that this fundamentalist movement is simply an effort to return our nation to what the founding fathers intended, though it is not what they intended.

In fact, many of America's revolutionary leaders were deists who blatantly rejected Christian doctrine, even when "swearing an oath" on a Christian Bible, a holdover from previous times. The Bible Washington swore on was, by the way, a Masonic Bible, essentially the same text but symbolizing significant deviations in belief. Deists, such as Washington, Paine, Jefferson, Voltaire, Franklin, and Allen did not believe in the virgin birth, divinity, the resurrection of Jesus, or the divine inspiration of the Bible. They did not believe in the doctrine of exclusive salvation. They did not fear death but saw it as another part of nature (see Boller, 1963, p. 92). In his famous *Age of Reason*, the father of the American Revolution, Thomas Paine (1807/1996), referred to this doctrine when he said, "We must be compelled to hold this doctrine to be false, and the old and new law called the Old and New Testament, to be impositions, fables and forgeries" (p. 134). Paine say in such impositions an unnatural rational for the oppressive politics that caused the injustices of European life and that would continue to be perpetrated on the American Indians. Furthermore, he contrasted the European worldview with the life and worldviews of the Indigenous Peoples he observed. "Among the Indians," he wrote, "There are not any of those spectacles of misery that poverty and want present to our eyes in the towns and streets of Europe" (p. 282).

Vine Deloria Jr. (1992) agreed with Paine's concern. He argues in his classic *God is Red* that a polarity exists between Native religiosity and Christianity, as it is practiced in the U.S. especially, because of Christianity's relative disregard for the sacredness of "place." The Indigenous understanding of geography, Nature, landscape, and other aspects of place are crucial aspects of Indigenous spirituality that lead to a balance and peacefulness not generally seen in Western civilizations during the past 5,000 years.

In an effort to "solve" the problems that such fundamentalism has brought to silencing the voice of Indigenous People and its contribution to world health and peace, I wish to introduce a new consideration that might be able to reconcile Christianity to both itself and to Indigenous spirituality. In brief, my hypothesis suggests that original Christian thought, based on the purported teachings of Jesus of Nazareth, represented an understanding of both the physical and the spiritual in balance. However, political structures put into places less than 100 years after the death of Jesus established an authoritarian version of these teachings, one based on the "physical" aspects only. At the same time, an opposing understanding of the teachings asserted a more "spiritual" aspect and this group was branded by the other as heretical. The point is that the Gnostic interpretations which were advocated by early followers of Jesus but were seen as heresy by those that established the organized religion actually coincide with Indigenous spirituality. For example, both see authority only in personal reflection; both embrace the feminine; both reject the doctrine of original sin, on so on.

If one accepts this split within Christianity not as oppositional factors, but potential complementary ones, then Indigenous spirituality can offer a way for Christianity to regain its balance in ways that will avoid the violence perpetrated in its name. Indigenous stories and myths offer such a way, especially as relates to "twin" stories.

Every culture has stories of twin heroes, with the twins reflecting the complementarity of body and spirit; of solar and lunar; of male and female principles. For example, the Navajo stories about the twins, Monster Slayer and Child Born of the Water, show how important it is for these opposing energies to work together in harmony. In fact, most Indigenous cultures have similar stories about twins that work together to fight the monsters (that ultimately reside within us). In fact, most cultures have such stories, however, many of the twin stories from Western cultural myths have evolved in such a way as to have the twins fighting one another or with the solar twin overpowering the lunar one. For example,

Cain slew Abel, Romulus overshadowed Remus; Hercules became more honored than Iphicles.

Thus, playing out the myths of the separated twins, Christianity has emerged primarily as the "solar" twin: active, heroic, intent on mastery. Adherents must believe in the physical resurrection; only Jesus and belief in his physical reality can bring eternal salvation. This "religion of the sun" prevails over Gnostic Christianity—the spiritual twin that reveals "god" in all things and accepts the spiritual mystery at the heart of creation. Thus, Indigenous spirituality may be one of the forces that can reunite the Christian twins! The dominant, assertive "above Nature" cultures, under the banner of Christian fundamentalism, including Islamic and Jewish versions, may be the "twin" of the more reflective, creative Indigenous spiritual traditions based upon Nature. With such a rebalancing, the "fifth world" of peaceful relationships that the Hopi predict may have a chance to manifest. This is the spirituality of people of the water, the people who:

1. See reflection on lived experience, on intuitive spiritual awareness, and on cultural traditions that "make sense" for the greater good as the only true authority in life.

2. Believe that animals are fellow creatures, not lowly ones.

3. Put the community above selfish individualism or ambition and hold that cooperation, not competition, is the natural dynamic in life.

4. Maintain an even balance of power between men and women.

5. Respect the development of children, who are considered sacred, with a higher degree of permissiveness and positive peer pressure.

6. Recognize and respect the significance of everyone in the community.

7. View criminals as people out of balance who need to be brought back into the community, rather than as villains.

8. Value self-sacrifice, generosity and courage as ideals for adulthood.

9. Believe that honesty and integrity are too important to allow for deception.

10. Understand that the spirit life—good heart, love of neighbor as your brother, sister, mother, father, grandparents—is at the heart of spiritual practices.

11. Assert that generosity is the greatest virtue and the highest expression of courage and

12. Recognize the interconnectivity between humans and Nature as the ultimate reality.

The gift of American Indian spirituality to contemporary education is its ability to move educational theory beyond classroom doors and literally into the sun and under the moon. There can be little doubt as to the contribution to peace on earth from its perspectives as we have seen. Non-Indians do not need to change religions or participate in unique tribal ceremonies and rituals to benefit from this enlargement. If given their due, however, these spiritual assumptions force us to recall forgotten realities. With this memory, we are more likely to do what we can to break down the concrete walls protecting the destructive institutions that surround us.

Another way to say this is that if we embrace some of the spiritual assumptions of our First Nations, then education will stop being something that stands separate from spiritual life. We will ponder why we choose the subjects we teach and if there are more important priorities. We will learn new ways to engage people in matters of significance.

If teachers enter a classroom without this sense of Spirit, they will have difficulty nurturing its natural growth in the children. If parents remain unwilling to reflect on the significance of experience, their children will likely ignore such meaning as well. If community members assert absolute answers from uninvestigated authority that crush continual, open-minded inquiry and dialogue, creative impulses nurtured in spiritual schools may become lost outside of them.

One way to help young people in schools to carry "spiritual education" from classroom to community comes from learning how to think about thinking, one of the ways Indian people come to understand whether or not—and, if so, how—life experience dovetails with sacred truths. Children who practice metacognition begin to know themselves in ways that allow for consistent application of spiritual values in any setting. This self-awareness brings a degree of individual freedom which alone can bring true cooperation with others, with the whole. It is the function of education to help individuals discover their own psychological hindrances to the expression of natural love, not impose another's way of thinking or behaving. Eventually, children who are taught to continually reflect on their own thinking come to understand their spiritual connections to the communities around them. They become the community and then the community itself becomes spiritual. In my book *Primal Awareness* (Jacobs, 1998) I offer a mnemonic for remembering the major influences on our beliefs and how indigenous interpretations of these influences can help keep us on a spiritual path where transformation is more important than memorizing facts or rigidly defined knowledge that is common to most curricula. "FAWN" reminds us that these influences relate to fear, authority, words, and Nature. The most important of these now for our times has to do with our relationship with Nature.

As I have stated several times earlier, a sacred view of Nature is foundational to American Indian reflection on experience and significance. It is
a key for spiritual education in our modern world. Not surprisingly, it also
plays a key role in metacognition, or thinking about thinking. Sam Keen
(1994) says in his book *Hymns to an Unknown God*, "One way to define
modernity is to trace the process by which nature has been desacralized
and God has moved indoors" (p. 27). Western education, though it has
much we can respect, has too often placed humans over Nature. In the
Phaedrus, Socrates, the father of Western philosophy, says, "I'm a lover of
learning, and trees and open country won't teach me anything, whereas
men in the town do" (Plato, 1982, p. 479). Anthropocentrism has nourished our materialism and technological success, but our reasoning minds
have ironically become unreasonable. Our actions take us in the opposite
direction of logical, moral, ethical, and spiritual priorities.

Defining spirituality as that which is significant in the most sacred
sense means realizing the truth about our relationship with Nature. We
see ourselves as a part of Nature and see Nature as part of us. Through
deep concentration, meditation, ritual, observation, art, music, and stories, we can achieve an appreciation of the great complexities of Nature.
We see it not as something to be feared, but as something wonderful. This
leads to a sense of oneness with rather than separation from the source of
life that is Nature. We are less inclined to ignore, retreat from or destroy
Nature, and more likely to learn from her diverse lessons.

When thinking about thinking and embracing this "primal awareness"
of Nature, we can rediscover the origins of love. This requires going
beyond normal thinking into states of consciousness that allow us to tap
into the universal wisdom that exists in Nature. We spontaneously love the
colors, the energy, and the beauty that fill our senses. We regain sensa-
tions that ultimately give us the multidimensional capability for genuine
and harmonious loving relationships. Without a constant affiliation with
Nature in our thinking, we are kept from reaching our potential for
unconditional love.

Perhaps Nature's unparalleled ability to create balance amidst chaos is
part of the reason. Whatever the answer, we know that Nature as teacher is
a factor in why wilderness treatment programs for troubled youth tend to
succeed, why pristine wilderness vacations can renew our spirit, and why
Indigenous cultures emerged as cooperative systems that emphasized
equity and art. In fact, the concept of art in education when understood
in light of American Indian spirituality can be a model for teaching.
Imagine what might happen if we all saw teaching as an art form, not art
as conceived in western culture as a diversion or entertainment, but a creation from the heart and soul. We could trust teachers to be creative,
rather than stifle their creativity with mile-wide, inch-deep curriculum

and mandates for standardized testing. From Nature we might understand the fury of art as a creative force that like life itself should not be contained by an overemphasis on comfort and convenience. We might come to appreciate that "life as art," like a beautiful sand painting, is at once both profound and impermanent; with this realization, we may live life more fully.

We understand that each day may be our last on this beautiful planet and that the vibrations we create have the potential to provide our children's children with a world that has not lost its health, beauty, and peacefulness. If we allow it and nurture it, American Indian education can help us all realize this spiritual awareness. With it all educators will feel free to emphasize authentic self-reflection; to remember Nature as teacher; to see teaching as art; and to give significance to that which truly matters. As did native children from around the world for tens of thousands of years, all children may come to "honor the teacher of spirit within themselves and the natural world." This is the educational legacy of Indigenous people, a legacy that constantly reminds us that we are all related and to do violence to another is to do violence to ourselves. It is imperative that this legacy and its message be revitalized for life's sake. Consider these approaches to conflict resolution common to Indigenous societies as an alternative to war:

1. Replace a focus on retribution, hierarchy, and laws with a focus on authentic transformation.
2. Emphasize win-win outcomes over win-lose outcomes.
3. Incorporate spiritual awareness, not religious orthodoxy, into pedagogy.
4. Widen the circle of responsibility and blame for problems to include links in the chain generally not considered.
5. Begin to see responsibility as more important than rights.
6. Make the earth and its creatures more important than materialism in your life.
7. Understand the relationship between violence and shame.
8. Make the commitment to restore balance more important than commitments to exact revenge or punishment.

I realize I have made some strong statements about the potential for Indigenous spirituality to make a contribution to world peace and that some might find me guilty in both my critique of Western culture and religion and in my praise of Indigenous spirituality of romanticizing the Indigenous. Allow me to address this concern with a quote from my chapter in the *Encyclopedia of American Indian History, Volume II*, edited by Bruce Johansen and Barry Pritzker about the "myth of the noble savage."

> One of the most enduring, ironic, and perhaps damaging of the concepts used to describe American Indians is represented both by the idea of a "noble savage" and by the phrase, "myth of the noble savage." In the first instance, the oxymoronic pairing of words and the myth that has surrounded them put Native peoples in an untenable social position. In the second instance, they myth idea has been used to dismiss the legitimate contributions, worldviews and qualities of Indigenous People. (p. 441)

The myth of the noble savage has been but one of the European ideas that served to colonize and oppress American Indians. Even in contemporary times, the media has made American Indians appear as anything but who they really are: a perfect side-kick for a White hero; a dangerous foil for the military might of other White heroes; or a romantic artifact of the past. In my celebrating and advocating for Indigenous spirituality as an important way of understanding ways to achieve world peace, I fully recognize that all peoples of every race have the same potentiality for moving in both positive and negative directions, and that Indigenous individuals and societies can be as ignorant and violent as any other society. However, the facts speak for themselves as to how the spiritual foundations of Indigenous Peoples have managed to uphold traditions of peacefulness and I entertain no romantic myths about this possibility. In fact, I think that if we do not begin to embrace the vision of "the seventh generation" as it common for Indigenous Peoples and substitute it for the corporate quarterly profit report, we are all in big trouble. *Mitakuye Oyasin* (We are all related).

REFERENCES

Boller, P. F. (1963). *George Washington & religion*. Dallas, TX: Southern Methodist.

Carmody, D., & Carmondy, J. (1993). *Native American religions*. New York: Paulist Press.

Deloria, V. (1994). *God is red*. Golden, CO: Fulcrum.

DeMeo, J. (2008). Peaceful versus warlike societies in pre-columbian America: what do archaelology and anthropology tell us? In Four Arrows (Ed.), *Unlearning the language of conquest*. Austin, TX: University of Texas Press.

Four Arrows. (1996). *Unlearning the language of conquest: Scholars expose anti-Indianism in America*. Austin, TX: University of Texas Press.

Jacobs, D. T. (1998) *Primal awareness: A true story of survival, transformation, and awakening with the Raramuri shaman of Mexico*. Rochester, VT: Inner Traditions International.

Johansen, B. (2008). Adventures in denial. In Four Arrows (Ed.), *Unlearning the language of conquest*. Austin, TX: University of Texas Press.

Keen, S. (1994). *Hymns to an unknown god*. New York: Bantam.

Leavitt, G. C. (1977). The frequency of warfare: An evolutionary perspective. *Social Inquiry, 47*, 49-58.

McGaa, E. (1990). *Mother earth spirituality: Native American paths to healing ourselves and our world*. San Francisco: HarperSanFrancisco.

Paine, T. (1996). *The age of reason*. Pomerory, WA: Health Research. (Original work published 1807)

Plato. (1982). Phaedrus (R. Hackforth, Trans.) In H. Cairns & E. Hamilton (Eds.), *The collected dialogues of Plato* (p. 479). Princeton, NJ: Princeton University Press.

Smith, H. (1991). *The world's religions*. San Francisco: Harper Collins.

Trevor-Roper, H. (1965) *The rise of Christian Europe*. London: Thames & Hudson.

Van der Dennen, J. M. G. (1995). *The origin of war: The evolution of male-coalitional reproductive strategy* (2 vols.). Groningen, The Netherlands: Origin Press.

Warrior, R. A. (1989, September 11). Canaanites, cowboys and Indians: Deliverence, conquest, and liberation theology today. *Christianity and Crisis*.

PART II

PEACE EDUCATION,
TEACHING AND LEARNING, AND SPIRITUALITY

CHAPTER 9

CONTEMPLATIVE PRACTICES IN COUNSELING AND EDUCATION

A Course in Nonviolent Intervention for Counselors and Teachers

Nathalie Kees

INTRODUCTION

Counselors and teachers are on the front lines of working with people who are in conflict or have experienced emotional and physical violence and trauma. People are often drawn into these professions by their compassionate and caring natures. Compassion can soon turn into "compassion fatigue" however as counselors and teachers become overwhelmed with the intensity and duration of the emotions they experience in their work with clients and students (Kees & Lashwood, 1996; Stebnicki, 2008). From a place of compassion fatigue, counselors and teachers may rush toward solutions, quick fixes, and advice giving with their clients and students,

Spirituality, Religion, and Peace Education, pp. 149–162
Copyright © 2010 by Information Age Publishing
All rights of reproduction in any form reserved.

when what is needed may simply be empathic listening and compassionate witnessing as first steps in the discernment of right action.

Providing counselors and teachers with the skills and techniques needed to transform compassion fatigue into quiet stillness, deep, empathic listening, and right action is often overlooked in training programs. The purpose of this chapter is to describe a course developed for counselors and teachers at Colorado State University in which contemplative practices from the major spiritual and religious traditions are presented experientially by spiritual teachers and practitioners in the fields of counseling and teaching. These contemplative practices serve as pathways toward nonviolent, compassionate interventions with clients and students. Experiencing diverse spiritual traditions and practices also allows students of this course to expand their understanding of different cultures and develop more universal perspectives when working with clients and students who are different from themselves. Increased perspective taking is an essential element in practicing nonviolent counseling and teaching interventions (Brantmeier, 2008; Harris, 1999). In the second part of this chapter, I will provide direct applications of three of these contemplative practices into the work of counselors and teachers. Last, I will discuss the relationship between contemplative practices in counseling and education and peace education.

CONTEMPLATIVE PRACTICES

Contemplative practices are those practices which enable us to quiet our minds, emotions, physical bodies, and spirits in an effort to increase awareness of, and connection to, our true nature. Through this increased awareness, we are able to move toward understanding our interconnectedness with all beings, empathizing with the experiences and emotions of others, and, from this place of heightened compassionate awareness, discern appropriate, right, or compassionate action (Hanh, 1991; Palmer, 1990).

Through their extensive research with prominent teachers of contemplative practices, the Center for Contemplative Mind in Society has delineated seven categories of contemplative practices. These include; (1) stillness practices, (2) movement practices, (3) creation process practices, (4) activist practices, (5) generative practices, (6) ritual/cyclical practices, and (7) relational practices (For examples of practices within each of these categories see http://www.contemplativemind.org/programs/cnet/practices.html). While a spiritual or religious perspective is not necessary to engage in contemplative practices, many of these practices have their origins in the world's major spiritual and religious traditions.

Contemplative Practices in Counseling and Education

The incorporation of contemplative practices into counseling and education has drawn increasing scholarly interest over the past 20 years. In the fields of counseling and psychology, one type of contemplative practice, mindfulness, is being tested for its effectiveness in the treatment of chronic pain, stress, anxiety, depression, personality disorders, and eating disorders (Allen, Blashki, & Gullone, 2006). While research in this area is still developing, and additional rigor such as more controlled studies, larger sample sizes, and replication studies need to be incorporated, the initial research findings show promise for mindfulness techniques as effective therapeutic interventions (Allen et al., 2006).

One of the areas of psychotherapy that is embracing contemplative practices is behavioral therapy, with newer, mindfulness-based behavior therapies being considered the "third wave of behavior therapy" (Corey, 2009, p. 254). These newer therapies acknowledge the mind-body connection, helping clients develop present moment awareness by utilizing relaxation, visualization, and mindfulness techniques in order to manage physiological, affective, and behavioral symptoms. Three of these approaches include dialectical behavior therapy (DBT) (Linehan, 1993), used often with personality disorders such as borderline personality; mindfulness-based stress reduction (MBSR) (Kabat-Zinn, 1990), used to reduce anxiety and stress; and mindfulness-based cognitive therapy (MBCT) (Segal, Williams, & Teasdale, 2002) used in treating depression. Other contemplative practices such as meditation, silence, and contemplative prayer are being used in psychotherapy with individuals, couples, and families, and in counselor training (Blanton, 2007; Gale, 2009; Jankowski, 2006; Newsome, Christopher, Dahlen, & Christopher, 2006; Van Meter, McMinn, Bissell, Kaur, & Pressley, 2003).

In the field of education, contemplative practices such as silence, meditation, mindfulness, and creative contemplation are being used in classrooms from elementary to university level, in public as well as private schools, in physics classrooms as well as humanities (Hart, 2004; Hill, 2006; Palmer, 2007; Zajonc, 2006). Poet Laureate of the State of Connecticut, Marilyn Nelson, uses meditation and contemplative writing techniques with cadets in her poetry course at the United States Military Academy at West Point (Nelson, 2001) and in her course on the poetry of war and peace at the University of Connecticut. She states, "I strive to teach not technique, but attitude. I ask my students to explore several ways of listening for, and listening to, silence. I hope that they will develop a contemplative attitude and learn how to hear silence" (Nelson, 2006, p. 1733). From this place of awareness and attention, her students describe experiences of increased connection with, and empathy for, others, nature, and what is happening in the present moment. Some of her students told her of experiences as they were deployed in Iraq and talked about how they became involved in civil affairs projects in villages including helping to build and improve schools and clinics.

Nelson's work is part of a larger project begun by the Center for Contemplative Mind in Society in 1996 to offer fellowships to higher education instructors interested in incorporating contemplative practices into their college courses. The Center now has 120 fellows in 80 colleges and universities across the country (Bush, 2006). The Center also held a national conference on contemplative practices and education at Teachers College, Columbia University in 2005. A special issue of the *Teachers College Record* resulted from that conference and provides information regarding many of the fellows' work of integrating contemplative practices into education (Hill, 2006). Clifford Hill, the editor of this special issue, also discusses how the work of contemplative education is impacting social change, increasing tolerance, and educating for peace (Hill, Herndon, & Karpinska, 2006).

One question that arises is; how does one incorporate contemplative practices into public education and still maintain the separation of church and state? Arthur Zajonc, professor of physics at Amherst, answers this by stating that contemplative practices do not teach the "what" of spirituality but are part of the "how" of knowing and therefore essential components of all education, research, and empirical study (Zajonc, 2003). We understand something by bringing our full attention and awareness to it. We seek to understand before intervening. This is the foundation of contemplative counseling and education.

Parker Palmer (2007), author and consultant to educators all over the country, comes from a Quaker tradition of silence, questioning, and direct experience of insight. Based on this tradition, Palmer suggests that, in our present world of public education based on testing and accountability, a few moments of silence at the beginning of a class period can be considered a radical act yet can create an atmosphere where students and teachers are able to collect themselves and form what he calls a "community of knowers" ready to contemplate and study the big questions and truths of any discipline. Both Zajonc and Palmer suggest that we help students ask and consider the big questions that do not have easy, readily available answers yet impact us all, such as; How do we act in our daily lives in the face of such disparate access to food, water, and other resources worldwide? How do we maintain an open and compassionate heart in the midst of our own and others' suffering? How do we discern right and appropriate action given our limited viewing point? (Palmer, 1998). The following course is one I designed to help counselors and teachers, clients and students begin to contemplate some of these important questions and formulate their own plans for right and compassionate action.

THE COURSE

In 2000, I began development of a graduate level course for counselors and teachers in training in which various contemplative practices from the major spiritual and religious traditions would be presented, experienced, and applied to the fields of counseling and education. Some of the contemplative practices incorporated into the course include; (1) mindfulness, tonglen, and walking meditations from Buddhism, (2) centering prayer, labyrinth walking, and pilgrimage from Christianity, (3) yoga nidra meditation from Hinduism, (4) dances of universal peace and chanting from Sufism/Islam, (5) Ho'oponopono from native Hawaiian tradition, (6) mystical Kabbalah from Judaism, (7) silence and the clearness committee from the Quaker tradition, and (8) rituals and practices from Wiccan and Pagan traditions.

Spiritual teachers from these various traditions, who are also professionals in the counseling and teaching professions, serve as guest presenters in the class. These experts provide authenticity as they take students through directed experiences of the contemplative practices, provide background information on the historical, spiritual, and religious origins of the practices, and offer practical application strategies from the fields of counseling and education. The lives and works of spiritual teachers and peace activists such as Peace Pilgrim, Thich Nhat Hanh, Scott and Helen Nearing, Jane Goodall, Aung San Suu Kyi, and Rosa Parks are also included in the course as role models for right action. Students develop plans for application of course content to their elected fields.

Following, I will expand upon just a few of these contemplative practices and how they apply to the fields of counseling and education. Application to peace and reconciliation work will also be discussed. Included are the practice of tonglen from Buddhism, Ho'oponopono from native Hawaiian tradition, and pilgrimage and labyrinth walking from Christianity. Each practice will be related to skills necessary for counselors and teachers in their work as nonviolent practitioners and conflict mediators.

Tonglen as a Path to Empathy and Compassion

Tonglen is a Buddhist practice of expanding one's awareness of suffering and transforming that suffering into compassion for oneself, others, and the world. According to Buddhist nun and teacher, Pema Chodron (2001):

> *Tonglen*, or the practice of sending and taking, reverses [the] process of hardening or shutting down by cultivating love and compassion … instead of running from pain and discomfort, we acknowledge them and own them fully. Instead of dwelling on our own problems, we put ourselves in other people's shoes and appreciate our shared humanity. Then the barriers start to dissolve, our hearts and minds begin to open. (pp. 3-4)

As with many contemplative practices, the steps of the tonglen process appear simple yet can be difficult to master. The first step is to open one's heart and mind by connecting with an image, feeling, or sense of openness or space. Connecting with an image such as the vastness of the blue sky is one recommendation. In the second step, we practice breathing in difficult feelings or 'textures' such as darkness, heaviness, or sadness and breathing out feelings of lightness, spaciousness, or openness (Chodron, 2001). It is important to allow ourselves to fully experience the difficult feelings before we then transform them with the out-breath into lightness or spaciousness. From this practice of fully experiencing difficult feelings, we increase our capacity for compassion, empathy, and transformation.

Step three involves practicing this in and out breath with people and situations in your own life. You may begin with people you love who are suffering, breathing in their pain and hurt and sending them compassion and love with the out breath. You can also use any difficult feelings you may be having and transform them into compassion for all who are feeling similar feelings. In step four you practice tonglen for all sentient beings, realizing that suffering is a universal feeling and that our practice of tonglen can send spaciousness, compassion, and love to all those in need (Chodron, 1994). Through this practice we can learn to fully empathize with others, allowing ourselves to completely feel what they may be feeling, knowing that our compassionate presence may help them feel less alone as we send out love and expansiveness with each out breath.

Let us apply this practice to an example from the fields of counseling and education. A young person is engaged in self-mutilation through cutting him or her self with a razor or knife. It may be difficult for a counselor or teacher to empathize with this person without experiencing fear, revulsion, or confusion about what motivates this behavior. Through the practice of tonglen, the listener can breathe in the internal pain of the cutter and breathe out space for exploration of what motivates or drives these actions. Opening this compassionate space can be very revealing. People who self-mutilate are often trying to create an outward representation of their internal, emotional pain. Self-mutilation can represent a cleansing or releasing of internal pain or an attempt to obliterate emotional pain through competing physical pain (Smith, 2006). It has even been suggested that cutting may serve the purpose of "atoning for one's real or imagined sins" similar to other forms of self injury, deprivation, or flagellation found in many religious traditions (Plante, 2007, p. 53). Dr. Plante suggests that for some, "Cutting serves as a declaration of war on the unwanted aspect of self, affording the teen a temporary sense of power and pride" (p. 53).

Moving into judgment and quick fixes is a typical reaction when working with this population. Often we want to stop their pain and self-injury in an attempt to escape our own pain as witnesses to their acts of violence toward themselves. Practicing tonglen while working with the self-injurious teen can create space for a "cease fire" of the behavior, allowing for other nondestructive forms of emotional release, catharsis, and healing through empathic, non-judgmental listening and caring interventions.

Ho'oponopono, Forgiveness, and Conflict Resolution

In the summer of 2006, Dr. Ihaleakala Hew Len traveled at his own expense from California to Colorado to present to my contemplative practices class a modernized form of an ancient native Hawaiian healing practice called Ho'oponopono. Dr. Hew Len was taught this practice from his spiritual teacher, or Kahuna Lapa'au, Mormah Nalamaku Simeona in 1982 and used it for many years in his work as a staff psychologist at the Hawaii State Hospital for the criminally mentally ill. He currently teaches this practice all over the world, including the United Nations, as a peacemaking and conflict resolution tool and therapeutic intervention for individuals, families, organizations, and communities (http://www.hooponoponotheamericas.org/peace-of-i.htm). A good deal of research has been conducted over the past 30 years on the usefulness of this spiritual practice as a multicultural therapeutic intervention and as a conflict resolution and peacemaking process (Andres, 2002; Boggs & Chun, 1990; Forisha, Wright, & Tucker, 2005; Hurdle, 2002; Ito, 1985, 1999; Merry, 2001; Omuro-Yamamoto, 2001; Patten, 1994; Shook, 1985).

Ho'oponopono is a philosophical way of being in the world and relating to self and others. While the conceptual framework of Ho'oponopono is more complicated than can be described here, the basic practice requires us to accept full responsibility for ourselves and all that happens in the world. Ho'oponopono suggests that we, and every other sentient being and/or piece of matter in the world, are part of divine creation and therefore interconnected, not only in this lifetime but through our ancestors and relatives as well. When problems or difficulties occur, rather than externalizing blame, practitioners of Ho'oponopono use various spiritual tools to clear their own personal and historical connections to, and responsibility for, the problem. Because the problem or difficulty exists and we are all interconnected, we are all involved and can begin the process of resolution through the practice of Ho'oponopono.

The most basic practice is to repeat the phrase "I am sorry, please forgive me" to oneself at all levels of consciousness. In this way, the problem begins to be resolved or cleared at an intrapersonal level and can move from there to the interpersonal, global, and universal levels. Practitioners of Ho'oponopono use these and other "cleaning" tools on a continuous basis as a way of healing themselves and, through our interconnectedness, healing others and the world.

Dr. Hew Len and others connected to the Foundation of I, Inc. are teaching these practices to non-native Hawaiians as well in an effort to engage the world in the peacemaking process. The practice has been a part of my contemplative practices class since its inception in 2000. As counselors and teachers practice their own healing and clearing, they begin to open space for peace, forgiveness, and reconciliation for their clients, students, and organizations as well.

In interpersonal conflicts, it only requires one person to begin the reconciliation process. Rather than waiting for the "perpetrator" to admit guilt and apologize, anyone can begin the reconciliation process by accepting their connection to the conflict and, by saying "I'm sorry, please forgive me," the healing process is begun. This is not to suggest a "blame the victim" mentality or a "martyr" stance. Instead, paradoxically, the practice of Ho'oponopono empowers those involved, including the injured party, mediator, counselor, or teacher, to take the initiative and begin the healing process. If one's goal in practicing Ho'oponopono is to elicit an apology from another however, then the practice becomes yet another form of violent intervention and is typically unsuccessful. The practitioner keeps their focus on self responsibility and creating a space for whatever healing may need to occur.

Pilgrimage, Labyrinth Walking, and Right Action

In the words of the late Peace Pilgrim, "A pilgrim is a wanderer with a purpose. A pilgrimage can be to a place—that's the best known kind—but it can also be for a thing. Mine is for peace, and that is why I am a Peace Pilgrim" (Friends of Peace Pilgrim, 2004, p. 25). Peace Pilgrim's pledge was to "walk until given shelter, fast until given food, remaining a wanderer until mankind has learned the way of peace" (p. 4). Her message was simple, yet one we still have not learned, "This is the way of peace: Overcome evil with good, falsehood with truth, and hatred with love" (p. 26). She took a vow of simplicity, "I shall not accept more than I need while others in the world have less than they need" (p. 51). Peace Pilgrim walked for almost 30 years, crossing the United States seven times, spreading her message of peace. She owned only the clothes on her back and a few items in her pocket. She says she rarely went for more than a day or two without being offered food or shelter and that these acts of generosity showed us all that peace and goodness are possible. Few of us are as committed a pilgrim as Peace Pilgrim was, yet each moment of our lives can be thought of as a pilgrimage, either to a sacred site or for a just cause.

For thousands of years, pilgrims of many faiths have made pilgrimages to sacred sites all over the world. Making at least one Hajj, or pilgrimage to Mecca, is a lifelong goal of devout Muslims. Christians make pilgrimages to miraculous sites such as Lourdes, Medjugorge, and Santiago de Compostela (Repath, 2007). Hindus make the "grand pilgrimage circuit of the Ganges—tracing it along one bank from its source to its mouth, then returning along the other bank from its mouth to its source" (Leviton, 1994, p. 26). Dr. Lauren Artress (2006) states that "The tradition of pilgrimage is as old as religion itself" (p. 31). Dr. Artress has spent her life studying great pilgrimage sites such as Chartres Cathedral in France and reviving the pilgrimage tradition of walking the labyrinth as one form of pilgrimage.

The labyrinth is an ancient symbol with a recorded history dating back to 2500 B.C.E. (Artress, 2006). The labyrinth differs from a maze in that the labyrinth has only one path in and out, whereas a maze has many false starts. Artress states that the maze "engages the mind" and "challenges the choice-making part of ourselves" (p. 51). The labyrinth, on the other hand, "presents us with only one, but profound, choice" and represents the choice to "walk a spiritual path" (p. 52). During the eleventh, twelfth, and thirteenth centuries in Europe, the Christian church chose seven cathedrals as pilgrimage sites and inlaid labyrinth designs into the cathedral floors. The labyrinth at Chartres Cathedral is the last intact example. Pilgrims could walk the cathedral's labyrinth as a spiritual practice or as a substitute for making a pilgrimage to distant sacred sites, such as Jerusalem, when expense and war made traveling prohibitive. For the past twenty years, Dr. Artress has trained facilitators and conducted groups of pilgrims to walk the labyrinth at Chartres Cathedral and in 1991, she and her non-profit organization, Veriditas, installed a replica of the Chartres labyrinth at Grace Cathedral in San Francisco. Her work has spread the practice of walking the labyrinth throughout North America and labyrinths can now be found at many churches, healing centers, and hospice organizations across the United States (www.veriditas.org).

As part of the course in contemplative practices at Colorado State University, students walk the labyrinth as a practice in mindfulness meditation. Hospice of Larimer County has installed an outdoor replica of the Chartres labyrinth and it is open to the public to use at any time. In the hospice setting, walking the labyrinth provides solace and quiet for those who have lost loved ones or are in the midst of difficult end-of-life decisions. Students in the course look forward to our time at the hospice labyrinth as an opportunity to integrate all of the teachings and practices they have experienced in the course thus far. As they walk the labyrinth, students begin to imagine how their insights and awareness will manifest in their work as counselors and teachers. From a place of quiet and solitude, students begin to realize how they may become agents for right action within their chosen professions.

Another use of the labyrinth as a tool for peace, forgiveness, and healing is the reconciliation labyrinth created by Clare Wilson, a White South African, as part of the peace and reconciliation movement in South Africa (http://www.labyrinths.co.za/). This double sided labyrinth was designed for the purpose of acknowledging the very different places from which the oppressed and the oppressor begin in the reconciliation process. The labyrinth helps individuals increase their understanding of the other's perspective and perhaps, if willing to join together in the center, they may exit together with the possibility of a third or new path.

The two people enter the labyrinth from separate entrances. At the midpoint they cross and follow the others' path. At another point they can choose either to exit the labyrinth or to join together in the center which represents a place where their hearts can open to one another. At the center, silent contemplation, meditation, reflective listening, asking for forgiveness or rituals of reconciliation and making amends can take place. The participants can then choose to exit the labyrinth through a common path which represents a shared vision or resolution. There are currently over 30 reconciliation labyrinths throughout South Africa and its use has spread to other countries including the United States (http://www.transformationcenter.org/labyrinth.htm).

The reconciliation labyrinth can be used with anyone in conflict or where a third path is needed. In the fields of counseling and teaching, this could include; couples work, working with parents and children, restorative justice, divorce mediation, and school related conflicts, to name a few.

CONTEMPLATIVE PRACTICE AND PEACE EDUCATION

The Dalai Lama has been quoted as saying, "If we are to make peace in the world, we must first make peace in ourselves" (Hill et al., 2006, p. 1915). This is the foundation of the course in contemplative practices which I have described here. The Dalai Lama's words provide us with hope, but not necessarily a guarantee. Inner peace does not automatically translate into right action or peaceful coexistence. The literature is beginning to make a case however, that inner peace is the vital starting point for any truly nonviolent intervention. A moment spent in silence, contemplation, and empathy can provide a much more stable basis from which steps toward compassionate right action can be taken. Without this moment for increased awareness and understanding, we can often do more harm than good, even when our intentions are meant to be helpful.

Counselors and teachers are in particularly advantageous positions to help their clients and students learn the contemplative approach to peacemaking. As Maria Montessori (1972) said, "Preventing conflicts is the work of politics; establishing peace is the work of education" (p. 30). Counselors and teachers are already instrumental in engaging clients and students in the activities of peacemaking and peace education described by Harris (1999) including, but not limited to, conflict resolution and mediation, communication skills, anger management, nonviolence, caring, empathy, and empowerment. One example comes from the Center for Safe Schools and Communities in Erie, CO. As part of this nonprofit organization, Sara Salmon (2003) has developed "The PEACE Curriculum." The letters in PEACE stand for *P*arent empowerment, *E*mpathy training, *A*nger management, *C*haracter education, and *E*ssential social skills. This curriculum is helping to create safer schools throughout the United States and is also being used in other organizations such as hospitals and detention centers.

The field of counseling is realizing the important role counselors play in peace education and peacemaking. Gerstein and Moeschberger (2003) describe the role of professional counselors in building cultures of peace. Their recommendations are based on the work of a group of psychologists who met at the Sixth International Symposium on Contributions of Psychology to Peace and created a special issue of *Peace and Conflict: Journal of Peace Psychology* on building cultures of peace (Brenes & Wessells, 2001). Gerstein and Moeschberger recommend that counselors "develop a systemic lens" including an understanding of global economics and politics, environmental science, peace studies, and non-western models of counseling (p. 117). In this way, counselors can make more effective use of "psychoeducation, prevention, lobbying, and modeling" as non-violent means for building cultures of peace (p. 118). In many ways our work is just beginning. Connecting the work that counselors and teachers are already doing with the important work of peace education can only strengthen all of our efforts and bodes well for continuing progress toward global peace.

CLOSING

In one of his first books, *To Know as We are Known: Education as a Spiritual Journey,* Parker Palmer (1993) states that "to teach is to create a space in which the community of truth is practiced" (p. xii). In this way, having the courage to contemplate truth within a larger community becomes a radical act. And, as stated earlier, to begin a class or counseling session with a few moments of silence can also become a radical act for peace. But from these few moments of silence, a space can be created in the classroom or counseling office where students and teachers, counselors and clients can become more fully present to themselves, each other, and the tasks at hand. And from this place of connection, we can begin to discern the right and appropriate actions that fulfill the promise of our peacemaking roles as teachers and counselors. The course in contemplative practices at Colorado State University is just one example of how this is being attempted.

REFERENCES

Allen, N. B., Blashki, G., & Gullone, E. (2006). Mindfulness-based psychotherapies: A review of conceptual foundations, empirical evidence and practical considerations. *Australian and New Zealand Journal of Psychiatry, 40,* 285-294.

Andres, B. S. (2002). A qualitative phenomenological analysis of the critical incidents in the native Hawaiian peacemaking process of "ho'oponopono." *Dissertation Abstracts International, 63*(4-B), 2048.

Artress, L. (2006). *Walking a sacred path: Rediscovering the labyrinth as a spiritual practice.* New York: Riverhead Books.

Blanton, P. G. (2007). Adding silence to stories: Narrative therapy and contemplation. *Contemporary Family Therapy: An International Journal, 29*(4), 211-221.

Boggs, S. T., & Chun, M. N. (1990). Ho'oponopono: A Hawaiian method of solving interpersonal problems. In K. A. Watson-Gegeo & G. M. White (Eds.), *Disentangling: Conflict discourse in Pacific societies* (pp. 122-160). Palo Alto, CA: Stanford University Press.

Brantmeier, E. J. (2008). Building intercultural empathy for peace: Teacher involvement in peace curricula development at a U.S. Midwestern High School. In J. Lin, E.J. Brantmeier, & C. Bruhn (Eds.), *Transforming education for peace* (pp. 67-92). Greenwich, CT: Information Age Publishing.

Brenes, A., & Wessells, M. (Guest Eds.). (2001). Psychological contributions to building cultures of peace [Special Issue]. *Peace and Conflict: Journal of Peace Psychology, 7*(2), 99-107.

Bush, M. (2006). Foreword. *Teachers College Record, 108*(9), 1721-1722.

Chodron, P. (1994). *Start where you are: A guide to compassionate living.* Boston: Shambhala.

Chodron, P. (2001). *Tonglen: The path of transformation.* Halifax, Nova Scotia: Vajradhatu.

Corey, G. (2009). *Theory and practice of counseling and psychotherapy.* Belmont, CA: Thomson Brooks/Cole.

Forisha, B., Wright, C., & Tucker, M. (2005). Toward a culturally and spiritually consonant treatment of native Hawaiians: An integration of family therapy and Ho'oponopono. In K. M. Hertlein & D. Viers (Eds.), *The couple and family therapist's notebook: Homework, handouts, and activities for use in marital and family therapy* (pp. 195-206). New York: Haworth Clinical Practice Press.

Friends of Peace Pilgrim. (2004). *Peace Pilgrim: Her life and work in her own words.* Santa Fe, NM: Ocean Tree Books.

Gale, J. (2009). Meditation and relational connectedness: Practices for couples and families. In F. Walsh (Ed.), *Spiritual resources in family therapy ()* (2nd ed., pp. 247-266). New York: Guilford Press.

Gerstein, L. H., & Moeschberger, S. L. (2003). Building cultures of peace: An urgent task for counseling professionals. *Journal of Counseling and Development, 81,* 115-119.

Hanh, T. N. (1991). *Peace is every step: The path of mindfulness in everyday life.* New York: Bantam Books.

Harris, I. M. (1999). Types of peace education. In A. Ravid, L. Oppenheimer, & D. Bar-Tal (Eds.), *How children understand war and* peace (pp. 299-317). San Francisco: Jossey-Bass.

Hart, T. (2004). Opening the contemplative mind in the classroom. *Journal of Transformative Education, 2*(1), 28-46.

Hill, C. (2006). Introduction. *Teachers College Record, 108*(9), 1723-1732.

Hill, C., Herndon, A. A., & Karpinska, Z. (2006). Contemplative practices: Educating for peace and tolerance. *Teachers College Record, 108*(9), 1915-1935.

Hurdle, D. E. (2002). Native Hawaiian traditional healing: Culturally based interventions for social work practice. *Social Work, 47*(2), 183-192.

Ito, K. L. (1985). Ho'oponopono, "to make right": Hawaiian conflict resolution and metaphor in the construction of a family therapy. *Culture, Medicine and Psychiatry, 9*(2), 201-217.

Ito, K. L. (1999). *Lady friends.* Ithaca, NY: Cornell University Press.

Jankowski, P. J. (2006). Facilitating change through contemplative prayer. In K. B. Helmeke & C. F. Sori (Eds.), *The therapist's notebook for integrating spirituality in counseling: Homework, handouts and activities for use in psychotherapy* (pp. 241-249). New York: Haworth Press.

Kabat-Zinn, J. (1990). *Full catastrophe living: Using the wisdom of your body and mind to face stress, pain, and illness.* New York: Dell.

Kees, N., & Lashwood, P. (1996). Compassion fatigue and school personnel: Remainingopen to the affective needs of students. *Educational Horizons, 75*(1), 41-44.

Leviton, R. (1994, Winter). Designing your pilgrimage: What you need to bring. *The Quest,* 25-29.

Linehan, M. M. (1993). *Cognitive-behavioral treatment of borderline personality disorder.* New York: Guilford Press.

Merry, S. E. (2001). Rights, religion, and community: Approaches to violence against women in the context of globalization. *Law & Society Review, 35*(1), 39-88.

Montessori, M. (1972). *Education and peace*. Chicago: Regnery.

Nelson, M. (2001). Aborigine in the Citadel. *The Hudson Review, 53*(4), 543-553.

Nelson, M. (2006). The fruit of silence. *Teachers College Record,* 108(9), 1733-1741.

Newsome, S., Christopher, J. C., Dahlen, P., & Christopher, S. (2006). Teaching Counselors self-care through mindfulness practices. *Teachers College Record, 108*(9), 1881-1900.

Omuro-Yamamoto, L. K. (2001). Ho'oponopono: A phenomenological investigation of a native Hawaiian harmony restoration process for families. *Dissertation Abstracts International, 62*(4-B), 2114.

Palmer, P. J. (1990). *The active life: Wisdom for work, creativity, and caring.* San Francisco: Harper & Row.

Palmer, P. J. (1993). *To know as we are known: Education as a spiritual journey.* San Francisco: HarperCollins.

Palmer, P. J. (1998, Dec-Jan). Evoking the spirit in public education. *Educational Leadership*, 6-11.

Palmer, P. J. (2007). *The courage to teach: Exploring the inner landscape of a teacher's life.* San Francisco: Jossey-Bass.

Patten, T. H. (1994). Ho'oponopono: A cross cultural model for organizational development and change. *The International Journal of Organizational Analysis, 2*(3), 252-263.

Peace Pilgrim (2008). *Steps toward inner peace.* Shelton, CT: Friends of Peace Pilgrim.

Plante, L. G. (2007). *Bleeding to ease the pain: Cutting, self-injury, and the adolescent search for self.* Westport, CT: Praeger.

Repath, A. (2007, Spring). El Camino de Santiago: An ancient pilgrimage leads us on the journey within. *Light of Consciousness*, 44-60.

Salmon, S. (2003). Teaching empathy: The PEACE curriculum. *Reclaiming Children and Youth, 12*(3), 167-173.

Segal, Z. V., Williams, J. M. G., & Teasdale, J. D. (2002). *Mindfulness-based cognitive Therapy for depression: A new approach to preventing relapse.* New York: Guilford Press.

Shook, E. V. (1985). *Ho'oponopono: contemporary uses of a Hawaiian problem-solving Process.* Honolulu: University of Hawaii Press.

Smith, C. (2006). *Cutting it out: A journey through psychotherapy and self-harm.* London: Jessica Kingsley.

Stebnicki, M. A. (2008). *Empathy fatigue: Healing the mind, body, and spirit of professional counselors.* New York: Springer.

Van Meter, J. B., McMinn, M. R., Bissel, L. D., Kaur, M., & Pressley, J. D. (2003). Solitude, silence, and the training of psychotherapists: A preliminary study. In T. W. Hall & M R. McMinn (Eds.), *Spiritual formation, counseling, and Psychotherapy* (pp. 175-184). New York: Nova Science.

Zajonc, A. (2003, Winter). Spirituality in higher education: Overcoming the divide. *Liberal Education*, 50-59.

Zajonc, A. (2006). Love and knowledge: Recovering the heart of learning through contemplation. *Teachers College Record, 108*(9), 1742-1759.

CHAPTER 10

FINDING PEACE VIA RECONCILIATION AND AWAKENING

12-Step Programs, Religion, Spirituality, and Peace

D. Brent Edwards Jr.

INTRODUCTION

While this book explores the relationship between religion, spirituality, and peace education from multiple perspectives and religious traditions, this chapter focuses on a particular type of spiritual program that receives little to no attention in the literature on these three concepts—12-step programs, such as Alcoholics Anonymous (AA), Narcotics Anonymous (NA), or Gambler's Anonymous (GA), to name a few. Given that these programs are spiritual in nature and are designed to lead to the development of an inner peace, there exists a need to examine more closely how these programs conceive of these concepts and, subsequently, what we can

Spirituality, Religion, and Peace Education, pp. 163–184
Copyright © 2010 by Information Age Publishing

learn from them. Specifically, then, this chapter seeks to answer the following two questions:

1. What do 12-step programs—which are spiritual in nature—say about religion, spirituality, and peace individually and in relation to one another?
2. How can these programs inform education and curricula that treat the three broad but inter-related concepts of religion, spirituality, and peace?

One might wonder how or why 12-step programs are relevant to a discussion of religion, spirituality, and peace. Simply describing these programs as spiritual in nature most likely triggers more than a few puzzled looks, which does not come as a surprise since very little is known about these programs generally. Limited understanding is helped by the negative stigma typically associated with such programs, as well as by their anonymous nature. Nevertheless, membership in these programs is growing exponentially: The Substance Abuse and Mental Health Services Administration, an agency in the United States Department Health and Human Services, recently estimated that 5 million people—or 2% of the U.S. population—attended one of these self-help programs during 2008 (United States Department of Health and Human Services, 2008). AA—the largest and most well known of these programs—reports more than 2 million members across the world (over 600,000 of which are outside the United States and Canada) (Alcoholics Anonymous Fact File, n.d.). NA, which branched off from AA in the 1950s, reported 200 registered groups in 3 countries in 1978; in 2007, NA reported 25,065 registered groups holding 43,900 weekly meetings in 127 countries.[1]

In response to their growth and success, as well to general ignorance about these programs, this chapter, in addition to attempting to answer the two questions posed at the outset, will present and explain the process embedded in the 12 Steps and reflect on what these programs suggest for education and curricula for religion, spirituality, and peace. The next section reviews prior research before investigating the literature of 12-step programs and reflecting on implications for education curricula and programs.[2]

PRIOR LITERATURE

Though there is a growing body of research and thinking on peace education (Harris & Morrison, 2003; Lin, 2006; Lin, Brantmeier, & Bruhn, 2008), few scholars address the interrelationship of religion, spirituality, and peace education. Some scholars do, however, examine the relationship between peace education and varying religious traditions (Gordon & Grob, 1987; Jackson & Fujiwara, 2008). Separately, the connection between spirituality and education has been the topic of investigation (Lantieri, 2001; Mayes, 2005), as has spirituality and the human condition (Helminiak, 1996), spirituality and religious tradition (Helminiak, 2008), and even the relationship between spirituality and peace with just and ethical economic development (Alters, 2008). Though authors in these areas bring to the fore themes that are relevant to a discussion of three concepts of religion, spirituality, and peace education—including religious plurality (Helminiak, 2008; Jackson & Fujiwara, 2008), dialogue (Kim, 2008; Doorn-Harder, 2008), understanding across religions (Baidhawy, 2008), harmony (Schweitzer, 2008), and reflection and reflexivity (Mayes, 2005; Weissman, 2008)—there is persistently a missing link in that the authors discuss these themes in terms of various concept pairs, but not all three.

More than an attempt to address this missing link, this chapter furthers and expands the focus of the authors in this area. In terms of peace education, it begins, as do Jackson and Fujiwara (2008), with the assumption that: "Peace education is as much about self-understanding and interpersonal relationships as it is about dealing with issues of peace and justice in society and globally; personal and social issues are seen as interrelated" (p. viii). It is for this reason that underinvestigated 12-step programs serve as the unit of analysis, because they lead to both inner and outer peace, dealing first with the personal, and then the personal in relation to the external.

At the same time, in terms of religious education, this chapter addresses the "need for more sophisticated ways of analyzing different approaches [to religious and peace education], which transcend the simple distinction between confessional, [or based in a religious tradition,] and non-confessional, [meaning based in state-run education,]" (Jackson & Fujiwara, 2008, p. xi). This chapter addresses that need by analyzing programs that are based on anonymity and voluntary involvement, and which are not controlled or supervised by either religious or governmental entities.

Last, on the connection between spirituality and education, this chapter continues the important work of Mayes (2005), who, through exploring the spiritual foundation of teaching and learning, proposes an "intuitive pedagogy." On the role of the teacher he writes: "To teach spiritually ... requires that the teacher constantly work at developing her intuitive capacity—in how she relates to both her subject-matter and students" (p. 39). Similarly, "the student comes expecting external information—but the teacher requires internal transformation; she requires the student to be 'cut through' by the 'bowstring' of the curriculum as the sine qua non of moral and spiritual growth" (p. 44). The process of the 12 Steps provides a concrete example of one way for teachers to develop their intuitive capacity, while at the same time providing a map from which the teacher can draw to facilitate the internal transformation of the student.

Surprisingly, though 12-step programs generally—and AA specifically—have been the subject of much research, most of this research has been in areas unrelated to religion, spirituality, and peace education, pertaining instead to the fields of counseling, addictions treatment, substance abuse, psychiatry, psychology, public health, and, in some cases, theology. Research within these fields looks at specific elements or alternative applications of these recovery programs in relationship to the development of spirituality (Aiken & Sandoz, 2005; Galanter, 2006; Harbaugh, 2007; Hart & Huggett, 2005; Sandoz, 2004; Sloan, 1999; Swora, 2004; Zylstra, 2006). While a number of scholars have examined the spiritual aspect (or spiritual development as a result) of 12-step programs, it is always in relation to addiction or alcoholism (Arnold, Avants, Margolin, & Marcotte, 2002; Bliss, 2007; Forechimes, 2004; Galanter et al., 2007; Hart, 1999; Li, Feifer, & Strohm, 2000; Mathew, Georgi, Wilson, & Mathew, 1996; McGovern & McMahon, 2006; Miller & Bogenshulz, 2007; Monahan, 2005; Morjaria, 2002; Tonigan, 2007; Watkins, 1997; Zemore & Kaskutas, 2004). The findings are encouraging: Members of 12-step programs exhibit higher levels of spiritual orientation than do the control groups, as measured by the importance they give to private spiritual thought, effort given to living life according to personal religious beliefs, whether spirituality results in a more balanced life, and the extent to which their "whole approach to life is based on [their] spirituality" (Galanter et al., 2007, p. 263). Such studies, nevertheless, restrict their target population to addicts and do not attempt to generalize their findings to those who do not identify as members. None comes from or extrapolates to the field of education, except for one (Matthews, 1998). In this case, however, the study draws lessons from 12-step programs along the lines of spirituality and then applies them to the creation of a curriculum for addictions counseling. The present chapter takes a different tack by beginning with the literature of 12-step programs and extrapolates outward to see what this literature has to offer the development of a curriculum that encompasses religion, spirituality, and peace education.

DEFINING RELIGION, SPIRITUALITY, AND PEACE

The literature of 12-step programs does not provide lengthy definitions of these concepts. Where they are mentioned, much is left open to interpretation. Such room for interpretation is a hallmark of these programs.

Members understand the principles in their own terms by talking to other members and visiting various groups where dialogue around such concepts occurs. Emphasis is on individual understanding for each member so that they can share about their own understanding and how the process of the 12 Steps has produced benefits—and ultimately a spiritual awakening—in their own life. As such, the definitions provided here reflect the fullest extent to which they are defined in the literature of these programs; they will most likely not satisfy those who prefer clearly defined concepts.

Twelve step programs separate the concept of spirituality from that of religion. The introduction to one 12-step program states: "We are not a religious organization. Our program is a set of spiritual principles" (NA, 1988, p. xvi). A number of the 12 Steps, however, do deal with the topic of a God or a Higher Power. Clarification of the difference between religion and spirituality is essential:

> It bears emphasizing that we should never confuse religion with spirituality. In [this program], they are not the same at all. [This program] itself is not a religion. It offers a set of spiritual principles, and uses a concept referred to as "God," a "Higher Power," or a "Power greater than ourselves" for members to use as a path out of active addiction. The spiritual principles and the concept of a Higher Power can go along with a member's personal spiritual path that he or she follows outside of [this program], or those principles and the concept of a Higher Power can serve as a spiritual path all by themselves. It's up to each member. (p. 108)

Another 12-step program puts it a little differently while still communicating the same idea:

> [God] means different things to different people. To some of us, it is a God of an organized religion; to others, it is a state of being commonly called spirituality. Some of us believe in no deity; a Higher Power may be the strength gained from being a part of, and caring for, a community of others. There is room in [this program] for all beliefs. We do not proselytize any particular view or religion. In [this program] each of us discovers a spirit of humility and tolerance, and each of us finds a Higher Power that works for us (Marijuana Anonymous [MA] World Services, n.d.).

These programs are unambiguous about their status: they are not religious organizations. Members are only encouraged to find a Higher Power that works for them; it does not have to be a God associated with an organized religion. One exceptional statement from the above quote is that a Higher Power can even be "the strength gain from being part of, and caring for, a community of others." This is evidence of their openness towards defining a Higher Power. The only guidelines offered by such programs with regard to an understanding of a Higher Power are that the Higher Power is "loving and caring and greater than [the individual]" (NA, 1998, p. 24).

Through such statements 12-step programs attempt to diffuse the extremely touchy subject of religion by making room for all religions and all conceptions (or lack thereof) of a Higher Power. This includes atheists and agnostics, since what 12-step programs refer to as a Higher Power may simply be "the strength gained from being a part of, and caring for, a community of others" (MA World Services, n.d.). One's Higher Power could be collective goodwill and does not have to be a deity or other omnipotent being. Furthermore, 12-step programs write: "We may discover that we're very sure what God isn't for us, but not what God is, and that's okay" (NA, 1998, p. 21). This even speaks to the position of the agnostic who neither confirms nor denies the existence of a God.

Despite the assertion by 12-step programs that they are based on "a set of spiritual principles," the index of one program's central text shows that the term "spirituality" is written on only four pages within the 12 Steps (NA, 1988, p. 284). Pursue the referent pages and one finds that the term is used without definition: One page speaks of being "spiritually bankrupt" (p. 20); another states that individuals "grow spiritually" (p. 25); the third states that members "do not recover … spiritually overnight" (p. 27); and in the final listing one reads that, in Step Five, members "begin to awaken to spiritual reality" (p. 32). Perhaps more telling is the fact that the same index, before listing page numbers for the term "spirituality," completely redirects the individual to the terms "acceptance," "faith," "giving," "hope," "humility," "love," "service," "surrender," and "tolerance." What this indicates is that spirituality, as far as 12-step programs are concerned, is not something fixed or amenable to definition. It also indicates that spirituality—or experiencing spirituality—is the result of the application of spiritual principles, such as those mentioned here.

This application happens as one works the 12 Steps, which are inextricable from spiritual development: "Many of us have wondered how this spiritual awakening comes about…. While there may be great variations within our experience about this awakening of the spirit, we all agree that it results from working *the steps*" (NA, 1993, p. 113). Explicating what is meant by "spiritual awakening," then, requires an explication of the 12 Steps; the next section encompasses this.

"Peace" is left open to interpretation to a large extent. The word is not mentioned until Steps 11 and 12. Step 11 speaks of an "inner peace" in relation to "quieting the mind through meditation" (NA, 1988, p. 45). Meditation is a way to communicate with and draw on one's Higher Power. "When we remove our selfish motives and pray for guidance we find feelings of peace and serenity" (p. 46). Step 12 simply speaks of an "increase in peace of mind" (p. 48) as a result of practicing "unconditional love, selflessness, and steadfastness" (NA, 1998, p. 122). Though the Steps do not explicitly mention peace until Steps 11 and 12, each Step, as a part of the process, contributes to increasing peace.

To this point, what is clear is that the value of such programs is not in the definitions they provide, but rather in the principles-based process of understanding and application they represent—especially since it is through internalizing, living, and applying such principles that members come to know peace and experience spiritual awakening. Peace and spiritual awakening are not end-points in that they are achieved permanently at the conclusion of working through the 12 Steps, but rather changing states of mind and emotion connected to one's actions and the extent to which one is able to live the principles embedded in the 12 Steps. In order to fully grasp the peace and spiritual awakening inherent in the 12 Steps, it is necessary to explicate how each contributes to the overall process.

THE PROCESS OF 12 STEPS

This section delineates the process of the 12 Steps, showing how peace and spiritual awakening increase through the process as a result of the underlying principles.[3] Table 10.1 presents the language and principles of each 12 of the Steps.

Step 1: Step 1 is the response to the insanity and unmanageability of drug addiction. Once the individual steps out of denial, recognizes the damage and harm of their addiction, and becomes truly ready to stop repeating the given behavior, he or she is ready to integrate into their lives the principles of honesty, open-mindedness, willingness, humility, and acceptance (NA, 1998, p. 6). By admitting to and accepting the insanity and harm of addiction one experiences incredible relief because it means that the fight against drug use is over. Being humble enough to admit defeat, open-minded enough to try a new way of life, and accepting enough to let go of the struggle is difficult, but it is also liberating because it means that hope, possibility, and a measure of peace replace powerlessness and desperation. More generally, the principles of powerlessness and acceptance result in more peace in one's life because they entail letting go of the people and circumstances beyond one's control.

Step 2: To counter the power over the individual that addiction has, members identify a number of different potential sources as their "Higher Power," which could help them "relieve their obsession to use" (NA, 1998, p. 23). At this point, some think of the group that they frequent as their "Power;" for others, it is the 12-step program as a whole; yet others name it God, or follow the convention of their religious affiliation. It is only

Table 10.1.   Language and Principles of the 12 Steps*

Step	Language	Principles
1	We admitted we were powerless over our addiction, that our lives had become unmanageable.	Honesty, Open-mindedness, Willingness, Humility, Acceptance
2	We came to believe that a Power greater than ourselves could restore us to sanity	Open-mindedness, Humility Willingness, Faith, Trust,
3	We made a decision to turn our will and our lives over to the care of God as we understood him	Surrender, Willingness, Faith, Trust, Commitment
4	We made a searching and fearless moral inventory of ourselves.	Willingness, Honesty, Courage, Faith, Trust
5	We admitted to God, to ourselves, and to another human being the exact nature of our wrongs.	Trust, Courage, Self-honesty, Commitment
6	We were entirely ready to have God remove all these defects of character.	Commitment, Perseverance, Willingness, Faith, Trust, Self-acceptance
7	We humbly asked Him to remove our shortcomings.	Surrender, Trust, Faith, Patience, Humility
8	We made a list of all persons we had harmed and became willing to make amends to them all.	Honesty, Courage, Willingness, Compassion
9	We made direct amends to such people wherever possible, except when to do so would injure them or others.	Humility, Love, Forgiveness
10	We continued to take personal inventory and when we were wrong promptly admitted it.	Self-discipline, Honesty, Integrity
11	We sought through prayer and meditation to improve our conscious contact with God as we understood Him, praying only for knowledge of His will for us and the power to carry that out.	Commitment, Humility, Courage, Faith
12	Having had a spiritual awakening as a result of these steps, we tried to carry this message to addicts and practice these principles in all our affairs.	Unconditional Love, Selflessness, Steadfastness

*Language taken from NA's "Basic Text" (1988, p. 17); principles taken from NA's Step Working Guide (1998).

necessary that one believe that a Power exists on which they can draw for support, nothing else. Step 2 increases the peace that one comes to know by developing faith that a Power exists that can help them with issues beyond their control.

Step 3: After coming to believe that a Power greater than oneself does exist, the Third Step asks the individual to trust in that Power, to turn one's will and life over to the *care* of that power.[4] For members of 12-step programs, this is essential, as it provides a counter to the "destructive force" of addiction (NA, 1988, p. 24). Each individual making the decision for themselves to engage with their conception of God is vital since doing so opens them up to receive the benefits of that positive force. "If we take time to think and seek direction before acting, we no longer have to run on our own self-centered will" (p. 28). Indeed, making the decision to reflect and seek direction before acting is a huge change in behavior for most people, especially addicts. The specifics of how one goes about seeking direction are up to the individual, as is their conception of God. What is important is that a decision is made, that an action is taken, and that one's heart and spirit are involved. It should be noted that this is not an intellectual exercise. Given that the only requirements for a Higher Power are that it be "loving, caring and greater than oneself," very little in the way of intellectual activity is involved. What matters is action.

A previous section of this paper clarified what 12-step programs mean by use of the term God or Higher Power. Each individual has "complete personal choice and freedom" (NA, 1993, p. 30) with regard to how they understand and communicate with their Higher Power, even if that means defining only "what God isn't" and not "what God is" (NA, 1988, p. 21).

Peace, acceptance, and contentment further result from Step 3, from surrendering to the guidance and *care*—not control—of a Higher Power:

> We begin to see positive results from the decision we have made. We begin to notice changes. While the circumstances of our lives may not change, the way we deal with those circumstances does. Because we have made the decision to allow spiritual principles to work in our lives, we may notice a sense of relief. We are being relieved of a burden we've carried far too long: the need to control everything and everyone. We begin to react differently to the situations and people around us. As we gain acceptance, we cease to struggle against life on life's terms. Striving to maintain and build our surrender, we are better able to live and enjoy life in the moment. (NA, 1993, p. 32)

As one believes in the process and practices the principles of the first three steps, acceptance, trust, and faith provide both a new perspective on one's life and the courage and strength to begin to address such things as "fear, anger, guilt, self-pity [and] depression" (NA, 1988, p. 26). This Step, then, is a lynchpin in the process—it provides the love, strength, and courage to carry on with the rest of the 12 Steps, to change the behavior that detracts from one's quality of life, as well as the faith that, no matter what, everything will be okay, which together greatly increase the level of peace and serenity.

Step 4: Step 4 is about laying "bare the unresolved pain and conflicts in our past so that [one] is no longer at their mercy" (NA, 1998, p. 31). Doing so requires courage and honesty, and is done by taking a "moral inventory." Here, "the word, 'moral' has nothing to do with specific codes of behavior, society's norms, or the judgment of some authority figure" (p. 33). Instead, a moral inventory is a process of "self-appraisal" (NA, 1993, p. 39) through which one discovers their "individual morality, ... values and principles (NA, 1998, p. 33). This is done by writing, and is characterized in the following way:

> We simply look at our instincts, our desires, our motives, our tendencies, and the compulsive routines that kept us trapped.... An inventory allows us to look at our basic nature with its flaws and its strengths. We look not only at our imperfections but also at our hopes, our dreams, our aspirations, and where they may have gone astray. (NA, 1993, p. 39)[5]

The result of writing and reflecting on resentments, feelings, guilt, shame, fear, relationships, sex, abuse, assets, and secrets is not only new found understanding, perspective, and clarity on one's pattern of behavior, motives, and feelings, but also the sense of relief that follows from processing all of the intense emotions, memories, resentments and secrets that have accumulated over a lifetime. With the clutter removed from one's spirit, they are better able to identify "the pure and loving spirit that lies at the core of [their] being" (p. 47). A new and deeper acceptance of oneself follows from this step as clearing away the "wreckage of the past" is accompanied by an opening of one's spirit and the ability to live in today.

Step 5: By admitting the exact nature (i.e., the underlying character defect) of one's wrongs to oneself, to another human being and to one's Higher Power, a person releases themselves from the bondage of the past, experiences true honesty, and ensures that denial does not stifle the process of spiritual development.[6] Significant developments result from having the courage and self-honesty necessary to make such an admission—namely, compassion, unconditional love, and intimacy (NA, 1998, p. 48). One's sense of self-worth and confidence increase because they are neither rejected nor judged. The willingness to be open with others also increases as a result because one is not as afraid to be themselves. This is a manifestation of the new freedom and trust that this step engenders. Step 5 is thus instrumental in the process of the 12 Steps in that it results in peace on a personal level via peace with one's past, which enhances peace in the moment because one is distracted less by memories of yesterday.

Seeing, as well, that one is not rejected for who they are is energizing and opens one up to be available in today for themselves and for the benefit of other people, no longer preoccupied by old experiences.

Step 6: Once one has made the decision that they sincerely desire to change their behavior by addressing their character defects, such as fear, self-centeredness, selfishness, anger, laziness, procrastination, lust, and so forth, they have worked half of Step 6. Working the other half necessitates becoming ready to work with their Higher Power towards that end: "To be entirely ready is to reach a spiritual state where we are not just aware of our defects; not just tired of them; not just confident that the God of our understanding will remove what should go—but all of these things" (NA, 1998, p. 34). Reaching this state of readiness is significant because it means that one is prepared to change the behaviors that detract from their quality of life (and peace) in the present.

Step 7: Step 7 invokes the principles of humility and patience by calling upon the individual to ask for help from their Higher Power in the life-long task of removing character defects and changing one's personality. "We approach this Power greater than ourselves to ask for the freedom to live without the limitations of our past ways" (NA, 1988, p. 35). Through prayer—however one chooses to define or engage in such behavior—and action, shortcomings are removed and replaced by actions whose genesis is love, selflessness, and concern for others, which continues to increase peace and awaken one's spirit.

Step 8: One applies the humility learned in the Step 7 by making a list that details all persons that an individual has harmed. The result of making this list, coming to terms with the untreated harm lingering in the present, and becoming willing to make the necessary amends is fourfold: First, one comes to understand that judging the faults of another will not make them a better person; second, as one realizes the need to be forgiven, they tend to become more forgiving; third, it becomes harder to intentionally harm others; and, fourth, the need to avoid those one has harmed or live with a sense of guilt or shame dissipates. Again, honesty and courage fortify the peace one experiences in the present by treating the pain of the past (NA, 1998, p. 76).

Step 9: Humility, love and forgiveness are the core of Step 9, as individuals make amends when the opportunity presents itself. This typically involves nothing more than humbly asking for understanding of past wrongs. The result of making amends is that one is freed from the weight of the past. More often than not, one is greeted with unconditional love upon making an amends. While experiencing this unconditional love "will rejuvenate [one's] will to live," simply mustering the courage to make the amend leads to "a lot of spiritual growth" in the form of humility and patience, which begin to characterize interpersonal interaction as the guilt and shame of the past is replaced with understanding and forgiveness (NA, 1988, p. 40). Reconciliation fuels awakening as one's spirit is freed from the past, energized by a sense of gratitude about the present, and excited about the increasingly positive and selfless interpersonal interactions.

Step 10: This step builds upon the skill learned in Step 4—that of taking one's inventory—and applies it to daily life: "Continuing to take a personal inventory means that we form a habit of looking at ourselves, our actions, attitudes, [and] relationships on a regular basis" (NA, 1988, p. 41). When an apology or an amend is necessary, fault is promptly admitted. This process ensures (a) that one does not fall into patterns of harmful behavior and (b) that one remains free to live "in the here and now, [free] from ourselves and the past" (p. 43).

Step 11: At this point, one increases awareness of their Higher Power and their ability to use that Power as a source of strength. This is done through prayer, described as "asking for God's help," and meditation, described as "listening for God's answer" (NA, 1988, pp. 44-45). These *actions* bring about "an inner peace that brings us into contact with the God within us" (p. 45). The phrase "conscious contact" refers to one's "conscious awareness of [their] link to a Higher Power," which can be experienced in many ways, including

> when we experience something in nature, such as a forest or an ocean; through the unconditional love of our sponsor or other ... members; through the feeling of being anchored during difficult times; through feelings of peace and warmth; through a coincidence that later on we see as having led to some great good; through the simple fact of our recovery; ... through our ability to listen to others; ... and countless other means (NA, 1998, p. 111).

Establishing contact is a first step to understanding the will of one's Higher Power, which must also be clarified given the sensitive nature of the topic, and the fundamental role that understanding this idea has for applying Step 11 to one's life:

> "God's will for us is the ability to live with dignity, to love ourselves and others, to laugh, to find great joy and beauty in our surroundings. Our most heartfelt longings and dreams for our lives are coming true. These priceless gifts are no longer beyond our reach. They are, in fact, the very essence of God's will for us." Our personal vision of God's will for us is revealed in how our lives might be if we were consistently living with purpose and dignity. (p. 112)

Thus, one becomes aware that the essence of God's will is for each person is to live with dignity and purpose, to love oneself and others, to find joy in their lives, and to realize their dreams. One must continue to draw on their Higher Power for the strength and courage to carry out that will, as change can be uncomfortable and fear of the unknown can be paralyzing. Maintaining courage in the face of change and fear is perhaps the most difficult aspect of this step; nevertheless, the principles of faith and courage help one live a life of integrity:

> We need not be so afraid of losing friends or having relationships change or even having our lives profoundly affected because we know that we're being cared for. We have faith that if we have to let go of old friends because what they're doing is unhealthy for our spiritual development, we'll form new relationships with people whose values we share. (p. 114)

Leaving one's comfort zone, letting go of the known, attempting to change, and accepting new circumstances can be difficult, but when one is able to call upon the strength of their Higher Power the result is spiritual development that "offers unlimited growth," and "a peace we never imagined possible" (NA, 1988, pp. 43-44). A combination of reconciliation and courage throughout the process of the steps brings one to this point, a point characterized not only by peace, but also by an awakening of the spirit.

One can understand this "spiritual awakening" as the result of the work of the previous 11 steps, which have prepared one for and made possible this awakening. Indeed, getting to a place where one is free of the burdens of the past, is unafraid of the future, and can live in the moment with both the sense that their Higher Power is caring for their life and the knowledge that they are trying to understand and follow the goodwill of that Higher Power imbues one with hope and gratitude. What is remarkable, however, is that, at this point, 12-step programs emphasize most the idea that an individual "must give freely and gratefully that which has been freely and gratefully given to [them]"—namely, love and support in the process of trying to recover and work the 12 Steps—because that is the only way to maintain the spiritual awakening and peace that one comes to know in Step 11 (NA, 1988, p. 47). Continual application of the principles yields continued spiritual awakening and peace.

Step 12: The last Step acknowledges that the previous 11 Steps have, over time, led to "an awakening of a spiritual nature," and states that the task at hand now is (a) to share what one has learned through their journey, supporting the individual who still suffers, and (b) to continue to apply the principles learned throughout the process in all areas of one's life. The willingness to carry the message, help those who still suffer, and work with those who are trying to figure out the process of the 12 Steps emanates from the gratitude that one feels as a result of personally experiencing a spiritual awakening and the mental, emotional, and spiritual benefits the process of the 12 Steps carries. By making oneself a "spiritual instrument" the effect is that the individual—while still working to apply the principles in their own life so that they can know spiritual growth and peace of mind—simultaneously contributes to the realization of spiritual growth and the development of peace in the lives of others. More people become exposed to, receive help with, and implement spiritual principles in their lives, ultimately increasing the inner and outer peace present in the world.

Individuals continue to apply the principles of the 12 Steps to the best of their ability indefinitely, and, as one grows, repetition of the steps incorporates new and different areas and situations into the reflective process (such as work, relationships, etc.). Familiarity with the underlying principles results in the individual becoming more adept at applying them and noticing "subtleties of meaning" (NA, 1998, p. 117). Depth of understanding and breadth of application results in heightened spiritual awakening and increased levels of peace and goodwill in one's life, and the lives of others. This is the ripple effect of the never-ending process of the 12 Steps—that they not only lead to spiritual growth and peace for the individual, but that they also bring about positive changes in the lives of others. Underpinning this Step are the principles of unconditional love, selflessness, and steadfastness (p. 122).

TWELVE STEP PROGRAMS, RELIGION, SPIRITUALITY, AND PEACE

This section briefly explores answers to and limitations facing the second question posed by this chapter. The suggestions provided here are not exhaustive and represent only an initial response.

Initially, there is the matter of place, which contains two aspects. First, the context should be characterized by "empathy, honesty, caring, sharing, and service," as is the case with the meetings of 12-step programs. The key to this is that such an atmosphere fosters trust, openness, and dialogue—prerequisites for teaching and learning about religion, spirituality, and peace. Second, 12-step programs successfully (through carefully crafted traditions and principles for governance) organize and operate an anonymous association of individuals. It is not that any entity dealing with such topics need be anonymous or volunteer in nature, but rather that nontraditional forums (i.e., forums outside of public education and organized religion) may represent the most suitable avenue for exploration of such topics and the development of associated curricula, at least given the current climate and regulations around the discussion of religion in school in the United States or other countries. More specifically, this speaks to Jackson and Fujiwara's (2008) point regarding the need to explore neither state-run nor religious organizations for the implementation of curricula based in such topics as religion, spirituality, and peace.

With regard to curricula, 12-step programs rightly accommodate the divisive issue of religion through respect for—both—all choices of religious affiliation and all conceptions of a Higher Power—an important aspect given the number of wars, past and present, that stem from intolerance of religious differences. Guided by how 12-step programs facilitate the growth of their members, students would be asked to come up with their own understanding of key concepts through dialogue with others—whether it be that of a Higher Power, spirituality, peace, or anything else. Along with student-generated knowledge via discussion, reflection on principles in relation to the lived experiences of students would be essential because doing so makes the process of learning, and the knowledge that results, more meaningful. What's more is that such curricula—based on reflexive processes—inherently address what Mayes (2005) discusses in relation to a spiritual pedagogy—namely, student internal transformation, as opposed to external information. Table 10.2 begins the process of reflection on the possibilities that 12-step programs hold for curricular development by presenting a suggested 12 Steps for a Life of Peace and Spirituality for those who are not members of 12-step programs. Further work by scholars might explore the merit of these suggested steps for a variety of educational settings and purposes, in addition to the formulation of specific curricular materials to accompany them.

As mentioned earlier, Mayes (2005), in his discussion of spiritual pedagogy, states that such a pedagogy "requires that the teacher constantly work at developing her intuitive capacity—in how she relates to both her subject-matter and students" (p. 39). Absent from that discussion, however, is mention of either the need for the teacher to develop spiritually first, or any suggestions for how the teacher is to go about that development. This is a critical area for further exploration, especially given that the nature, dynamics and fruitfulness of the relationship between the teacher, the subject-matter, and the students changes with the personal and spiritual development of the teacher. As such, the process of the 12 Steps not only has relevance for teachers directly in that they must first experience the process of those Steps, understand themselves and develop spiritually before they can facilitate such development in their students, but also for teacher education programs in that such spiritual processes and development should inform them. Furthermore, going through such a process individually and with one's students places a different light on the purpose and direction of education, keeping the

Table 10.2.   Twelve Steps for a Life of Peace and Spiritual Awakening

Step	Language
1	We let go of things we cannot control.
2	We come to believe that a Power greater than ourselves can help us.
3	We turn our will and our life over to the care of a(our) Higher Power(s), as we understand It (Them).
4	We make an honest and thorough self-appraisal of past behavior.
5	We share the exact nature of our behavior with a(our) Higher Power(s), ourselves, and another person.
6	We become ready and willing to have our Higher Power(s) remove our defects of character.
7	We ask and work with our Higher Power(s) to remove our character defects.
8	We make a list of all persons we have harmed and become willing to make amends to them all.
9	We make direct amends to individuals we have harmed wherever possible, except when to do so injures them or others.
10	We continue to take a personal inventory and when we are wrong promptly admit it.
11	We improve conscious contact with our Higher Power(s), seeking only knowledge of Its(Their) will for us and the power to carry that out.
12	Having had a spiritual awakening as a result of these steps, we try to carry this message to others and to practice the principles of these steps in all areas of our life.

emphasis on principles-focused and student-centered education within a holistic framework.

Along these lines, a holistic approach to education provides a complement to the technically-focused, fact-heavy curriculum that currently predominates at most levels of education—but especially the elementary through secondary levels—by promoting a reflexive process that leads not only to personal spiritual development, but also to acceptance of and concern for others. Such a holistic curriculum—holistic in that it considers the spiritual and emotional state of the child in addition to the intellectual—would necessarily teach students to practice a process of self-reflection and self-improvement, identify and communicate their feelings, be of service to others, forgive and be forgiven, and develop trust in a Higher Power, among other things. Sadly, while preparing students with the skills to deal with the emotional and spiritual aspects of their beings is something that many curricula around the world currently lack, possessing such skills is what leads to peace and spiritual awakening personally and interpersonally by informing the way individuals interact with themselves and others on spiritual, emotional, and intellectual levels.

Because, as a regional website for one 12-step program affirms, the goal of these programs is that the underlying principles be made available in local languages and in accordance with local culture (NA Latin American Zonal Forum, n.d.), 12-step programs are amenable to transformation into curricular materials in all parts of the world. The focus is on understanding principles, not on reifying dogma. That the steps are based on principles that local members of these programs adapt to their language and culture is a hallmark of these programs. The teaching of principles—as opposed to ideological truths, for example—equips the student with not only knowledge but also skills and understanding that is applicable across time and space. Emphasis on principles is a strength for both the individual and a boon to 12-step programs to be translated into education-related curricula.

Using 12-step programs as an inspiration for a curriculum on religion, spirituality and peace is not without its limitations, however, and there are four issues not yet mentioned. First, the 12 Steps presuppose a history of drug use and a genuine desire to learn to apply and live by the principles to the best of one's ability. With regard to the former, it is for this reason that the 12 Steps should not be taken whole, but rather adapted to particular contexts and educational settings. With regard to the latter, proponents might point out that simply because an individual is not intent on applying the principles to a specific behavior or situation in the immediate term does not mean that they should not be exposed to or equipped with the tools to manage the emotional and spiritual aspects of their being. Exposing students to the underlying principles and familiarizing them with the reflexive process may still have positive effects in the future.

Second, in large part, the 12 Steps represent a process of reconciliation and may not be appropriate, if taken as is, for translation to public school curricula. The corrective process of the Steps may be more appropriate for alternative education settings, such as adult education, education for troubled youth, or tailored extracurricular programs. In the end, whether all or only a portion of the Steps inform curricula or serve as topics for dialogue and discussion, what matters is that the underlying principles be the focus of attention, not the explicit teaching of Steps themselves. Living the principles, not memorizing the Steps, leads to peace and spiritual awakening.

Third, matters of religion, spirituality, and morality (as in moral inventory) are politically contentious topics. Even though these programs are not religious and allow for any conception of a Higher Power one chooses—including defining that Power as "the strength gained from being a part of, and caring for, a community of others"—the prospect of including such topics in public schooling is certain to be controversial (MA

World Services, http://www.marijuana-anonymous.org/faq.shtm). There is a fine line between (a) teaching about, and creating opportunities for discussion of, topics related to religion and spirituality, and (b) proselytizing or preferencing one's own beliefs. Regardless, more dialogue and understanding, as well as a search for more and better ways to discuss religion, spirituality and peace, is what is needed.

Fourth, though the 12 Steps state that "the language of … recovery literature is not meant to determine a member's spirituality" (NA, 1998, p. 109), the use of the masculine gender (Steps 3, 7, and 11), along with the Christian roots of this tradition, is problematic. Additional research on how the 12-step programs are implemented and tailored to varying cultural and religious contexts around the world (how would, for example, Buddhists respond to the 12 Steps?) represents an important area of future research generally, and could illuminate how non-Christian societies interpret or adapt the gender bias. In the least, such programs should, as I have done in proposing a 12 Steps for a Life of Peace and Spiritual Awakening, alter their convention to be not only gender neutral, but also to be more explicitly open to multiple deities, or none at all.

CONCLUSION

This chapter covers a lot of ground in attempting to answer the two questions posed at the outset. It has reviewed the literature of 12-step programs to explicate how the process of the 12 Steps is designed to lead to both the development of inner and outer peace and the experience of a "spiritual awakening." The most essential aspect of this process, however, is the development of a relationship with a Higher Power, the definition of which is up to the individual, so long as that Power is loving, caring, and greater than the individual. One thing should be clear from the 12-step literature that this paper explores regarding the principles upon which they are based: In order to experience the benefits, the individual must go beyond understanding and move to the realm of implementation. That is to say, as one incorporates into their life the principles on which the 12-step process is based, the amount of peace and spiritual development in one's life increases, leading eventually to an awakening of the spirit. Neither of these states is fixed, however; the literature of such programs emphasizes that only through continual application to the best of one's ability in all areas of one's life does one continue to experience peace and spiritual awakening.

This chapter also considers how such 12-step programs can inform various aspects of education, as well as the limitations associated with attempts to use the process of the 12 Steps for inspiration in relation to educational context, curricula, pedagogy, and language. Education based on self-understanding, inspiration, principles, and process (as opposed to memorization) is lacking in education currently; the process of the 12 Steps, and the hope, freedom, and love that characterize it, serve as a starting point for improvement and an example from which to draw lessons. Indeed, nurturing the spirit through education is necessary; by ignoring the spirit, we not only hamper its growth, we impede its awakening.

NOTES

1. While AA was the first 12-step program, originally started in 1935 in Akron, Ohio, many other such programs have been developed to treat addiction to other substances, such as Narcotics Anonymous (NA), Cocaine Anonymous (CA), Marijuana Anonymous (MA), Gamblers Anonymous (GA), and Overeaters Anonymous (OA), among others.

2. Due to its most inclusive view of addiction, which includes any mind or mood altering substance, this chapter draws primarily from the literature of Narcotics Anonymous. The central text of NA, which contains a discussion of the Steps and Traditions, among other topics, does not have a name and is known informally as the "Basic Text" (NA, 1988).

3. Although the language of 12-step programs is unfamiliar and foreign, readers are asked to have patience with what may strike them as difficult or uncomfortable language. In order to focus on the underlying content of each step, it may help to mentally substitute terms such as addiction with the phrase "unhealthy behavior."

4. Although this Step refers to God as having a male gender, the literature of Narcotics Anonymous states that, "It's important … to understand that the language of NA's recovery literature is not meant to determine a member's spirituality" (NA, 1998, p. 109).

5. Writing the inventory is especially important since the information will be used again in steps five through nine.

6. Making the admission to one's Higher Power, in addition to another person, is essential because:

   > This is a spiritual program, and our whole purpose is to awaken spiritually. Our willingness to approach our Higher Power openly with our past and who we are is central to our recovery…. When we reveal something about ourselves, we draw closer to our Higher Power and experience the unconditional love and acceptance which springs from that Power. (NA, 1993, p. 54)

REFERENCES

Aiken, A. A., & Sandoz, J. C. (2005). Changes in levels of ego strength and spirituality of recovering alcoholics in AA. *American Journal of Pastoral Counseling*, *8*(1), 47-59.

Alcoholics Anonymous Fact File. (n.d.) Retrieved February 14, 2009, from http://oas.samhsa.gov/2k8/selfHelp/selfHelp.cfm

Alters, E. K. (2008). *Spiritual awakening: The hidden key to peace and security, just and sustainable economics, a responsible European Union.* Leuven, Belgium: Peeters.

Arnold, R. M., Avants, S. K., Margolin, A., & Marcotte, D. (2002). Patient attitudes concerning the inclusion of spiritual principles into addiction treatment. *Journal of Substance Abuse Treatment, 23,* 319-326.

Baidhawy, Z. (2008). Building harmony and peace through multiculturalist theology-based religious education: An alternative for contemporary India. In R. Jackson & S. Fujiwara (Eds.), *Peace education and religious plurality: International perspectives* (pp. 1-16). New York: Routledge.

Bliss, D. L. (2007). Empirical research on spirituality and alcoholism: A review of the literature. *Journal of Social Work Practice in the Addictions, 7*(4), 5-25.

Doorn-Harder, N. (2008). Teaching religion in the USA: Bridging the gaps. In R. Jackson & S. Fujiwara (Eds.), *Peace education and religious plurality: International perspectives* (pp. 87-100). New York: Routledge.

Forcehimes, A. A. (2004). De profundis: Spiritual transformations in Alcoholics Anonymous. *Journal of Clinical Psychology, 60*(5), 503-517.

Galanter, M. (2006). Spirituality and addiction: A research and clinical perspective. *American Journal on Addictions, 15*(4), 286-292.

Galanter, M., Dermatis, H., Bunt, G., Williams, C., Trujillo, M., & Steinke, P. (2007). Assessment of spirituality and its relevance to addiction treatment. *Journal of Substance Abuse Treatment, 33,* 257-264.

Gordon, H., & Grob, L. (Eds.) (1987). *Education for peace: Testimonies from world religions.* Maryknoll, NY: Orbis Books.

Harbaugh, J. (2007). Integrity through twelve-step spirituality. *Human Development, 28*(3), 29-35.

Harris, I. M., & Morrison, M. L. (2003). *Peace education.* Jefferson, NC: McFarland.

Hart, K. E. (1999). A spiritual interpretation of the 12-steps of Alcoholics Anonymous: From resentment to forgiveness to love. *Journal of Ministry in Addiction & Recovery, 6*(2), 25-39.

Hart, K. E., & Huggett, C. (2005). Narcissim: A barrier to personal acceptance of the spiritual aspect of Alcoholics Anonymous. *Alcoholism Treatment Quarterly, 23*(4), 85-100.

Helminiak, D. A. (1996). *Human core of spirituality: Mind as psyche and spirit.* Albany, NY: SUNY Press.

Helminiak, D. A. (2008). *Spirituality for our global community: Beyond traditional religion to a world at peace.* Lanham, MD: Rowman & Littlefield.

Jackson, R., & Fujiwara, S. (Eds.). (2008). *Peace education and religious plurality: International perspectives.* New York: Routledge.

Kim, C. (2008). Contemporary religious conflicts and religious education in the Republic of. In R. Jackson & S. Fujiwara (Eds.), *Peace education and religious plurality: International perspectives* (pp. 17-30). New York: Routledge.

Lantieri, L. (2001). *Schools with spirit.* Boston: Beacon Press.

Li, E. C., Feifer, C., & Strohm, M. (2000). A pilot study: Locus of control and spirituality beliefs in Alcoholics Anonymous and Smart recovery members. *Addictive Behaviors, 25*(4), 633-640.

Lin, J. (2006). *Love, peace and wisdom in education: Vision for education in the 21st century.* Lanham, MD: Rowman & Littlefield Education.

Lin, J., Brantmeier, E., & Bruhn, C. (Eds.) (2008). *Transforming education for peace: A volume in peace education.* Charlotte, NC: Information Age.

Marijuana Anonymous World Services, Frequently Asked Questions. (n.d.). Retrieved February 16, 2009, from http://www.marijuana-anonymous.org/faq.shtml

Matthews, C. (1998). Integrating the spiritual dimension into traditional counselor education programs. *Counseling and Values, 43*(1), 3-18.

Mathew, R. J., Georgi, J., Wilson, W. H., & Mathew, G. V. (1996). A retrospective study of the concept of spirituality as understood by recovering individuals. *Journal of Substance Abuse Treatment, 13*(1), 67-73.

Mayes, C. (2005). *Teaching mysteries: Foundations of spiritual pedagogy.* Lanham, MD: University Press of America.

McGovern, T. F., & McMahon, T. (2006). Spirituality and religiousness and alcohol/other drug problems: Conceptual framework. *Alcoholism Treatment Quarterly, 24*(1/2), 7-19.

Miller, W. R., & Bogenshulz, M. P. (2007). Spirituality and addiction. *Southern Medical Journal, 100*(4), 433-436.

Monahan, M. (2005). A faith that works. *Human Development, 26*(1), 12-18.

Morjaria, A. (2002). The role of religion and spirituality in recovery from drink problems: A qualitative study of Alcoholics Anonymous members and South Asian men. *Addiction Research & Theory, 10*(3), 225-256.

Narcotics Anonymous. (1988). *Narcotics Anonymous* (5th ed.) [Basic Text]. Van Nuys, CA: World Service Office.

Narcotics Anonymous. (1993). *It works how and why: The twelve steps and twelve traditions of Narcotics Anonymous.* Chatsworth, CA: Narcotics Anonymous World Services.

Narcotics Anonymous. (1998). *The Narcotics Anonymous Step Working Guides.* Chatsworth, CA: Narcotics Anonymous World Services.

Narcotics Anonymous Latin American Zonal Forum. (n.d.). Retrieved March 2, 2009, from http://65.98.89.98/~fzlatino/

Narcotics Anonymous World Services. (n.d.). Retrieved February 14, 2009, from http://www.na.org/basic.htm

Sandoz, J. (2004). *Exploring the spiritual experience in the 12-Step Program of Alcoholics Anonymous: Spiritus Contra Spiritum*, Lewiston, NY: The Edwin Mellen Press.

Schweitzer, F. (2008). Religious individualization: New challenges to education for tolerance. In R. Jackson & S. Fujiwara (Eds.), *Peace education and religious plurality: International perspectives* (pp. 75-86). New York: Routledge.

Sloan, H. P. (1999). *God imagery and emergent spirituality in early recovery from chemical dependency: Ana-Maria Rizzuto and the Alcoholics Anonymous twelve steps.* Unpublished Dissertation, Graduate Theological Union.

Swora, M. G. (2004). The rhetoric of transformation in the healing of alcoholism: The twelve steps of alcoholics anonymous. *Mental Health, Religion & Culture, 7*(3), 187-209.

Tonigan, S. (2007). Spirituality and Alcoholics Anonymous. *Southern Medical Journal, 100*(4), 437-440.

United States Department of Health and Human Services, Office of Applied Studies. (2008). *The national survey on drug use and health: Participation in self-help groups for alcohol and illicit drug use: 2006 and 2007.* Retrieved June 3, 2009, from http://oas.samhsa.gov/2k8/selfHelp/selfHelp.htm

Watkins, E. (1997). Essay on spirituality. *Journal of Substance Abuse Treatment, 14*(6), 581-584.

Weissman, D. (2008). Jewish religious education as peace education: From crisis to opportunity. In R. Jackson & S. Fujiwara (Eds.), *Peace education and religious plurality: International perspectives* (pp. 49-62). New York: Routledge.

Zemore, S. E., & Kaskutas, L. A. (2004). Helping, spirituality and Alcoholics Anonymous in recovery. *Journal of Studies on Alcohol, 65*(3), 383-391.

Zylstra, R. (2006). The use of spirituality in alcohol recovery. *Southern Medical Journal, 99*(6), 643.

CHAPTER 11

THE PLACE OF SPIRITUALITY IN THE LIFE AND WORK OF ISMAILI TEACHERS OF CENTRAL ASIA

Sarfaroz Niyozov and Zahra Punja

INTRODUCTION

Teaching is globally becoming a technically inefficient, managerial job aimed at achieving successful test results and monetary reward. There is a global cry that teaching is losing connection with soul, mind, and heart, and its calling for service and empowerment (Love, 2002; Miller, 2000). This chapter tells the story of teachers who work with extremely low salaries, without properly heated and furnished classrooms, updated textbooks, and enough food and clothing for their students and their own families. What makes some teachers continue serving their students, communities, states, and religious and secular authorities when their own status is degraded, their freedom curbed, and life impoverished? Are there

Spirituality, Religion, and Peace Education, pp. 185–207
Copyright © 2010 by Information Age Publishing
All rights of reproduction in any form reserved.

teachers who see teaching much more than fixed content to be transmitted, more than pedagogy devoid of emotion and passion and more than tests to be passed?

These are the stories of teachers' life and work from Central Asian mountainous area of Badakhshan in Tajikistan and the Northern Areas and Chitral district in Pakistan. The area is a highly mountainous, rural part of the larger Central Asia with highest peak and glaciers of the world. Living on "the roof of the world," the people in Northern Areas of Pakistan and Tajikistan's Badakhshan have many cultural, historical, and religious affinities. Among these affinities are the mountainous terrain, once a crossroads of the ancient Silk Road, as well as a common religious origin of the teachers; these are Ismaili Muslim teachers, followers of the *Aga Khan*, whom they call a Living Imam.[1]

Ismailis are a Shi'i branch of Islam. They represent a small minority within the wider Muslim community (Daftary, 1990). They live in over twenty-five countries including Afghanistan, Pakistan, and Tajikistan (Nanji, 1987, p. 179). The Living Imam and the Imam's institution (called Imamat) are central to Ismaili doctrine, history, and life worlds. The Imam is believed to be the direct descendant of Prophet Mohammed through his daughter Fatima and Ali, his cousin and son-in law. Within the Ismaili doctrine, the Imam is divinely—inspired, infallible, protected from mistakes and sins, capable of knowing the future of the humanity. Thus, for Ismailis, Ali and the subsequent 48 Imams from his progeny have the Prophet of Islam's "power of spiritual guidance and initiation" (Nasr, 1988a, p. 103).

According to the Shi'a Ismaili interpretation of Islam, Ali is perceived as the first Imam, assigned to be the leader of Muslim community, indeed the leader of all believers (*Amir al-Mu'minin*), and designated by the Prophet himself (Tabatabai, 1988, pp. 159-160). In Shi'a Islam, Imam is a hereditary position. The current Imam of the global Ismaili community is His Highness Karim Aga Khan IV, known as global leader and philanthropist, and the head of the Aga Khan Development Network (AKDN) (www.akdn.org). Obedience and submission to the Imam is a guiding principle in the Shi'i Isma'ili faith. Like other Muslims, Ismaili theologians also do not separate the *din* and *dunya*, that is, the religious and worldly, extending the power of the Imam into both domains of his followers' life. The Aga Khan (1976) puts it as follows:

> history and the correct interpretation of the Imamah require that the Imam, while caring first of all for the spiritual well-being of his people, should also be continuously concerned with their safety and their material well-being. (Aga Khan IV, 1976, p. 3, as cited in Keshavjee, 1998, p. 48)

While devotion to the Imam serves as an important motivator for teachers' lives and work, these teachers' lives have been affected by more than Ismaili ideas and authorities. The areas' historical memory includes pre-Islamic Zoroastrian, Buddhist, various Islamic, Mongol, Russian, Soviet and post-Soviet discourses (Foltz, 1999; Nanji & Niyozov, 2002). Even though these forces have changed and shifted, the energy they provide is based on similar messages of selfless service and a moral calling. In addition, these teachers' capacity to exert agency though using their critical engagement with these forces and drawing lessons from their experience and history, didactic literature, tradition, and their professional roles, have all contributed to the development of their larger vision of teaching. This broader vision affects their pedagogy, relationships, and leadership as they continue preparing their children and communities for a global society (Johnson, 2009). The spiritually-infused stories of these teachers speak to the life and work of millions of teachers who see teaching as a complex moral, ethical, and spiritual task of making a difference in the lives of their students and communities (Fullan, 2002). We illustrate this by showing how teachers articulate their views of their communities, their commitment to teaching, and their relationships inside and outside their schools.

THE DATA SOURCES AND METHOD

The empirical data for the study comes from qualitative doctoral theses on teachers' life and work in Tajikistan (Niyozov, 2001) and Northern Pakistan (Afzal Tajik, 2004; Ashraf, 2004). The data were connected to what we might call elements of spirituality. At the same time, we acknowledge that (1) spirituality comes in different forms and cannot be reduced into certain operational definitions (Carr, 2003), (2) it is not easy to distinguish between a spiritual and nonspiritual or less-spiritual person because spirituality is not just about declaring arthritic values and theories; and (3) spirituality is equally embedded in one's actions and their impact.

The chapter begins with a brief journey into an understanding of spirituality from the Shi'a Ismaili interpretation of Islam.[2] The paper's second section exposes teachers' voices from the above-mentioned studies to show the practices of spirituality lived in a complex, paradoxical, and pragmatic profession such as teaching. The final section shows the data's implications for teacher development and research on teaching.

SPIRITUALITY-BEYOND THE CONTESTATION

Spirituality is a contested social construct (Carr, 2003; Miller, 2000; Tacey, 2004). Some have strictly associated spirituality with religion, the metaphysical, and the divine (Belousa, 2006; Sayani, 2005; Shahjahan, 2005), others have rejected religion's monopoly over spirituality (Carr, 2003; Krupskaya, 1982; Kovel, 1994) and still others have aligned it to nature (Taylor, 2001). While we focus on Ismaili Muslims' spirituality, the teachers' worldviews, pedagogies, relations, and roles suggests the need to go beyond religious/natural/secular polemics. One is able to find some common aspects and elements that are mentioned in the discussion on spirituality in education.

Shi'i Ismaili Muslim Concept of Spirituality

Religious spirituality stems from the spirit, soul, which is believed to be divine, invisible, immaterial and from the "domain of God" (*ar-ruhu min amri rabbi*). This spirit/soul is eternal; it is the driving force that pushes the body, which is seen as its cage, to move and perfect itself so that when the body is perished, the soul returns to its origin. This soul, as Rumi eloquently puts it, longs for return; it is suffering from the separation, from the hardship of the limiting body and worldly life embroiled in corruption and unworthy temptations. The worldly life is soul's test in its journey to the perfection. It is neither Eastern or Western, does not come from water and or from the soil, it is neither from Iraq and nor from Khurasan, says Rumi in his famous poem: It is from the beloved and will return to thee.

In Islam, spirituality ("*ruhaniyat* or *ma'nawiyat*," Nasr, 1988b, p. xvii) is not only connected with the principle of unity (*tawhid*) of God (Nasr, 1987), but also to the realization that in Islam, spiritual development is synonymous with nearness to *Allah*. According to Nasr (1987),

> spirituality has rejuvenated Islamic society over the ages and produced countless men and women of saintly nature who have fulfilled the goal of human existence and brought joy to other human beings. It has caused a flowering of some of the world's greatest art, ranging from gardening to music, and made possible the appearance of some of the most outstanding philosophers and scientists whom the world has known. It has also carried out a discourse with other religions where circumstances have demanded. It has always remained at the heart of Islam and is the key for a deeper understanding of Islam in its many aspects. (p. xviii)

For Brohi (1987):

> Spirituality means, in fact, the attainment of higher levels of being .... asserted by the revealed Word of God.... Spirituality has no other meaning and it has no other content apart from this link that man has with this process of realizing the truth of the revealed Word of God. This process of

accepting on faith the religious truth is an essential prerequisite for securing the awakening of inner powers and hidden resources of man in order to be able to witness the higher truths in terms of experience. (pp. 22-23)

The Ismaili Imam is also one of those Muslim leaders who promotes dialogue, tolerance, pluralism, civil society, education, and cooperation between various cultures as central elements of Islamic spirituality. During his visits to Badakhshan, he emphasized that his *murids* (followers) should resolve differences through dialog and negotiation, not through the use of guns and violence. He also emphasized that his followers should not produce, trade, or consume drugs. To the contrary, generosity, humility, forgiveness, peaceful resolution of conflicts, observance of laws of the land, avoidance of harmful social habits such as the use of drugs and guns are repeatedly endorsed as ethics of Islam. In so doing the Imam used a *Qur'anic ayat*

Who so ever kills a human being [as punishment] for [crimes] other than manslaughter or [sowing] corruption in the earth, it shall be as if he has killed all mankind, and who so ever saves the life of one, it shall be as if he had saved the life of all mankind. (The Qur'an, Sura Al-Ma'idah, verse 32)

The Imam also invited his *murids* to provide unconditional voluntary services to him and his community as an Islamic tenet. He endorsed the righteousness of the values of justice, sharing, caring, cooperation, and helping the needy:

It would be traumatic if those pillars of the Islamic way of life, social justice, equality, humility and generosity, enjoined upon us all, were to lose their force or wide application in our young society. It must never be said generations hence that in our greed for the material good of the rich West we have forsaken our responsibilities to the poor, to the orphans, to the traveller, to the single woman. (Aga Khan IV, 1967, quoted in Niyozov, 2001, p. 280)

While Ismailis are expected to follow the guidance of the Imam, which is seen as the straight path, they are also expected to use their "rational and intellectual faculty and ... human reason (*aql*) to its fullest potential under the guidance of the Imam" (Nanji, 1987, pp. 184-185).

In Ismailism, worldly duties called *zahir* are considered to provide the "arena in which the context for a spiritual life is shaped" and "without action in it, the spiritual quest is regarded as unworthy" (Nanji, 1987, p. 197). The 48th Imam of the Ismaili Muslim community, Sir Sultan Mohammed Shah, Aga Khan III in his autobiography book *Memoirs of the Aga Khan* described Ismaili spirituality wherein he says:

In our ordinary affection one for another, in our daily work with hand and brain, most of us discover soon enough that any lasting satisfaction, any contentment that we can achieve, is the result of forgetting self, of merging subject with object, in a harmony that is of body, mind and spirit. (cited in Nanji, 1987, p. 197)

The Imam in this sense leads the Ismaili community through "divine command" (Nanji, 1987, p. 197) and shoulders the responsibility for continual guidance throughout the ages and time. The Shi'i Imams have been argued as the *A'raf* which mean "the summit of knowledge" (*ma'rifat*) (Corbin, 1988, p. 181). The Imam's intellect has been described as "a spirit that surpasses, while comprising, the activities of the rational mind, as well as encompassing domains not nowadays associated with the intellect, domains such as moral comportment and aesthetic sensibility" (Shah-Kazemi, 2006, p. 22). By Imam's being perceived by Ismailis as the "summit of gnosis" (p. 22), their guidance, direction and practices are believed as representing the path to light and knowledge. The goal here is to participate in intellectualization (*aql*) until one becomes "one with intelligence (*aql*)" (Corbin, 1988, p. 185). In sum, the Ismaili imam has tremendous power. He implements his power through personal and institutional means (such as orders, guidances, speeches, and structures, e.g., Religious Education Boards, the Aga Khan Development Network etc. See Aga Khan, 2008; also www.akdn.org). Later in this chapter, we will illustrate how this is reflected in the teachers' professional lives in various contexts.

TEACHNG AND KNOWLEDGE IN ISMAILI ISLAM

Like in the rest of Islamic traditions, here too, teaching is noble and anyone who teaches knowledge and is faithful and has a high and exalted status spiritually. Halm (1997) explains: "Knowledge (*ilm*) and wisdom (*hikma*) are, according to Ismaili belief, gifts from God, revealed to humanity through His prophets" (p. 17). In the Ismaili idea of knowledge, teaching and learning are tied to community service:

Knowledge means life; learning means resurrection from the death of ignorance; knowledge is a good entrusted by God to human beings (*amana*) who must not selfishly keep it to themselves but instead pass it on. Learning and teaching are a divine mission: the man who is spiritually resurrected through learning has the duty to bring his neighbor back to life as well. (p. 20)

Teaching is considered as prophetic mission and the ideal image of a teacher is one of the prophets, Imams, Sufi sheikhs, and luminaries.

Ta'lim (instruction/education) is at the heart of the Ismaili message across the history. Ismaili imams deemphasize the secular-religious and scientific —profane divide and consider all knowledge as united, coming from God. The role of humans is to discover that knowledge and use it with ethics and humility. More knowledge should lead to more humility, closeness to God, to becoming more peaceful, and less materialistic, said Nasir Khusraw (1378), one of the luminaries- teachers in Ismaili history. Nasir Khusraw is an eleventh century poet and preacher. He is believed to have spread the Ismaili faith in Badakhshan, organized its structures, wrote major treatises in the local (Dari) language, and became a legendary-miracle performing saint (Hunsberger, 2000). Until now, Nasir Khusraw is revered as the saint Ismaili figure in the Central Asian Ismaili community, the community's identity mark, its pride and an ideal person (Niyozov & Nazariev, 2005). Among many things, Nasir has called people to use their intellect, serve justice, seek knowledge, and their Imam's satisfaction. He was eloquent about knowledge's power, "If you persist in the search of knowledge, your head will reach leadership; And if your life's tree bears fruits of knowledge, you will subdue the azure wheel of heavens (as cited in Niyozov & Nazariev, 2005, p. 17).

The relationship between teacher and pupil in the Ismaili faith is also seen as a spiritual one. Imam Ja'far al-Sadiq (765 C.E.D) preached:

> Study in order to acquire learning, and to adorn yourself with it; cultivate dignity and goodwill; treat with respect those who teach you and those whom you teach. Do not make learning oppressive to anyone, and do not permit your vanity to destroy the effects of what is really good in you. (Halm, 1997, p. 61)

To summarize the above, the Imam, Ismaili doctrinal principles, and Ismaili luminaries have all affected the life and work of the teachers in the community for centuries. Following we will show examples of these influences in the teachers' worldviews, pedagogy, and relationships.

SPIRITUALITY IN PRACTICE: MORAL DUTY TO SERVE AND CARE

Regardless of the changed times and difficult conditions, many teachers in Tajikistan and Northern Areas of Pakistan have continued to see teaching as a serious duty and moral responsibility. Although they complained about the lack of care for themselves, our study found teachers believed they should not leave teaching. One teacher described this commitment:

> Teachers are a source of spirituality, culture, education and the future of the society. We work so that the children live better than we and our community

do not fall back to the level of Afghanistan. In 70 years, we have moved so much ahead and we do not want our people to become ignorant again. Both the prosperity of the society and its backwardness are our concerns. (Niyozov, 2001, p. 230)

Their notion of teaching has surpassed the years of transformation; it reflected the teachers' egalitarian, humanistic values in time of social polarization of their post-Soviet communities. They continued to be accountable and principled in a time of chaos and dramatic changes. They preferred being poor despite noticing that their poverty has made them "dervishes of the 20th century," and has adversely affected their prestige among their community and their students. They continued serving and helping everyone, with little appreciation and acknowledgement and indeed with increasing contempt for them as moralists, guardians of honesty, law, and justice. They continued to worry about the community and society in a time when many people focus on their personal and selfish interests. A Tajik teacher put it this way:

When I look at these children, my heart breaks. They had nothing to do with the collapse of the USSR. Like the teachers, they too were innocent victims of the events. Their childhood was even more disturbed. Unlike our times, many of these children have not seen sweets and toys. What sort of a heart one should have to not attend the school? (Niyozov, 2001, p. 222)

Learning from Soviet and post-Soviet experiences, Niyozov's Nigin and Sino (i.e., teachers) believed that teaching was a form of anti-politics to enable students to stand against demagogues:

Teaching is making students aware of the politicians, their sweet words and promises. Unlike politicians, I do not misuse the children, do not manipulate them, and do not cheat them. If I do so, I will harm my own reputation and I will do harm to the profession. (Niyozov, 2001, p. 147)

Connecting this to the post-Soviet corruption, lawlessness, absence of regulation and accountability in the market economy, Sino hoped that a better future was possible:

I cannot tell these students to cheat, steal, kill or sell drugs. The values that I talk about never die and never get old. I hope we are going to have a country where there is law and which is also blessed by *Mawlo*.[3] The key to this is preparing people with ethics and knowledge. That is what the Imam tells us now and that is what the Communists told us before. It will take time when the number of these people becomes larger than those corrupted. I believe that good is going to win. The current victory of bad is temporary. We may not win

materially and physically, but we can cause a deep psychological blow to the
bad, make it feel ashamed and put down. (Niyozov, 2001, p. 178)

In Hunza of Northern Pakistan, Ashraf's (2004) teachers saw teaching as:

> a sacred profession. It is the teacher who gives the students a light of learn-
> ing … pays an important role in making a child's life…. Teaching is a pro-
> phetic profession. It is kind of a jihad where we try to enlighten individuals
> with learning [by struggling against ignorance]. (pp. 193-194)

Rabia (Ashraf's another teacher) echoed this sentiment by arguing that,
"I am not just doing my duty, it is *khidmat* (honorary service) to the community" (Ashraf, 2004, p. 194). Duty is like "I come, teach and go away"
(p. 215). *Khidmat* is not for money, it is *fi sabili-llah* (in the service of God).
At another time, she reinforced this belief by stating, "I consider myself
fortunate that here is the community, completely illiterate, and I [can] do
service for them." While honorary service was one of the major reasons
teachers taught, the other benefit was the great respect they received from
the community where one teacher Zehra said, "It is good especially for
women…we get lots of respect, people respect us" (p. 198).

In Chitral of Pakistan, Afzal Tajik's (2004) teacher educator (Karim)
built his preaching and teaching and training on a spiritual connection
with the Imam and the Qur'an and not on the material incentives his
trainees' gain from teaching—whether it be money or grades:

> Through making reference to the holy Qur'an and sermons of the Imam, I
> try to make the teachers realize that becoming a teacher is a great responsi-
> bility; but teaching in the institutions which belongs to the Imam doubles
> the responsibility.[4] They should always keep in mind that their work is a
> kind of worship. When they realize this, they work beyond their limits. Such
> a realization springs from within but one has to invoke it in them. (Afzal
> Tajik, 2004, p. 168)

Working as Agents of Justice, Unity, and Peace

The teachers felt that their roles as teachers extended beyond the classrooms and they were often times called by their community to be healers,
social worker, and advisors. In Chitral, Karim felt he had God-given
abilities to help resolve problems between different people. He used a prophetic saying, "The ink of a scholar is holier than the blood of a martyr"
(Afzal Tajik, 2004, p. 177) to justify his work. Like him other Ismaili teacher
educators in Chitral volunteer at different levels of the teaching profession,
such as school management committee members, chairs, and members of

regional and local education boards, and as community representatives. Karim stated, "What keeps these teachers and the volunteers working so hard is their spiritual attachment with their Imam" (p. 163). Despite the little pay and long work hours, teachers continue to serve unstintingly:

> Although we [teachers] taught in a one-room school and were paid only 500 rupees (c.US$9) per month, we immersed ourselves in our work so deeply that we never felt deprived or disgruntled. There was a kind of enjoyment, playfulness and satisfaction in what we were doing. There was something spiritual between our students and us. We cared for them and for our work—and that always brought about satisfaction and motivation to us. (p. 164)

Karim's moral persuasion strategy in teacher development draws similarity to that of Starratt and Guare's (1995) definition of spirituality, "expressed in everything we do; it is the reflection of our inner, honest, probing self; it is the expression of our tender, receptive, and hoping heart" (p. 200). Karim felt that teachers who teach beyond the call of duty and who have a deep connection to their professional lives usually uphold spiritual and moral attitudes towards change: "The depth involves their unwavering commitment, passion and love for what they do and the way they do it" (Afzal Tajik, 2004, p. 161). Karim strongly felt that change in the teaching profession would not occur unless more teachers embraced the moral dimensions of teaching. For him, this involved believing that teaching is a divine mission, having a positive impact on the students, and becoming role models for the students and community at large. For this teacher, the moral and ethical qualities teachers need to have are honesty, justice, fairness, integrity, humility, empathy, and open-mindedness. Karim said:

> To bring about a change one needs to work with full mind, whole heart, and complete body and soul. We need teachers who will proudly say, "I am a teacher. I am in a prophetic profession. I do not care about my salary, promotion and other things. It is my duty to make this school a better place for my students". I think this kind of thinking, emotions and sense of volunteerism cannot be aroused without a strong spiritual attachment with the profession. (p. 163)

In Tajikistan, Sino believed that teacher should have an encyclopedia of knowledge to fulfill his duties as a teacher:

> When we say teacher, we assume knowledge. By teacher, I mean the most knowledgeable person in the village. Like a technician working for hours behind a machine, teachers work with ideas that way. A teacher should be an encyclopedia and knowledgeable about many subjects. (Niyozov, 2001, p. 147)

Working through miserably low pay, the deterioration of civil society, a rise in corruption and, ethnic tensions, Sino and his fellow teachers worked for peace and justice in their multiethnic communities. Sino narrated that he had Kyrgyz neighbors and noticed that their young child, whenever he saw Sino and his children:

> hid himself or ran back inside his home. One day I suddenly turned up right in front of him. I talked to him in Kyrgyz and gave him a candy. He looked with wondering eyes: Look, this man of whom I was scared all the time, speaks Kyrgyz, smiles and even gives me candy. We gradually became friends and visited each other. I told this story at a large meeting in 1995, where I refuted the parents' accusation of our school causing ethnic tensions. (pp. 178-179)

Sino also noticed that a senior government official was conspiring to plant the animosity between Tajiks and Kyrgyz. Sino as the Tajik school's head and a community leader rallied his Tajik and Kyrgyz fellows and religious leaders and resolved the conflict before it was too late:

> This would have been a real disaster. Kyrgyz from Alay[5] valley would have come here and there would have been bloodshed as there was with the Uzbeks in 1990.[6] The road to Osh would have closed. The humanitarian supplies would have been suspended and we would have all died here. (Niyozov, 2001, p. 179)

The teachers worked for a society free from guns and drugs. They discussed and criticized the use of guns and drugs with parents, used the living examples of those who ended up badly with drugs and guns, and employed the warnings of the Aga Khan, who suggested that the ethics of faith have no room for socially harmful activities. The Tajik teachers had personally experienced the damages of the post-Soviet conflicts: loss of relatives, influx of refugees, poverty and hunger, and the events in Afghanistan and Chechnya. Peace was crucial for building roads to China, new jobs, and purification of the society from drugs, corruption, and guns. Nigin, after noticing how the post-Soviet ethnic nationalism has turned yesterday's Soviet brothers and friends into adversaries, has worked for peace:

> Once I said Uzbeks were our brothers; now people talk of them as occupiers of Samarqand and Bokhara. If I talk today about Russians as brothers and friends, the youth of the village and my students do not like it.[1] I do not want to be a liar again, because of someone else's mistakes. How can I talk about Samarqand and Bokhara so as to avoid a conflict between Tajiks and Uzbeks? How can I state that we have a law-abiding, democratic and secular society, when there are drugs, corruption and nepotism? (Niyozov, 2001, p. 242)

Sino believed in a humanistic and multicultural education:

> You noticed how many nationalities and ethnicities we have got here in Murghab. We should make it a tradition to celebrate the days of each ethnicity here. One day for Wakhan, the other for Rushan, another day have a Kyrgyz cultural event. I should promote education that teaches respect, peace, justice and internationalism. By internationalism I mean the equality of people despite their geographical locations, languages, races, and religions. (p. 179)

Nigin worked for a society of sharing and helping the needy:

> If I eat and do not worry about the life of my neighbours, what is the use of my life. If my neighbour is in hardship, that is my hardship. We need each other, because there is no sound from one hand. (Niyozov, 2001, p. 283)

She despised nepotism and corruption as slaps in the face of genuine education, peace, justice, and spirituality:

> Imagine a poor child prepares himself all life, works day and night. Then someone else who had enjoyed all life gets to the university by giving a bribe or using a connection. I have developed hatred for those who do all this. I feel humiliated and slapped in the face. I just wonder how patient people we are. I know which of my students is capable of what. When you see your good student has failed you curse the Earth and the sky. I pray that the Imam saves us from this at the new university. (Niyozov, 2001, p. 288)

Teachers' Multiple Roles

Teachers in the mountainous rural communities of Central Asia were educational and community leaders whose work transgressed boundaries of classrooms, schools, and communities. Afzal Tajik's teacher educators in Chitral had multiple roles, such as teachers, change agents, village leaders, and board members. All these raised their own expectations of themselves and developed their leadership qualities such as honesty, professionalism, integrity, fairness, and communication skills. Called *Molim, Muallim, or Ustod* (teachers) by the youth and adult alike, they were teachers to all in the community. They worried about their students and society, and the impact of the conflicts, the Afghan war, and recent market–related changes on the future direction of their communities. These multiple roles and images reflected expectations and continuities that crossed the historical periods and political formations. Table 11.1 shows teachers views of their images and roles in society.

The teachers' visions and missions included engaging the local cultures. They called for including the local in the curriculum:

> During the Soviet times we learnt about USA, Russia and the Roman Empire, which were too far and too old. But we knew nearly nothing about our neighbour Afghanistan. I would include the view of mountains, the traditions of the people of Badakhshan, the needs of Badakhshan and the problems we face today. We have several small ethnic groups and languages here in Badakhshan, which have little respect for and understanding of each other. We need to know about ourselves before knowing others. Why are there so many languages here? Why are we despite our high level of education so poor? Why did we follow blindly our populist leaders?

Here, we should start the history of Tajik people from the history of Badakhshan. We should have a special topic on famous Pamiri people and

Table 11.1.   Teachers' Views of Their Images and Roles (Adapted From Niyozov, 2001, p. 307)

Domains	Examples and Indicators
Professional	Source of knowledge; Warner of students about politicians; Teller about good and bad; Curriculum developer; Critics of reforms; Advisers to parents on schooling and justice; Defenders of students against abusive parents; Fighters for their admission to universities; Keeper of students' secrets and personal confessions; Counsellors about their future aspirations and professions; Subject matter specialists; Writers of articles on professional topics; Teacher trainers;
Moral-spiritual	Moral guardians; Sources of spirituality; Attendants and performers of religious ceremonies; Teachers of Ta'lim (Ethics and Knowledge[a]); Defender of their Imam and his work; Fighters against corruption, drug, guns, and bigotry; Promoters of honesty, ethics, caring and sharing of food and clothes;
Political	Conductors of census and referenda; Propagandists for states and Imam; Volunteers during the religious and national events; Peace makers between Tajiks and Kyrgyz and among the Tajiks; Identifiers of corrupt politicians; Members of political parties and groups;
Economic	Teachers of the farmers and shepherds; Farmers; Traders in the new market; Laborers for the rich/mafia; Sellers of retails in the local markets; Laborers in Russia; Businessmen;
Administrative	Head of the school; Head of method unit; Class teacher; Member of village organization;

a. Centralized Ismaili religious subject produced by the Institute of Ismaili Studies, consisting of a package (textbook, teacher guide, students' activity book, and parents' guide) and taught across globe in the local languages by Ismaili teachers (professional or voluntary) see www.iis.ac.uk

their contribution to Tajik history. We in the school take the children to the spring of Nasir Khusraw, bring in a veteran of the war and work, or a local scholar, arrange a visit to Shotemur Museum here, and to the Ethnographic Museum in Khorog. On our own efforts, time, energy and expenses; No one pays us for that. No one thanks us. But we have been doing this since Soviet times and we believe it is important for the children learning. (Niyozov, 2001. p. 233)

According to these teachers, the future of their Central Asian rural Ismaili communities was no more dependent on the farming, industrial work, and patriarchal relations. There was not enough land and space for plants here. They believed that their students should be able to move and work anywhere they wanted. To be able to survive and live and dignified life in other places, they needed to pursue learning and seeking knowledge:

Here nature is stronger than human beings and it shows that strength all the time. Our grandparents had private land and planted all over the mountains. Our population was many times smaller, yet we have always suffered from hunger, cold, and lack of food. Knowledge is the only wealth and a way out for the people of the Pamirs. The Soviets also realised this and emphasised education. Lenin said, learn, learn and learn again. Education enabled us to live anywhere we wanted. (Niyozov, 2001, p. 245)

Modeling Leadership

Modeling fairness, excellence, integrity, caring, and sharing was another spiritual quality of these teachers. Sino stated that he put all his energy into work in the most difficult times after the immediate Soviet collapse. It so doing, he overcame emotional challenges:

I never missed any of my 8 teaching hours in a week and learnt to work with both those I liked and disliked. I had to do too many things to ensure the school is working. Only then can you demand work from others. I also headed the committee for distributing humanitarian aid.[8] I refused to bow to the demands of my relatives to give them extra humanitarian aid and to provide a job to my sister. I was hurt by the gossips in the community and fed up with the demands from those above. But I did not give up my principles. (Niyozov, 2001, p. 174)

Similarly, Ashraf's (2004) Saira was out on the fields like the older traditional women tending to the cattle, cutting grass in the garden, and doing other farming duties. This made her an exceptional role model for young and old community members alike and she was highly regarded for this (p. 157). According to Nigin, teachers possessed some essential qualities, keeping people and society from losing the balance between the self and society:

> Teachers are the most honest, most educated and most important people in the society. They cannot bribe, cannot cheat and cannot make extra money at the expense of the students. If there is a force that could really promote knowledge and ethics in the society, this force is the teacher. (Niyozov, 2001, p. 213)

In Chitral, Karim was a teacher who passionately felt that teachers need to identify with the Present Living Imam and Prophet Mohammed to be effective reformers in their schools and communities. Karim's dressing was pious: Modest and dignified, similar to that of a prophet, saint, or priest. Karim himself was always dressed in a formal traditional gown called *Shalwar-Qameez*, a brightly colored scarf on his shoulders, a rosary in his hand. He always greeted elder and children with respect, patience and love. He spoke in a soft and gentle tone. He exhibited politeness, humility, and friendliness with his peers, community members, and strangers. During his visits to schools, he always offered prayers, and during his interactions with colleagues inside or outside school, he talks always made reference to Hadiths, the Holy Qur'an, and sermons of the Present Living Imam. The content of his lectures always involved the preaching of teaching as a holy profession, the moral aspects of teaching and teachers as nation builders, preachers and volunteers. At a workshop Karim was leading, he advised the teachers:

> You should remind yourselves that what kind of a teacher the Holy Prophet (Peace Be upon Him) was, how much salary He was getting, how many training programs He had attended. None, but He had commitment and devotion. We should follow Him as a role model if we are to do justice with our work. (Afzal Tajik, 2004, p. 167)

RELATIONSHIPS AS CENTRAL TO TEACHING AND LEARNING

The success of life and work in small, rural and mountainous communities bounded by language, kinship, religiosity, a clear concept of good and bad, economic and social interdependence, reverence for the elder and authoritative required deep sensitivity to relationships with the parents, students, and colleagues. The Table 11.2 provides Tajik teachers' voices on this.

Table 11.2.   Nature, Type, and Quality of Relationships

- If my students realize I care about them, they will listen to me, learn from me and even don't get angry when I shout at them or say be tough with them;
- To know whether I am doing a good job will be seen from the kind of relationship and attitude I face with those I work with;
- Everything has changed, but my relations have remained the same; I love children and miss them; I defend the students from the abusive parents;
- I believe in Chekhov's saying: "In a human being everything must be fine: the face, clothing, body, mind and soul" (Niyozov, 2001, p. 150).
- In our school we have decided to treat children as human beings;
- I really like this mutual understanding between the teachers themselves and with the students; students help me with preparing conferences;
- We decided to fight against the students being pulled into drugs and guns;
- We have decided to educate the community; students are our best messengers;
- In our school, if teachers insult the students, they too can be insulted;
- I feel hurt when someone has become rich and has forgotten his teacher;
- We work for the sake of the Imam; It is unconditional
- Here, a small mistake can poison relations with the parents. This can go on for generations.

The teachers' relations exhibited transparency and consistency across the contexts of home, school, classroom, and community. Their classroom was not a closed and private world, separate from the community and homes. Nigin and Sino in Tajikistan kept close relations with the parents, paid attention to the community's *sukh at gham* (happiness and sorrow), fought for their students against the university instructors and even against some abusive parents. They talked with the parents, did not join the local corrupt administration, or the local drug and gun mafias. Sino motivated the parents to speak up in parent-teacher meetings. He talked in public about improving Tajik-Kyrgyz relations and Nigin discussed intra-Tajik relations. Both participated in the Imam's visits, who during his visits to Tajikistan confirmed their vision: avoid drugs, do not use guns, search knowledge, resolve disagreements peacefully, observe the state's laws, continue teaching and leading their communities.

Relations were also important because they were very sensitive politically. These teachers taught children to whom they were connected by blood, faith, language, and land. Good, honest, and transparent relations meant living in peace, harmony, and counting on the community's support whenever needed. The teachers' relationships with the students and parents were grounded in a rich knowledge base. Their contexts gave birth to a rich historical knowledge about the students, their parents, the history of their families, their ancestors, their lifestyles, their relatives, their economic status, and their familial relationships. Teachers met their students' parents almost as often as they met their students. The knowledge thus accumulated and influenced the teachers' practice, relations with the students, judgment and expectations about them, and methods of working with them personally, instructionally and strategically.

Like their methodologies, teachers' relations were eclectic. The teachers could be soft or rude, laughing, or serious. They used praise, ridicule, threats, and requests. They employed family pride and blame; they might refer to their students' parents at time in ways that hurt the children and at other times in ways that boost their confidence. They believed that being constantly too nice to any student might cause as much damage as being continuously rude. The key to the success in relationships was *niyat* (intention) and communication, showing a long term care and goals on the part of the teachers. In sum, their relationship, pedagogy, and worldview were all geared towards modeling, and producing integrated, balanced and humble human beings. This comes through

> how you are dressed, what you say, how you treat the students, how you are groomed. Our work for three years without salary is an example of upbringing. We say, *Olim shudan oson odam shudan muskil* (It is easier to become a scholar/learned person than a human being). The Imam's advice is similar to what we have been telling the students: study hard, respect their friends, and elderly, and keep away from bad habits. Today the upbringing has bad effects coming from the street and the parents. That's why teachers should agree on upbringing. Teachers should be exemplary to their students. (Niyozov, 2001, p. 239)

CONCLUSIONS AND IMPLICATIONS

Given the failure of the existing managerial, technological, and rationalist models of teaching and education reform, there is an increasing attention in research and teacher education to study spirituality, including Islamic spirituality and its implications for learning and teacher development. Despite this increasing call by researchers and teacher educators, there is a significant dearth of research on spirituality in education (Miller, 2000; Shahjahan, 2005). A lot of research on spirituality in education is also theoretical and abstract, projecting the authors' wishes on how educators should be and look like. When the word "spirituality" is associated with religions such as Islam, and when the current media associates Islam with terrorism and violence, its connection with spirituality is not always accepted (Sayani, 2005, p. 656). To the contrary, this chapter has showed a spiritual and an empowering face of Islam. The chapter illustrated how an

Ismaili spirituality motivated teachers to see their work as inherently spiritual. Going beyond the deductive and rhetoric, these teachers' spirituality had a practical and pragmatic nature. It was exhibited in practices of selflessness, care, compassion, service to their students and communities; in voluntarism, generosity, and sharing; in developing a broader notion of teaching and in finding larger and plural meanings and purposes for staying in teaching in line with Palmer's (1997): "Good teaching cannot be reduced to technique; good teaching comes from the identity and integrity of the teacher" (p. 14). Spirituality is reflected in their struggle for peace, justice, honesty, reasonableness, harmony, unity, and equity (Ridge, 2008); in the use of moral, literary, religious, secular, and natural sources to back up one's vision, mission, and practice; in their self-analysis, open and fair-mindedness and constant search for new knowledge; in their bodies, minds and hearts, words and actions; in their worldviews, pedagogies and relationships.

The stories of the teachers' life and work in rural, mountainous Tajikistan and Northern Pakistan indicate the teachers' personal awareness of self and larger social issues, the vitality of their harmonious relations with the students and parents, their belief in larger goals, divine power, and sense of mission (Capper, Keyes, & Theoharis, 2000). These teachers see life inside and outside the classroom as interconnected at their village level; their call for tolerance and intercultural understanding shows the connectedness of human and nonhuman beings (Edwards, 2005). Their sense of teaching extends beyond technical method and objective content; it highlights ethics, relations, emotions, visions, goals, faith, politics, and passion. They come close to what Fullan (2002) said of educational leaders who possess a sense of spirituality whereby "they are not spiritual in theirs of God-like purity, but they are all too human as they recognize 'mixed motives' in themselves" (p. 3). The Central Asian teachers in this paper took on multi-purpose roles in their communities and school. They put their life on line for the sake of their students, community and society. In so doing they asked nothing in return.

The teachers connected spirituality with honesty and generosity; with selflessness, peace, dialogue, and love. These they learnt from Persian poets Rudaki, Nasir Khusraw and Rumi; from prophets like Moses, Jesus, and Mohammad, and from their Imams like Ali, Sultan Mohammed Shah (Aga Khan 3) and Shah Karim (Aga Khan 4) and others.[9] At the same time, these teachers did not follow authorities blindly. They used their intellect (Nanji, 1987) and learnt from their experiences. For them, actions and results mattered more than slogans and rhetoric:

> During Perestroika and Independence, I realised that the code of the constructor of communism[10] are similar to those of *javonmardi*[11] (chivalry) in

Islam. The problem is how to apply them in practice. I don't see that happening with either of them. (Niyozov, 2001, p. 261)

Like Henry Giroux (1992), these teachers ask to what end a religious or secular ideal is used and whose interests are being served and whether there is discrimination. Not everyone uses ethical authority or spiritual ideas with honesty and the common good in mind. There might be people who betray the ideals of justice, service, caring, equity, and compassion espoused by the grand ethical authorities and emancipatory theories. Together with the teachers, one worries whether such malfeasance will dissipate hope and vision, not only among the teachers, but among the community in general. The betrayal of such trust and hope by those in the official structures, including nongovernmental organizations (NGOs) is a betrayal of spirituality. It may make double standards, hypocrisy and cynicism the norms of the society.

Regardless, these teachers viewed their teaching as a calling, a prophetic mission, attending to the care and upliftment of their community. They viewed their work as part of a collective responsibility for the advancement and enlightenment of the community. For these Central Asian teachers spirituality is pragmatic and constructive: they connected the spiritual with the secular, tradition with change, the essential with the contextual, intellect with faith, and Western with Eastern. Their religious interpretation has allowed them to do so, playing an encouraging and transformative role in their lives (Giroux, 1992). It has provided hope and meaning to their life and work, and their motivation to change and improve themselves. The teachers' voices from this chapter reflect a love, respect, and devotion to the Aga Khan that have produced a readiness to sacrifice and endure. These qualities have been the most fundamental preconditions to the current government's, AKDN's and other NGO's successes in peace and development in Badakhshans of Tajikistan and Pakistan.

In conclusion, it is spiritual to view one's profession as a calling, a prophetic mission. As was discovered in this chapter, Ismaili teachers in Central Asia taught with their hearts, minds, bodies, and souls without expecting much in return. Nurturing spiritual teachers like the ones in this study, honoring their dignity, and retaining them in the profession is a key challenge and hope of global scale (Lee, 2000; Miller, 2000). Research and teacher development need to explore the subtle, deep, invisible, emotional, artistic, religious, and spiritual dimensions of teachers' identities. Teacher development needs to move beyond behaviors, content, and pedagogy, to appreciate teaching as a lived practice, as identity's mark, and as source of teachers' energy and existence. Teacher development needs to prepare teachers to examine their job's and their students' spiritual perspectives.

NOTES

1. In the local languages, the Imam is referred to as *Imom*, *Mawlo*, and *Hozir Imom* in the local language. The official discourse refers to him as *Mawlana Hazar Imam* or the Aga Khan.

2. Due to limitation on the space and this book's focus, we have eliminated a whole section on the Marxist spirituality (Carr, 2003; Fuller, 2001; Kovel, 1994), which we believe does exist and has played significant role in the lives of the teachers of Tajikistan (for evidences on this see Niyozov, 2001, pp. 119-275).

3. A term refers to the Imams in the Ismaili interpretation of Islam (e.g., Imam Ali, the Aga Khan).

4. Here the teacher refers to religious teaching outside secular schools to the community's children. Many secular school teachers are involved in religious instruction (*ta'lim*) in the community (for more on this see the www.iis.ac.uk).

5. Alay is a valley in neighbouring Kyrgyzstan.

6. Sino refers to the bloody conflict between the Kyrgyz and Uzbeks in and around Osh in 1990.

7. This view is based on the clashes between the Russian military and the youth of the village. While the military justifies its positions and posts by curbing the cross-border trafficking, the youth blame them for unsubstantiated harassment, restricting on freedom and killings. For example, many of the villagers, not only the youth, alleged that Russians border guards were involved in the death of the four young men from the village during my field work.

8. Mainly consisting of clothes, shoes, notebooks and pencils to enable the students and teachers attend and carry on the schools.

9. In case of the Tajik teachers, the teachers did not only recognize the influence of Marxist spirituality on their professional lives, but also connected it with those of the Ismaili elements. For an example, refer to page 28 of the chapter.

10. Code of ethics of the constructor of communism was a document regulating the principles upon which the ethics and behaviors of the Soviet citizen communist were to be grounded (see Long & Long, 1999).

11. Nigin referred to parts of the book Pandiyati Jawonmardi (Messages of Chivalry), (Ivanow, 1953).

REFERENCES

Afzal Tajik, M. (2004). *From educational reformers to community developers: The changing role of field education officers of Aga Khan Education Service Chitral, Pakistan.* Unpublished doctoral thesis. Ontario Institute for Studies in Education at the University of Toronto.

Aga Khan IV. (1967). Convocation address by His Royal Highness Prince Karim the Aga Khan at the Peshawar University on November 30th, 1967, Pakistan in *The Muslim world: Yesterday, today and tomorrow*, undated, publisher not listed. Retrieved from http://www.iis.ac.uk/learning/speeches_ak4/1994.htm

Aga Khan. (2008). *Where hope takes root. Democracy and pluralism in an interdependent world.* Vancouver, Canada: Douglas & McIntyre.

Ashraf, D. (2004). *Experiences of women teachers in the Northern Area of Pakistan. Unpublished doctoral thesis.* Ontario Institute for Studies in Education at the University of Toronto.

Belousa, I. (2006). Defining spirituality in education: A post-Soviet perspective. In M. De Souza, G. Durka, K. Engebretson, R. Jackson, & A. McGrady (Eds.), *International handbook of the religious, moral, and spiritual dimensions in education* (pp. 215-230). Secaucus, NJ: Springer.

Brohi, A. K. (1987). The spiritual significance of the Quran. In S. H. Nasr (Ed.), *Islamic spirituality: Foundations. Volume 19 of World spirituality: An encyclopedia history of the religious quest* (pp. 11-23). New York: Crossroad.

Capper, C. A., Keyes, M. W., & Theoharis, G. T. (2000). Spirituality in leadership: Implications for inclusive schooling. In J. Thousand & R. Villa (Eds.), *Restructuring for caring and effective education: Piecing the puzzle together* (pp. 513-530). Baltimore, MD: Brookes.

Carr, D. (2003). *Spirituality, philosophy and education.* London: RoutledgeFalmer.

Corbin, H. (1988). The meaning of the Imam for Shi'i spirituality. In S. H. Nasr, H. Dabashi, & S. V. Reza Nasr (Eds.), *Shi'ism: Doctrines, thought and spirituality* (pp. 167-187). New York: State University of New York Press.

Daftary, F. (1990). *The Ismailis: Their history and doctrines.* London: I. B. Tauris.

Edwards, M. (2005). The spirituality of others: A school administrator's vision. In C. Sheilds, M. Edwards, & A. Sayani (Eds.), *Inspiring practices: Spirituality and educational leadership* (pp. 97-112). New York: ProActive.

Foltz, R. C. (1999). *Religions of the Silk Road: Overland trade and cultural exchange from antiquity to the fifteenth century.* New York: St. Martin's Press.

Fullan, M. (2002). *Moral purpose writ large. The school administrator web edition.* Retrieved January 15, 2003, from http://www.aasa.org/publications/sa/2002_09/fullan.htm

Fuller, R. C. (2001). *Spiritual, but not religious: Understanding unchurched America.* New York: Oxford University Press.

Giroux, H. (1992). *Border crossing: Cultural workers and the politics of education.* London: Routledge.

Halm, H. (1997). *The Fatimids and their traditions of learning.* London: I. B. Tauris.

Hunsberger, A. (2000). *Nasir Khusraw: The ruby of Badakhshan. Portrait of a Persian philosopher, traveler and missionary.* London: I. B. Tauris in collaboration with the IIS.

Johnson, M. (2009, January). *Can post-Soviet education systems build knowledge-based societies?* Paper presented at the International Conference "The challenges of education reform: Central Asia in a global context" of the Harriman Institute at Columbia University.

Ivanow, V. (Ed.).(1953). *Panddiyat-i-jawanmardi* [Advices of manliness]. Bombay, India: The Ismaili Society Series.

Keshavjee, S. (1998). *Medicines in transition. The political economy of health and social change in Badakhshan, Tajikistan.* Unpublished doctoral thesis, Harvard University, Cambridge, MA.

Khusraw, N. (1378). *Diwani Nasiri Khusraw* (Diwan of Nasir Khusraw, in Persian). Tehran, Iran: Simoi Donish.

Kovel, Joel. (1994). Marxism and spirituality: An international anthology. *Monthly Review*. Retrieved April 13, 2009, from http://findarticles.com/p/articles/mi_m1132/is_n9_v45/ai_14862532/

Krupskaya, N. (1982). *On labour-oriented education and instruction*. Moscow: Progress Publishers.

Lee, C. O. (2000). Triple universal ethics for a new civilization. In C. Lee (Ed.), *Vision for a new civilization: Spiritual and ethical values in the new millennium* (pp. 161-169). New York: Won Buddhism.

Long, D., & Long, R. (1999). *Education of teachers in Russia*. Westport, CT: Greenwood Press.

Love, P. (2002). Comparing spiritual development and cognitive development. *Journal of college student development*, *43*(3), 357-373.

Miller, J. (2000). *Education and the soul: Toward a spiritual curriculum*. New York: SUNY Press.

Nanji, A. (1987). Isma'ilism. In S. H. Nasr. (Ed.), *Islamic spirituality: Foundations*. (pp. 179-197). New York: Crossroad.

Nanji, A., & Niyozov, S. (2002). The Silk Road: Crossroads and encounters of faiths. In C. Borden (Ed.), *The Silk Road: Connecting cultures, creating trust* (pp. 37, 39-41). Washington DC: Smithsonian Institution.

Nasr, S. H. (1988a). Shi'ism and sufism. In S. H. Nasr, H. Dabashi, & S. V. Reza Nasr (Eds.), *Shi'ism: Doctrines, thought and spirituality* (pp. 100-109). New York: State University of New York Press.

Nasr, S. H. (1988b). Introduction. In S. H. Nasr, H. Dabashi, & S. V. Reza Nasr (Eds.), *Shi'ism: Doctrines, thought and spirituality* (pp. xiv-xix). New York: State University of New York Press.

Niyozov, S. (2001). *Understanding teaching in post-Soviet, rural, mountainous Tajikistan: Case studies of teachers' life and work*. Unpublished doctoral thesis, Ontario Institute for Studies in Education at the University of Toronto.

Niyozov. S., & Nazariev, R. (Eds.). (2005). *Nasir Khusraw: Yesterday, today, tomorrow*. Collection of papers presented at the Millennium Conference of Nasir Khusraw in Tajikistan, Khujand: Noshir Publishing House.

Palmer, P. (1997). The heart of a teacher: Identity and integrity in teaching. *Change, 29*, 14-21.

Ridge, L. T. (2008). *Holistic education: An analysis of its pedagogical application*. Unpublished PhD dissertation, Ohio State University.

Sayani, A. (2005, November). Spirituality, school leadership and Islam. *Journal of School Leadership, 15*, 656-672.

Shah-Kazemi, R. (2006). *Justice and remembrance: Introducing the spirituality of Imam Ali*. New York: I. B. Tauris.

Shahjahan, R. A. (2005). Spirituality in the academy. *International Journal of Qualitative Studies in Education, 18*(6), 685-711.

Starratt, J. R., & Guare, R. E. (1995). The spirituality of leadership. *Planning and Changing, 26*(3/4), 190-203.

Tabatabai, C. (1988). The imams and imamate. In S. H. Nasr, H. Dabashi, & S. V. Reza Nasr (Eds.), *Shi'ism: Doctrines, thought and spirituality* (pp. 155-166). New York: State University of New York.

Taylor, B. (2001). Earth and nature-based spirituality (Part 1): From deep ecology to radical environmentalism. *Religion, 31*(2), 175-193.

The Qur'an. (2001). (Abdullah Yusif Al, Trans.). New York: Tahrike Tahsile Qur'an.

Tacey, D. (2004). *The spirituality revolution: The emergence of contemporary spirituality.* New York: Brunner & Routledge.

Wong, P. H. (2007). A conceptual investigation into the possibility of spiritual education. In C. Ota & M. Chater (Eds.), *Spiritual education in a divided world: Social, environmental and pedagogical perspectives on the spirituality of children and young people* (pp. 73-86). Abingdon, England: Routledge.

CHAPTER 12

DAOISM,[1] NARRATIVE INQUIRY, AND A CURRICULUM OF PEACE EDUCATION

Xin Li

The Dao that can be spoken about is not the Dao.
The name that can be named is not the Name (my translation).

These are the very first two lines of Chapter One in *Daode jing*[2] (Wang Bi version[3])—and perhaps the most popular Daoist teaching. I begin with these lines to disclaim any impartiality about Daoism (Taoism) in this chapter. Instead, I base my argument on my personal understanding of Daoism through 2 decades of narrative inquiry studies of Daoism in educational experience.

The central argument of this chapter is that Daoism may contribute to our philosophical understanding, spiritual pursuit, and educational practice of peace education. Furthermore, I argue that inner peace and peace with the outside world need to be approached holistically as one great peace. Aspects of Daoism can offer meaningful inspirations for how to reach such a great peace. The Daoist belief in the benevolent nature of all beings, its view on the dynamics between opposites, its intersubjective thinking and relating to self and others, I maintain, can inform

Spirituality, Religion, and Peace Education, pp. 209–225

contemporary efforts in peace education. Examples of educational practice grounded in such Daoist worldviews will be provided to illustrate my argument and connect theory to practice.

I will first provide a brief introduction to the term of Daoism, how I will approach it, and to the two Daoist texts I will analyze in this chapter. Next, I will examine Daoist concepts that I view might contribute to peace education through a few Daoist classical works, such as *Daode jing*, and *Zhuangzi*. Then, a narrative inquiry curriculum that teaches peace will be offered as one example. The chapter concludes with a call for a Daoist great peace in the theory building of peace education.

DAOISM: A PHILOSOPHY OR RELIGION?

There has been a persistent debate over the distinction between the Daoist philosophy and the Daoist religion. Only recently, scholars began to realize that the distinction was an interpretative problem, which has little to do with the divergence among the beliefs of Chinese Daoists. Kirkland (2004) explains that the two different terms were the result of the cultural and intellectual history of the interpretive category in modern times of the Western tradition. He further elucidates, "That category has a complex history, a history imbedded in the social, intellectual, and political conflicts within Chinese and Western culture alike" (pp. xi-xii). In *Daoism and the Chinese Culture*, one of the prominent Daoist scholars Kohn (2001) provides a comprehensive chronology about how Daoism evolves in Chinese history and interacts with the outside worlds, including the Western tradition. Kohn contends that the problematic distinction between the Daoist philosophy and the Daoist religion began by the early Christian missionaries in the nineteenth century when they came in contact with Daoism and could not reconcile its philosophical texts with its religious practices. Over the years, the Daoist philosophy was given the one-sided positive evaluation and the Daoist religion the rigid condemnation. The reprint of the *Daozang* in 1920s brought the attention of the international scholars to the multifaceted and highly complex nature of Daoism as a religion. Today Daoism is considered as the indigenous organized religion of China. It includes its philosophical foundations, health practices, sociopolitical visions, rituals, priestly hierarchies, protective talismans and exorcistic spells, spiritual medications, and ecstatic soul travels to the stars, and so on. Beginning with the works of Laozi and Zhuangzi around 400-600 B.C.E., Daoism went through several stages of organization and development and is still evolving in China today.

The study of Daoism so far, Kohn (2004) explicates, can be described as having been approached from four major angles: (1) philosophy—the study of the ancient texts *Daode jing* and *Zhuangzi* and their commentaries as well as the analysis of later Daoist texts from the viewpoint of philosophy or comparative mysticism; (2) history and literature; (3) ritual, and (4) practices and techniques. I study Daoism philosophically as in Kohn's first category. Thus Daoism in this chapter refers to the indigenous Chinese religion as a whole and my focus of study is on its philosophical foundations of *Daode jing*, and *Zhuangzi.*

Daode jing, which is believed to be written by Laozi between fourth to sixth centuries B.C., is considered as the foundational classic of Daoism taken broadly to include all forms of Daoist thought and practice. Inasmuch as Daoism forms a pillar of Chinese culture, the influence of the *Daode jing* is pervasive. The sheer number of commentaries devoted to the classic—some 700, according to one count, of which about 350 are extant (Chan, 1963, p. 77)—is itself a telling indication of its enduring popularity and hermeneutical openness (Chan, 2004, p. 1). Outside of China, *Daode jing* is the most translated work in world literature, next to the Bible (Mair, 1990, p. xi).

Zhuangzi is *sui generis* as a literary text, and its influence upon later literature has been enormous (Mair, 2004, p. 30). Philosophically and religiously, *Zhuangzi* has been instrumental in the development of Daoism and the Chinese culture. In the fourth century, 500 years after the death of its proclaimed author Zhuangzi, its terminology and vision of ecstatic freedom became a major contributor to the imagery and literary world of *Shangqing* (Highest Clarity) Daoism. *Zhuangzi* is influential in the adaptation of Buddhism into China, as well as in the fusion of Buddhist ideology and ancient Daoist thought in the formation of *Chan* (also translated as Zen) in Japan (Mair, 2004, p. 34).

DAOIST THINKING AND PEACE EDUCATION

Peace researchers have recognized Daoism as based on principles of peace. Harris and Morrison (2003) noted that Daoism believes in the fundamental goodness of human nature. Aggression is forbidden. Weapons are seen as an instrumental evil. Disarmament is preached. Ambition, political power, and worldly authority are opposed. Government is seen as a necessary evil. Unity is sought through an ardent love in universal brotherhood. "The follower of Daoism has a reverence for life, believes it is wrong to kill living things, and has a scorn for worldly striving after riches and wealth" (p. 42). These peace-relevant interpretations of Daoism are, in my humble opinion, very loyal to some of the Daoist classic texts, such as *Daode jing* and *Zhunagzi*, but do not provide adequate reasoning from those texts that support the beliefs. Therefore, it is my intention to proffer a more thorough analysis of the peace-relevant principles and their supporting ways of thinking from these two Daoist texts.

Benevolent Nature of All Human Beings

Unlike many religions that believe in evil or sinful nature of human beings, Daoism believes in the benevolent nature of all beings and reveres all forms of lives. Such belief is mostly imbedded as the foundation in Daoist classic texts. The last section in Chapter 57 of *Daode jing* could serve as such an example: "If I don't take action, people will transform themselves. If I remain still, people will correct themselves. If I don't interfere, people will enrich themselves. If I do not desire, people themselves will become simple as unhewn logs" (my translation).

Here, like in many other passages, *Laozi* does not directly address the nature of people or of unhewn logs. Yet the underlying assumption for non-action, stillness, noninterference, and no desire is that people are trustworthy. They possess the abilities of self-transforming, self-correcting, self-enriching, and self-becoming. These abilities, in Daoist frame of thinking, are signs of life and vitality. The "unhewn logs" that people will become stands for *pu* 朴. It is a metaphor for simplicity, a state of pure potential and perception without prejudices. In becoming *pu* 朴, people return to the primordial state of Dao where the true nature of the mind, free from knowledge that is composed of definitions, terms, and labels. Relying on this fundamental trust, a Daoist sage or an ideal Daoist would create an environment that fosters and releases these abilities that lie in the nature of all humans.

Daoism is not antiintellectual; nor is it against knowledge, definitions, or names. "The name that can be named is not the Name." That famous second line of the beginning chapter of *Daode jing* as I quoted at the outset does not say that the name should be abandoned. Instead, *Daode jing* continues as such: "The nameless is the origin of all. The named gives birth to all" (my translation). Laozi reminds us that naming is a necessary, useful and unavoidable process that helps us understand the reality, but the name and the reality are not the same—just as a map is not the territory.

Daoism is not antisocial or world-denying either. It supports periods of withdrawal for the sake of practicing simplicity and attaining an attunement with *Dao*. But ultimately, a Daoist is a catalyst of goodness in the society around him/her, and "filters the benevolent and creative powers of *Dao* into the world and by his/(her) very being makes the world a better place, one where *Dao* is heard more fully and can aid in the realization of universal goodness" (Kohn, 2001, p. 25).

Peace With the Outside World

Daoism does not believe in the dualism between inner world and out-side world, because it views the world as an integrated whole. Only for the purpose of organization of this chapter, I examine the Daoist teachings as "outside world" and "inner world." For "outside world," I loosely refer the reality outside of an individuals' physical, intellectual, and spiritual being and the relationship of human beings to other human beings, to society, to the natural environment, and to the universe, In contrast, I use "inner world" to indicate the reality of an individual' self-development, self-enrichment, self-cultivation, and the relation of a human being with him/herself.

Like many other religions in the world, Daoism believes in treating others the way one wants to be treated him/herself. It acknowledges the interconnectedness among human beings, other forms of life, the natural environment, and the universe; it rejects the idea of conquering others. What is unique about Daoism is that it gives this universal ethical principle an epistemological foundation and validates it as a way of thinking as well as living. As I referred earlier in this chapter, Daoism views concepts and their terms as useful tools for us to approach reality, but they are not the reality. In many chapters of *Daode jing*, Laozi further explains that concepts arise in contrast. Perhaps, the most famous of such reasoning is in Chapter 2, which begins as such:

> When the concept of beautiful comes into our mind,
> we must have noticed the contrary of it—ugly.
> When we are aware of kindness,
> we must have seen cruelty.
> Have and have not give birth to each other.
> Difficult and easy arise in each other's company" (my translation).

Following this way of thinking, self and others are two opposite concepts. Without one, the other would not exist.

However, Laozi warns us that we humans have a tendency to mistake a concept as the reality, reducing a self as completely different and separate from others. Thus, to use today's term, we objectify others or "other" oth-ers. Such "othering," I believe, is the beginning of violence and war. Laozi repeatedly reminds us that every self contains some of others, and vice versa. To relate to others, we need to first put ourselves in the positions of others as having equal legitimate centers of selves from which they experi-ence and view the world. Laozi (Chapter 54) has it as such:

> Know other persons through yourself.
> Know other families through your own family.

Know other villages through your own village.
Know other states through your own state.
Know the world through the world.
How do I know the world as such?
Through this (my translation).

Zhaungzi further develops this idea in many of his fables. The famous perhaps are "*Zhuangsheng Dreamt of Butterfly*" and "*The Joy of Fish.*" In "*Zhuangsheng Dreamt of Butterfly*" Zhuangzi puts himself in the position of a butterfly, imagines the world from its perspective, sympathizes with it. Does a butterfly dream? Does it dream about Zhaungzi? What is the reality; is Zhuangzi dreaming about a butterfly or is a butterfly dreaming about Zhuangzi? Or, perhaps both. In "*The Joy of Fish,*" Zhuangzi, walking along a riverside, sympathizes with the fish swimming in the river, as they both are happy. Challenged about the potential that his student may not know whether or not the fish is happy, Zhuangzi brings up the ultimate question of the human ability of understanding. Do we know for certain if, what, and how others know and feel? The greatest certainty is perhaps knowing what we know about ourselves and acknowledging that others may share something in common with us and also maintain something different from us. As Zhuangzi puts it "If there were no 'other,' there would be no 'I.' If there were no 'I,' there would be nothing to apprehend the 'other' " (Chuang Tzu, 1994, p. 13) That is the Daoist way of intersubjective knowing.

Based on the Daoist intersubjective knowing, every "I" in the world can be a point of reference from which "I" can know "other;" every "I" is an integral part of the world, and every "other" is part of "I." They are of equal importance and value. Therefore we should treat others the way we want to be treated. Conquering or defeating the "other" is not in the Daoist vocabulary, because to conquer "other" is to conquer part of "I."

It is important to note the historical context of these influential texts. Both *Daode jing* and *Zhuangzi* appeared during the periods of Springs and Autumns (770-481 B.C.) and of Warring States (468-221 B.C.). Both times were recorded as the most volatile and violent in Chinese history. With the arrival of iron-age technology, food production and population grew rapidly. So did hunger for power, weapons, and military forces. Fierce power struggles for dominance amongst multiple states escalated to violence and wars were rampant. It was in this social context that Laozi emphasized that military force is not the Dao and reminded us of the human suffering caused by greed, violence, weapons, and wars. In Chapter 31, for example, the Daoist position against weapons, killings of life, and wars is stated explicitly. "Weapons bring evil omens. Dao abhors it and a Daoist would not use it" (my translation). *Laozi* further clarifies that weapons should only be used as the last resort and should not be decorated because nobody should take delight in killing. If wars cannot be completely rejected, accept them as an evil necessity. More important and most enlightening in *Laozi's* message is the reminder of human suffering even in the case of victory and in time of celebration. "For killing of masses, we bewail with sorrow and grief; for victory in battles, we commemorate with mourning ritual" (my translation).

Please note the use of "evil necessity" and be reminded of the Daoist understanding about the difference between a word that is intended to represent a reality and the reality that could never be reduced to a pure concept. Daoism does not reject war or violence completely. Instead, it accepts it as the last resort. In other words, it acknowledges the possible benefit that may result from a war.

Inner Peace

The Daoist notion of inner peace is based on the faith in the benevolent nature of all human beings including oneself and also acceptance of both the positive and the negative aspects of oneself. Awareness of and efforts to balance between one's two sides are important. The Daoist inner peace is a process in which an individual constantly cultivates his/her ability to reach, beyond words and languages, thoughts and emotions that come to us in forms of language, for a primordial state of holistic self that is one with the outside world. That is a spiritual practice.

I discussed the Daoist belief in the benevolent nature of all human beings earlier and would like to emphasize here that all human beings includes oneself. Unlike many world religions, Daoism does not promote the feeling of guilt or fear for punishment on wrongdoing, nor plea for forgiveness. Each individual can find in him/herself opposite qualities as defined or named, such as kindness and cruelty, good and evil, strong and weak, rebellious and loyal, sweet and bitter, and the list goes as long as our vocabulary capacity takes us. Each of us should not be reduced to a mere concept or a name and concepts arise in pairs of opposites. This basic Daoist view of human knowing accepts each one of us as real and holistic beyond any names. The Daoist self-development and self-cultivation lie in our efforts to realize that real and holistic self. Along the way to that primordial state, however, we do not abandon the names or the languages upon which our intellect relies. We make attempts to understand them and make use of them in the way we interplay between opposite concepts, balance them in ourselves, and let this balancing motion transcend us.

How to balance ourselves? If we consider ourselves as being too cruel, we could try to embrace kindness. But does being too kind lead to cruelty? The answer, as my reading of Daoism stands, is yes. The reasoning is that once your kindness goes to the extreme, it may become unappreciated, unvalued, and loses its meaning as kindness. Once your kindness is not considered as kindness, it may lead to evil and cruelty in others as well as onself. Therefore, we need some adjustment and correction. For example, we sometimes choose to be unkind and apply tough-love to our children. Other times, we set up cruel and strict rules to our students, even in learner-centered classrooms. But eventually, our kindness for our children's healthy development and our students' successful learning experience may be better realized. The importance here, especially for those who are more used to the traditional Western either-or way of thinking, we do not abandon "kindness." Instead, we claim both.

Laozi (Chapter 28) puts it as such:

Know masculinity,
maintain femininity,
and be a ravine for all.
By being a ravine for all,
eternal integrity will never desert you.
If eternal integrity never deserts you,
you will return to the state of infancy.
...
Know whiteness,
maintain blackness,
and be a model for all.
If eternal integrity does not err, you will return to infinity.
Know you are innocent,
accept the wrong accusation,
and be a valley for all.
By being a valley for all,
eternity will suffice.
If eternal integrity suffices,
you will return to the simplicity of the unhewn log (my translation).

Besides the interplay between opposites, the passage above includes metaphors of low positions, such as ravine and valley. Taking low positions, or being modest and humble, is another important quality a Daoist would try to cultivate in him/herself. *Daode jing* frequently refers to peaceful images of water as soft and yielding, yet ultimately triumphant over such "hard" substances as rock. In Chapter 8, Laozi elaborates the metaphor of water as such: "The highest good is like water; water is good at benefiting the myriad creatures without claiming entitlement. It occupies the place of low rank that is loathed by the masses. Therefore, it is near to the Dao" (my translation). Being beneficial for others while remaining modest and humble is the Daoist's highest level of self-cultivation. Such self-cultivation is not in isolation. On the contrary, it emphasizes the interaction with the outside world in choosing one's humble position and unconditional goodness for the outside world. No reward should be expected, because, to benefit others is the same as doing good to oneself in the Daoist interconnected holistic universe. Being water is the Daoist choice of living.

A NARRATIVE INQUIRY CURRICULUM

In the late 1980s and early 1990s, I conducted a narrative inquiry about my own educational experience in China and Canada (Li, 1991). The inquiry led me to Daoism. It was Daoism, I found, that guided me through the maze of adolescent transition compounded by a major social catastrophe in modern Chinese history—the Cultural Revolution. Repudiated by the mainstream society, I was able to hang on to the faith in the benevolent nature of all human beings including others and myself. Exposed to the dark side of the world, I was able to keep in sight both negative and positive sides of the events taking place around me. Uprooted from a privileged social environment, I learned to see beyond my own loss, reach out to the opposite side—underprivileged, from whom I learned about life's giving. In contrast, I developed a strong consciousness of equality and social justice. My loss was turned into my gain. Deprived of schooling, I searched for education and curriculum outside of schools and self taught my missed secondary school curriculum. Influenced by the Daoist belief and behavior from my family and inspired by the Daoist wisdom in the underprivileged people, I made the best of life's giving in the difficult time, and improvised my experience into something that was educationally meaningful. Later, I realized, such Daoist improvisation was transferred to other difficult times, such as the early years of my immigration to the West. The Daoist improvisation—making the best out of life's giving even in worst situations—laid a foundation for my quest for inner peace and peace with the outside world.

In the 1990s, another narrative research embarked me on a journey to the Daoist intersubjective knowing (Li, 1998, 2002). In this research, I worked with others—a few Chinese women immigrants and adult students of mine. Together, we inquired about our life experiences in China and Canada. Daoism again, I found, guided me to put myself in their positions, view the world from their viewpoints, and understand their experiences as educational and meaningful for them, even, or I should say, particularly putting myself in the positions of others who had experienced social events from the opposite side of mine. Two former enemies, for example, told each other their stories of experience. Suspending our prejudices and judgments about the other, we listened to the details of each other's stories to their fullest possible extent. Shifting "I" into the position of "other," we tried to feel the other's joys and pains, and to dream the other's dreams and see the other's realities. Taking equal turns in our telling and listening, we were able to understand our former enemies sympathetically, and comprehend the other's experience that was originally remote and strange as that of a butterfly's dream and fish's joy in Zhuangzi's philosophical fables. However, we did not lose ourselves or become each other. We transcended the "I" and the "other," and became intersubjective selves. That is to say, in each of us, there is a little more of the other. This other is not the objectified or alienated "other" any more, but an other who is equally entitled to her subjectivity just like "I." The two have both gone through a process of intersubjective becoming and enemies were turned into friends.

In the past decade, I have developed the aforementioned research into a cross-cultural teacher education curriculum (Li, 2007). Over the years, I examined various aspects of the curriculum and its influence or even impact on pre- and in-service teachers' multicultural identity and cross-cultural competence. In a research project on a few in-service teachers from a deeply polarized class, the findings indicated that the curriculum was effective in bringing together teachers of different ethnic and social economic backgrounds (Li, 2005). It also had its ripple effect to public school classrooms in the ways of how these teachers teach their students with diverse cultural backgrounds in urban Los Angeles area. In another narrative inquiry (Li, 2006), I explored experience of people from opposing and even hostile cultural backgrounds; I found that such cultural backgrounds can be assets for people's intersubjective learning when opposites encounter and engage with each other in narrative inquiry. More recent research (Li, 2009) revealed that opposite cultural backgrounds may not only be an asset to the process of intersubjective becoming, but may also inspire cultural creativity. In the following section, I will briefly describe some important components of the curriculum that reflect Daoist knowing.

Unname the Named Through Thick Description

In the narrative inquiry curriculum of cross-cultural education I developed over the past decade, we do two types of things: we narrate and we inquire. We repeatedly tell, listen to, write, and read stories of life experiences. The purpose of all these activities is to inquire about our cross-cultural development in the past and project our future improvement. The inquiry is not the type of research in a traditional sense. It does not begin with a hypothesis, nor proceed with evidences to prove or disprove a theory. A narrative inquiry begins with open questions, such as "What is my cultural identity?" "Why did I teach the way I did?" "What or who influenced me the most?" Then in our effort to answer such open questions, we tell and write stories of our experience. Following the usual format of story writing, we focus on training the narrative inquirers to use a detailed and label-free language. Such a language, or *thick description* as I borrowed from the cultural anthropologist Geertz, offers us an opportunity to remove the preexisting labels and predefined terms that we have already attached to our experiences and takes us through a process of Daoist unnaming.

For example, in answering the first type of question, one may say: "I am White, and I have neither culture nor cultural identity." As Laozi says, "The named is not the Name." Nobody should be reduced to a mere name or concept. A thick description or a Daoist unnaming would not include any of the labels or the terms, "White" in this case. Instead, a full-blown story about the individual's cultural life is expected. This person may describe in detail his/her physical characteristics, what these characteristics have associated him/her with and brought to him/her in the upbringing, how individuals in his/her life and society have behaved in response to these characteristics, how he/herself have thought about and behaved in response to others' and the society's treatment of him/her regarding his/her physical characteristics. The list can go on and on, because the label "White" may mean different range of things for different people and a lot more than just physical characteristics for most. However, this unnaming process does not eliminate names or language(s) completely. Instead, it takes way vocabularies that are value-laden and abstract, and recovers the stories with a more concrete language, which is more open for interpretation, less inviting for argument or debate, and perhaps closer to the experience as how it was experienced. Stories written this way became our field text, or raw data as in the traditional research for analysis and synthesis later.

"I" and "Other" Interplay Through Story Sharing

The narrative inquiry curriculum includes structured interaction among the fellow inquirers. In pairs or larger groups, we share our stories. Sharing requires attentive listening, nonjudgmental response, and equal turn-taking in telling and listening. Such requirement is to ensure respect to "other" as if to "I," suspension of one's predetermined views and opinions, and equality of all. Often, for example, we observe how individuals interpret other's stories and offer their own quick, simple and biased interpretation and explanation even before they hear the end of the stories. Other times, individuals interpret other's stories as offensive to their own values and beliefs and decide to interrupt by offering their opinions or by arguing with the one who is telling the story. Such interruption treats the story-teller as "other." It indicates one's own perception is superior to other's, and sabotages the unnaming narrative process. But this has happened often in the particular environment where I taught. My understanding of such occurrence is that in a society where opinions—either public or private—are overvalued and argument and debate have been built into the entire public discourse, school curriculum no exception, it takes a long time and hard work to unlearn them. Following Daoist understanding, an intelligent person is empty-minded and receptive to, without prejudices, preconceived assumptions or judgment, new knowledge, may it be surprising or even shocking. We empty our boat before we may be able to load more.

Besides listening to and telling stories, narrative inquirers in this structured interaction are encouraged to respond to other's stories with their own stories of experience, however the connections may be, either by a specific topic, not necessary about the entire story, or by the specific time when the stories take place (see more in Li, 1998, 2002). And of course, all need to be in detailed and label-free language. When a listener finds parts of the stories not as detailed as it could be, he/she is encouraged to ask for more details. In such an interaction, stories become more and more detailed, and each participant's stories become more extensive, profound, and richer. Such interaction prepares participants to accept others as an equal center or subjectivity as oneself.

Intersubjective Becoming and Renaming

Intersubjectivity does not happen in isolation. As explained earlier, interaction between "I" and "other" is a must. But one such interaction is only the beginning. In order for "I" to see "other" as "I," multiple interactions are important. Narrative inquirers need to get into a habit of suspending "I" or emptying our minds and putting "I" in the position of "other" when listening to stories, and practice responding with stories and questions only for more details. This is a slow, long, and even painful process. Intersubjective understanding may not happen to some inquirers within the semester. It may occur to others but will not repeat after the semester is over. But most find it rewarding just to have experienced the process and record moments of their intersubjective understanding of "other" and "I" in composing their narratives of cross-cultural education as the final product from the experience.

Intersubjective becoming is an ongoing process and should never end. But our class has to end and our research has to be reported. Therefore we compose stories of our cross-cultural education. In this phase, similar to some other traditional research, we look for patterns and themes and sort out our stories accordingly. We also seek existing research literature associated with the theme to locate and guide our inquiry. Sometimes, we may need to further explore hidden stories. Other times, we may find it necessary to tell or listen to more stories that are found missing but important for the particular theme we identify as such in this phase of the inquiry. Eventually, we reconstruct our narratives that summarize our cross-cultural development and points out future directions. In another word, we rename our experience.

As Laozi recognizes that "the named gives birth to all." Our way of knowing, according to Daoism, relies on the names. We think through labels, symbols, and languages, without which we humans will be at loss in comprehending and communicating with the world around us. Without them, we will be even more confused at who we are and how we should behave in response to various cultural phenomena, people, and events in the world. However, this renaming does not undo the unnaming. It does take us back to the same old stories. Instead, it guides us to reach beyond the stories of past and create new meaning for our experiences in the future.

Opposites and Cultural Creativity

Over the years of developing this curriculum, I have also conducted a few studies to examine the effect and impact of the curriculum on the intersubjective learning of some participants. Participants in these follow-up studies reported intersubjective learning to various degrees (Li, 2005). One of the most surprising findings is that those who were from contrasting, opposing, and even hostile cultural backgrounds articulated a higher degree of intersubjective learning (Li, 2006). Does that mean opposite can be advantageous for intersubjectivity? I explored this question through studying two student teachers of opposite ethnic, social class and gender backgrounds (Li, 2008). At the beginning of the semester when they were in my class, they both expressed discomfort in each other's presence and requested not to work in the same group. As the semester went on, they told and listened to unnamed stories, and gradually accepted the "other" from the other's viewpoint. In turn, they learned about themselves. In untold or long forgotten stories, they each found different and opposite aspects of themselves. In each other's stories and in the presence of each other, they learned intersubjectively.

More interesting is that four years after they finished and left our program, we found they have become friends. They shared their ideas and strategies in teaching, and their two families spent time together. Their friendship has been the major support to each other in this era of extreme teacher-proof curriculum and high-stake testing. They both believed that their interaction was intriguing and a source of cultural creativity that they both experienced in teaching.

Creativity is defined, in the Western tradition, as "the interaction among aptitude, process, and environment by which an individual or group produces a perceptible product that is both novel and useful as defined within a social context" (Plucker, Beghetto, & Dow, 2004, p. 90). Daoism views creativity as an ontological experience of the ultimate truth and self-realization (Chang, 1963). Such an experience "transcends the knowledge which is composed by a system of labels and sees the real reality which is usually blocked by language, tradition, culture, and human needs" (Kuo, 1996, p. 200). It is spiritual. In other words, the Daoist view of creativity can be characterized as spiritual experience, whereas the Western view focuses on the final product. From the Daoist understanding of creativity, the two participants appeared to have experienced a cross-cultural self-realization ontologically through their interaction and friendship, transcended their prior knowledge about their cultural identities composed by a system of labels, and seen the reality of their complicated selves that was blocked by their previous respective traditions, cultures, and human needs. They have had a spiritual experience. In the Western definition of creativity, the result and product of their interaction and friendship the cross-cultural narratives they wrote at the end of the semester and their creative teaching later demonstrated novel combinations of both the familiar and unfamiliar, and such novelty is appropriate and useful in benefiting all, including themselves, their particular time, and place.

THE DAOIST GREAT PEACE

The example I offered above is not a curriculum of peace education by definition. However, following the Daoist belief in the benevolent nature of all humans, its understanding about how to achieve peace with the outside world, and inner peace, this cross-cultural teacher education curriculum has enabled people from opposing and hostile cultural backgrounds to interact peacefully, understand sympathetically, and discover cultural creativity together. It changes patterns of thought and behavior, transforms the human condition, creates peace in individuals, groups, classes at the university, public school classrooms, homeless centers, after school programs, and at-risk youths. One small program like this may continuously have a ripple effect that extends broad and deep into the structure of the society. Eventually it may bring 太平 or the Daoist Great Peace.

The notion of Great Peace can be traced as far back as to the First Emperor of the Qin dynasty (221-206 B.C.). However, it was in *Taiping jing* when the notion was most fully elaborated. *Taiping jing*, the Scripture on Great Peace is considered as the first religious text of Daoism, reconstructed from earlier versions between the second and fourth centuries (Kohn, 2004, p. 66). The term *Taiping* or Great Peace has been interpreted and used by politicians and thinkers in various dynasties. So has it been borrowed by peasant uprisings in Chinese history. However, as *Taiping jing* scholar Hendrischke (2006) points out, the aims and ways of thinking in *Taiping jing* cannot be identified with that of either the politicians or peasant rebels (p. 4). Instead, *Taiping Jing*, offers us a most comprehensive, coherent, and concrete picture of Great Peace: harmonious societies in tune with their natural environment and universe, and how it could be achieved.

Such Daosit harmonious societies require first and foremost respect and faith in the benevolent nature of each and all, Black and White, poor and rich, female and male, homosexual and heterosexual, Muslim and Christian, bilingual and monolingual, disabled and able, old and young. That is the prerequisite for basic human rights for all. Direct or physical violence, and structural violence constituted by systematic inequalities will both be abolished. Each is involved in self-cultivation to realize his/her primordial state and all are actively participating in benefiting others but humbly taking low positions. Social structures will be lateral instead of hierarchical. Every "I" puts him/herself in the position of "other," and understands sympathetically. Ways of thinking will be intersubjective instead of subjective or objective. Returning the inner peace and peace with the outside world back to the Daoist holistic peace brings us to cultural creativity. That is the Daoist Great Peace as a self-correcting, self-balancing, self-transforming living organism. That is what Daoism in my understanding can contribute to theory as well as practice in peace education.

NOTES

1. Daoism has also been translated as Taoism. Recent academic publications have adopted the translation of Daoism, such as the two volume *Daoism Handbook*. In keeping up with the current use of the term, I choose Daoism in this chapter, except in references.

2. I use *Daode jing* for 道德经 which has also been translated as Tao Te Ching, or the Scripture of the Way, and so on.

3. I use Wang Bi version of *Daode jing* for its general acceptance as one of the most complete version.

REFERENCES

Chan, A. K. L. (2004). The *Daodejing* and its tradition. In L. Kohn (Ed.), *Daoism handbook* (pp. 1-29). Boston, MA: Brill Academic.

Chan, W. T. (1963). *The Way of Lao Tzu*. Indianapolis, In: Bobbs-Merrill.

Change, C. Y. (1963). *Creativity and Taoism: A study of Chinese philosophy, art, and poetry*. New York: Harper & Row.

Harris, I. M., & Morrison, M. L. (2003). *Peace education* (2nd ed.). Jefferson, NC: McFarland & Company.

Hendrischke, B. (2006). *The scripture on great peace: The Taiping Jing and the beginnings of Daoism*. Berkeley, CA: University of California Press.

Kirkland, R. (2004). Introduction: Explaining Daoism-Realities, cultural constructs and emerging perspectives. In L. Kohn (Ed.), *Daoism handbook* (pp. xi-xviii). Boston, MA: Brill Academic.

Kohn, L. (2001). *Daoism and Chinese culture*. Cambridge, MA: Three Pines Press.

Kohn, L. (Ed.). (2004). *Daoism handbook* (Vol. I). Boston: Brill.

Kuo, Y-Y. (1996). Taoist psychology of creativity. *Journal of Creative Behavior, 30*(3), 197–212.

Laozi 老子 (400-600 B.C.). 道德经 通行本（王弼本）*Daode jing* (Wang Bi version). Retrieved from http://baike.baidu.com/view/16516.htm#4

Li, X. (1991). *Moments of improvisation in my life experience*. Unpublished master's thesis, University of Toronto, Toronto.

Li, X. (1998). *Becoming an intersubjective self: Teacher knowing through Chinese women immigrants' knotting of language, poetry, and culture*. Unpublished doctoral thesis, University of Toronto, Toronto.

Li, X. (2002). *The Tao of life stories: Chinese language, poetry, and culture in education*. New York: Peter Lang.

Li, X. (2005). A Tao of narrative: Dynamic splicing of teacher stories. *Curriculum Inquiry, 34*(3), 339–366.

Li, X. (2006). Becoming Taoist I and Thou: Identity-making of opposite cultures. *Journal of Curriculum and Pedagogy, 3*(2), 193–216.

Li, X. (2007). Multiculturize teacher identity: A critical descriptive narrative. *Multicultural Education, 14*(4), 37-44.

Li, X. (2009). Black and white may make a rainbow: Cultural creativity from opposites. *Multicultural Perspective, 11*(3), 1-7.

Mair, V. (1990). Preface. In L. Tzu (Ed.), *Tao Te Ching: The classic book of integrity and the Way*. New York: Bantam Books.

Mair, V. (2004. The Zhuangzi and its impact. In L. Kohn (Ed.), *Daoism handbook* (pp. 30-52). Boston, MA: Brill Academic.

Plucker, J. A., Beghetto, R. A., & Dow, G. T. (2004). Why isn't creativity more important to educationa psychology? Potentials, pitfalls and future directions in creativity research. *Educational Psychology, 39*(2), 83-96.

CHAPTER 13

PEACEMAKING
AND SPIRITUALITY

Bridging Faith,
Values, Understanding, and Life Skills

William M. Timpson

Spirituality is a topic that makes many instructors uneasy, especially within the social sciences. Because of the historic separation between church and state in the United States, educators at every level have struggled to know how best to incorporate what the various religions say about nonviolence. Especially during times of war, peace education is also problematic for teachers who fear that their patriotism will be challenged. Yet, religion has a very long, deep, and complex relationship with peace education and both can be important curricular foci for schools, colleges and universities. Emphasizing spirituality in my own classes allows me to avoid some of the controversies that surround religion and, instead, focus on those beliefs—and skills—that link our human existence with larger, unifying life enhancing forces in the universe.

While the Quakers and Mennonites have clear about their commitment to pacifism, other mainstream churches have struggled with "just war"

Spirituality, Religion, and Peace Education, pp. 227–239

theories. We also have many historic examples when church leaders and entire congregations have remained silent or complicit in the commission of barbarous actions by the state. Worse still are those instances when missionaries, for example, accompanied conquistadors from Europe into the Americas and used the church to bless those prospecting for riches while brutalizing the indigenous "heathen."

In my Honors seminar on Peacemaking at Colorado State University, these same tensions between religion, spirituality, and peacemaking have surfaced repeatedly, especially when we discuss the impact of the great peacemakers—Gandhi, Martin Luther King, Jr., Thich Nhat Hahn, and others—who drew much from formal religious tenets and practices. More specifically, I have used Bishop Desmond Tutu's (1997) book on the work of the Truth and Reconciliation Commission in South Africa, *No Future Without Forgiveness*. This honest, disturbing but ultimately heartening manuscript serves as a powerful argument for reconciliation from the horrors of apartheid through love, forgiveness, and acceptance.

In this Honors seminar, I also wanted to connect this history of peacemaking and these spiritual concepts to specific skill sets so that students can see the relevance of peace education in their own lives. We begin with communication, with the deep listening and empathy that supports forgiveness. We also work on the mechanisms of consensus for finding a unified way forward among disparate voices, learning how to slow the process of decision making to incorporate minority views and thereby attempt to make better and more creative decisions that have broader ownership.

For our readings, we also draw on Bill Ury's (1999) *The Third Side* and its many examples of skills that have helped to resolve conflicts in the workplace, between individuals and groups, and across ethnic, cultural as well as national divides. In David Orr's (2004) *The Last Refuge*, we hear a call for many of these same skills for an American public that has become lulled into a consumptive sleepwalk while the environmental crisis continues to build and the U.S. military stretches to protect "American interests" around the world. My own 2002 book, *Teaching and Learning Peace*, connects the work of the great peacemakers with the skills and understanding needed to build a positive classroom climate, encourage cooperation, and promote critical and creative thinking.

LESSONS FROM SOUTH AFRICA

It is in stories from South Africa, in particular, where my students see both the horrors of racist exploitation and the potential power of forgiveness. In Bill Moyers' (1999) videotape for PBS, *Facing the Truth*, they meet a one-armed white lawyer, Albie Sachs, taking us on a tour of the prison where he was detained month after month, tortured and humiliated because he had dared to work against the state's policy of apartheid. Later he was driven into exile and permanently maimed by a car bomb intended to silence his protests. Yet, instead of succumbing to a victim's paralysis and self-pity, Sachs returned from exile and joins the Truth and Reconciliation Commission's work, seeing the figurative "flowers" of democracy blooming out of the stump of his arm and insisting that the injury was worth the sacrifice. Here my students got to put in perspective their own struggles with forgiving people who have hurt them. Discussions about the real meaning of forgiveness now have a very real frame of reference.

In another scene we watch a theater group of Black South Africans taking on various roles in an effort to bring these issues out for public discussion. The "victims" of torture and their "family members" demand justice. The "soldiers" of the state ask for forgiveness. Someone says, "Let's just forget about all this and move into the future." Several yell back, FORGET? NEVER? Forgive? Maybe, but Forget? NEVER!" In our Honors seminar on Peacemaking, we talk about these complexities, the "emotional intelligence" needed to understand our own hurt in the present while simultaneously focusing on what is best for ourselves and others, now and in the future.

The spiritual aspect in this often surfaced in response to Bishop Tutu's reference to the Christian context of forgiveness in guiding his own reactions. While he struggled to understand those white South Africans who claimed to be Christians yet who either designed, supported, or benefited from apartheid, Tutu made frequent reference to the power of faith in underlying hope for the future, that the innate goodness in humans would see them and their country through the transformation to an inclusive, fair, and just democracy.

Because South Africans have talked about every aspect of postapartheid life through the workings of the Truth and Reconciliation Commission, including reconciliation and reparations, we often talk about the legacy of slavery in the United States and the history of efforts to exact an official apology from the government. Again, South Africa represents a powerful example of putting the concept of forgiveness into practice, how they discussed what was right and what was possible in a variety of public forums. Eventually, they came up with some criteria for amnesty as well as a sum for reparations that was approximately equal to U.S.$3,600 for every "victim" who could document his or her loss. In contrast, the federal government in the U.S. has been incapable of an apology for slavery, primarily because of the "threat" of legal action that might follow demands for reparations from slavery.

Bishop Tutu goes on the challenge the model of the Nurenberg Trials for addressing the worst aspects of the Nazi leaders in the Second World War. Instead of a preoccupation with questions of justice, judgments of guilt, and punishment, the South African Truth and Reconciliation Commission focused on requests for amnesty and forgiveness in return for admissions of guilt and apologies to victims and their families, all recorded and televised to a nation that never knew the whole story. On one side, there was state terror against its own citizens in an effort to sustain Afrikaner privileges and authority; on the other side were similarly brutal stories of rebel reprisals. For a supposedly Christian nation to face up to its violent and dark history was quite sobering, raising questions about the deeper meanings of spirituality.

The result of all this was a cathartic and sobering education for an entire nation. No one had known the full story before. Yet a bloody civil war that many people predicted was avoided and some significant credit must go to Bishop Tutu and other religious leaders who evoked the "better angels" of their fellow citizens. They used the Christian commitment to love and forgiveness to move through the hurts of the past toward a peaceful and inclusive future. Tutu (1997) then uses that special African concept of *ubuntu* to explain why an inclusive future was so important. Note how closely this concept parallels core principles in so many spiritual traditions:

> It is to say, "My humanity is caught up, is inextricably bound up, in yours." We belong in a bundle of life. We say, "A person is a person through other persons." It is not, "I think therefore I am." It says rather: "I am human because I belong. I participate. I share." A person with *ubuntu* is open and available to others, affirming of others.... Anger, resentment, lust for revenge, even success through aggressive competitiveness, are corrosive of this good. To forgive is not just altruistic. It is the best form of self-interest. What dehumanizes you inexorably dehumanizes me. It gives people resilience, enabling them to survive and emerge still human despite all efforts to dehumanize them. (p. 31)

CONNECTING THE PAST AND PRESENT

Historical examples have one level of impact. Connecting these to the present can reinforce important lessons learned. For this Honors seminar, I have made great use of resource people on campus and in the community. For example, in the Fall of 2007, Matshwene (Edwin) Moshia was a student at Colorado State University completing his PhD in soil and crop sciences and hoping to return to his native South Africa to play a lead role in moving his country toward more sustainable agriculture. As a Black he lived through the later stages of Apartheid and could talk to my students about that experience. He has also written about all this in his first book, *African Village Boy: Poverty and Bantu Education System of the Apartheid South Africa* (2006). What my students respond to is Edwin's upbeat determination to transform the traumas and tragedies that he survived into a clear commitment to bring something positive back to South Africa through his studies. Drawing in part on his faith, Edwin exhibits a profound forgiveness of his persecutors that is truly inspiring. In a handout he shared with my students, he wrote:

> I was born in the remote rural village in the Limpopo Province of South Africa. Gravel and thorny roads of the village are the daily paths on which village boys like me walked barefooted to shepherd livestock of our families. As a child in this village, agriculture was a main source of livelihood, and coupled with agriculture, religion was our one and only hope, our mainstay, for a better tomorrow.
>
> At present, I wish to become a leader in agricultural research for the betterment of not only commercial farmers but for our burgeoning group of co-operative farmers as well. The key for me is to ensure that our ability to address basic needs is not limited by a poor understanding of soil resources and plant nutrition, and that the health and integrity of the nation's resources and ecosystems are sustained.
>
> I am a product of a poverty-stricken family and a society which not only oppressed us but had no respect for our basic human rights. I was transformed by my own initiative, a strong sense of professionalism, an ability to quickly acquire new skills, a willingness to make every challenge a learning opportunity, and the ability to interact effectively with people in all walks of life. My own life is testimony to the fact that there are possibilities.

Another way to connect the past with the present is to identify current issues that have parallels to a discussion of spirituality and peace education. For example, South Africa's struggles began with the ascendancy of the apartheid government in 1948 and the linking of dissent with perceived or concocted communist threats during the Cold War. Resistance and protests continued and built to a crescendo during the 1970s, sparking increasing international condemnation and pressure. All of this culminated in the national election of 1994 when Blacks were first allowed to vote, and the subsequent convening of the Truth and Reconciliation Commission's first meeting in 1996. More than a decade later, however, are stories from other places that can help students see the relevance and meaning of all this history. For example, in a report by DeGroot (2008), we see that Rwanda is making a stunning recovery from the hell of genocide:

The statistics of the genocide are devastating. About 83 percent of the Tutsi population was murdered in a Hutu version of the Final Solution. The survivors carry terrible scars—physical and mental. Thousands of women still cope with the trauma of rape. Many were intentionally infected with HIV, itself a weapon of genocide.... (However,) Rwanda seeks admiration, not pity. And rightfully: The people should be seen as an example of the resilience of the human spirit, not of the despair that too often defines Africa.... The future is built on faith: Rwandans have convinced themselves that they were once a harmonious people and can be so again.... Rwanda provides stark contrast to the images usually emerging from Africa: instead of defeatism, there is dynamism; instead of pity, there is pride. If there is a bright future for Africa, it lies in the direction Rwanda points. (p. 9)

These are powerful stories to study for insights into the intersection of spirituality and peace education. For example, educators at every level of schooling can be invited to join with people throughout the community, regardless of their particular faith traditions, in a discussion of their collective future, connecting concepts like forgiveness to what we know about healing generally, to an analysis of resilience and harmony, to policies, and to practices that promote dynamism and pride.

TEACHING THE PROCESS OF CONSENSUS

Whether it is the concept of "*ubuntu*" that holds Africans together or the commitments needed to make forgiveness a reality in finding a peaceful way forward out of the horrors of the Apartheid past in South Africa, my Honors students see that spiritual ideals can find their practical applications in the mechanisms of mutual agreements by which Bill Ury fashions a "third side," or in the public awareness that David Orr insists must emerge to address our environmental threats. In my honors seminar on peacemaking I recognize that the concept of consensus with its related skill set can be taught, learned, and practiced. In several different books, I have described the role of consensus and effective communication generally for deepening student learning, especially when addressing difficult and complex issues (Timpson & Doe, 2008; Timpson, Dunbar, Kimmel, Bruyere, Newman, & Mizia, 2006; Timpson, Yang, Borrayo, & Canetto, 2005; Timpson, Canetto, Borrayo, & Yang, 2003; Timpson, 1999).

For example, in the Fall of 2007 our class happened to meet on the anniversary of the September 11 attacks in the United States. Wanting my students to apply our studies for the benefits of the campus community as a whole, I put the challenge to them in small groups and asked that they work toward consensus to decide upon some course of action. The only context I gave them was that the focus should begin with the Peace Pole that had been constructed just west of the Student Center on the first anniversary of the attacks. Standing some eight feet tall, this poll has the phrase "May Peace Prevail on Earth" written in eight different spoken languages including English, Russian, Hebrew, Arabic, Chinese, Japanese as well as sign language and animal paw prints.

Working with an established model of consensus, my students spent some time *defining* what would be appropriate on the anniversary of the attacks some 6 years later. After much discussion in small groups, they ultimately decided to "chalk" the walkways in the area with peace signs, sayings, challenges, and the like. They also picked up on my description of my visit to the Peace Park in Hiroshima where the atomic bomb exploded in 1945. In particular, I had told them how school children came from all over Japan to being chains of paper peace cranes to drape over the children's statue. Amid all the solid rock statues nearby, the children's statues comes alive with these chains of brightly colored paper cranes all containing thoughts for peace and reconciliation. Metaphorically, the faith of these children in a more peaceful world was not left calcified in stone but renewed regularly with this pilgrimage.

My own students also expanded their thinking to include some ideas for remodeling the area around the Peace Pole to reflect a larger commitment to peace and reconciliation, a campus "shrine" if you will, that could educate visitors as well as provide spaces for reflection, meditation and prayer. Then everyone jumped into *brainstorming* possibilities followed by some *assessments* of the quality of the ideas that emerged. Finally, I invited the director of the Student Center to hear from each group since he was eager to get some new ideas for the needed remodeling. The later stages of consensus—*deciding, implementing*, and *reevaluating*—would have to wait for the future. Following this exercise we debriefed what had occurred to reinforce what worked and what could have been improved.

What emerged were ideas for benches and plaques commemorating the great peacemakers, a Zen garden with calming water features nearby, as well as a labyrinth for walking meditation. Because of the inherent inductive process of consensus and its requirement for deep listening, new and creative ideas were able to surface. For example, when the focus turned toward landscaping, several students quickly argued for a selection process that would be "at peace" with the local bioregion, that is, xeriscaping or a sustainable design that recognizes existing moisture, weather, and soil characteristics. This kind of inductive process allowed them to connect their deeply held values with concrete actions.

TEACHING COMMUNICATION

As was abundantly clear during the consensus process we used for planning the "Peace Park," a different kind of listening was essential for finding common ground. The spiritual concept of forgiveness that was at the heart of Truth and Reconciliation process in South Africa required much arduous listening to reach agreement about solutions. Again, I emphasized that we could study, practice and apply modes of communication that lowered defenses among participants and simultaneously build bridges to understanding and common purpose, while honoring different experiences and beliefs. The process of uncovering those deeper truths helps connect people to some sense of the spiritual. In class we practiced *deep listening* by seeking first to *understand* others, by putting opinions on hold and helping others to *clarify* their thoughts, by using *reflective statements* to convey *empathy,* and by practicing *acceptance* even when we did not fully agree with another perspective. Wanting another meaningful context for the application of this deeper listening, I took my students over to the Vietnam Memorial Bridge near the Student Center on our campus. A plaque in the walkway on one side honors those who served in the military to defend the country; a plaque on the other side honors those who protested in defense of their country. I ask students to examine a current conflict in their lives, to look at it again from both sides, and to meet in the middle of the bridge to find "common ground." This kind of activity helps connect process skills with concrete events and personal values, reinforcing the skills needed to navigate our complex world and all its challenges while staying true to deeper spiritual beliefs.

TEACHING COOPERATION

Whether the reference is postapartheid South Africa, the enduring racial divides in the United States, or the challenges of reconciliation in the aftermath of war, the various conflicts that arise in any community require skilled negotiation. Working closely with others toward a goal has an almost magical way of breaking down old animosities and forging a more inclusive way forward. In his classic work on prejudice, for example, Gordon Allport (1954) describes how teamwork can help overcome learned stereotypes and promote positive feelings among people from very different backgrounds. Using various group activities that seek consensus about a shared assignment throughout a semester provides students repeated opportunities to discuss cooperation and reflect on what worked for that particular task and what could be improved.

Experiencing the benefits of a positive group experience reinforces these shared life-affirming values.

Knowing how to work effectively within a group context has the added benefits of helping facilitate *better and more creative decisions* as more diverse input is allowed to surface and challenge conventional thinking. We can learn how to live the "golden rule," treating others as we would want ourselves treated—or better yet, treating others as they would want to be treated (Bennett, 1998). Again, group assignments can provide students the chance to see this in action. However, it requires clarity and commitment on the part of the instructor to push beyond the experience of the activity itself and lead students to reflect on lessons learned. Too often, teachers neglect the importance of *debriefing* cooperative activities and mining the jewels just below the surface.

Understanding the concepts that underlie cooperation as well as the skills of consensus and communication, are essential for this transformation of what many think of primarily as "spiritual" into the realities of peacemaking and everyday life. For cooperation, that means understanding more about *mutual interdependence*, how our talents include our skills and expertise as well as the support we can give others and the assistance we can receive in an effort to maximize the potential for group success. This means understanding more about *synergy*, a powerful but elusive concept that describes those conditions where groups are able to function at very high levels. The whole becomes greater than the sum of the parts, when team "chemistry" blends individual talents toward new heights of performance.

Creating a variety of cooperative activities and goals for students underscores the concepts and skills needed for cooperation; it also offers opportunities for modeling and practice. Many instructors will, therefore, assign group projects to be completed outside of class. Students, of course, will routinely work together to study for exams, help each other with homework assignments, and so forth. Using some class time for group projects, however, requires time, skill and energy to do well. If instructors are wedded to efficient content coverage, they will not find much time to use cooperative activities in class. Their "faith" is in knowledge transmission, not the coconstructed understanding that energizes students and deepens learning.

When successful, students will often value these group projects as some of the most important aspects of a particular course. Yet, when groups struggle to work together to find a common goal, to negotiate responsibility for the various tasks, to find the time outside of class, then group projects can be very frustrating and counterproductive. Here again there are numerous opportunities for practicing those skills that help people address problems, communicate across differences, resolve conflicts and define a constructive way forward. These are the very same skills that can underlie our efforts to make real the spiritual aspects of peacemaking.

THE LAST REFUGE

In the opening lines of his seminal work on education and the environment, *Earth in Mind*, David Orr (1994), the academic son of a Baptist minister, notes how human population growth, our needs and manufactured wants comingle with development, industrialization, waste and pollution to consume the natural resources of the planet, outstrip its carrying capacity, and threaten its ability to support life. For example, according to Wackernagel and Rees (1996), if the rest of the world lived like Americans, the collective ecological footprint would be so large that we would need five to seven more planets to meet the human appetite for sustenance, safety, comfort and all that stuff. Here, concern for the natural systems that support all life moves beyond mere environmentalism and becomes a spiritual commandment as well, a way to unify all humanity within a reverence for what is life affirming. At the end of *The Last Refuge*, Orr argues for common ground and a common future.

> Ours is a time of both danger and opportunity. Effective and farsighted stewardship will make the difference between very different human futures. On one hand, better design and improved technology make it possible to increase resource efficiency, and decrease pollution radically, to establish sustainable prosperity, and to improve equity within and between generations for all the world's people. Failure to take full advantage of possibilities now before us will commit us to a darker future of increased political turmoil, terrorism, pollution, conflict over resources, adverse climatic change, and suffering. The time to make decisive changes is perilously short. (p. 140)

Above all he concludes, "it will require a change in how we see ourselves relative to other life forms and to future generations" (p. 149). Orr comes from a long line of preachers and we can hear the righteous anger as he rails at our political, economic, and moral failings to safeguard the earth that supports all life. These are stark predictions for any of us to consider and my Honors students struggle to grasp the enormity of them. Their youthful faith and idealism keep them upbeat. Yet, their hopes for the "good life" push many toward denial as a coping mechanism. Here the work of Dan Goleman on "emotional intelligence" and Howard Gardner on "multiple intelligences" prove useful, offering some understanding of how best to navigate through the intersection of complex and difficult topics like faith and peace that often evoke such strong feelings.

MULTIPLE INTELLIGENCES

Howard Gardner's (1999) critique of the traditionally narrow focus of formal education on the linguistic and logical-mathematical as mechanisms
for knowing leads easily to a consideration of other "intelligences" like
musical, spatial, and bodily-kinesthetic. Especially important for our discussion of spirituality and peace education is Gardner's insistence that
there is also both an "intrapersonal" as well as an "interpersonal" intelligence, where knowledge of self, communication and group dynamics
allows for larger, more inclusive discussions that can include faith, beliefs,
values, reactions, and emotions.

After completing his analysis of these seven basic "intelligences," Gardner also suggests that there could be an eighth, what he terms "spiritual/
naturalist," an ability that connects what David Orr worries we have lost, a
reverence for life that can transcend self-interest and our cultural concerns for the pursuit of happiness. Gardner (1999) writes:

> Even those who cannot identify with the spiritual realm or domain recognize
> its importance to most human beings.... (Books) about the spirit or soul
> crowd out those about memory or perception on the psychology shelves in
> bookstores. Regrettably, the majority of scholars in the cognitive and biolog-
> ical sciences turn away from questions of a spiritual nature, consigning this
> realm chiefly to the true believers and the quacks.... If the abstract realm of
> mathematics constitutes a reasonable area of intelligence (and few would
> challenge that judgment), why not the abstract realm of the spiritual? (p. 53)

Since public discussions of peace, violence, and war so often provoke
deeper conversations about the value of life and draw on articles of faith,
and in Christianity, for example, commandments to love one's neighbor
and to reject killing, Gardner's arguments lend support for embracing
both within education at every level:

> If we humans can relate to the world of nature, we can also relate to the
> supernatural world—to the cosmos that extends beyond what we can per-
> ceive directly, to the mystery of our own existence, and to life-and-death
> experiences that transcend what we routinely encounter. And, indeed, the
> realms of mythology, religion, and art have perennially reflected our efforts
> to understand the ultimate questions, mysteries, and meanings of life: Who
> are we? Where do we come from? What does the future hold for us? Why do
> we exist? What is the meaning of life, of love, of tragic losses, of death? What
> is our relationship to the wider world and to beings who lie beyond our
> comprehension, like our gods or our God? (p. 54)

Gardner is addressing issues, beliefs, and values that are especially
problematic for U.S. higher education and its historic preoccupation with

utilitarianism, vocationalism, and science. The constitutional separation of church and state has meant little formal attention to other values, beliefs, and attitudes that underlie education in a democratic society and why students pursue degrees. As attendance at mainstream church services continues to decline, the questions that students have about spirituality multiply. In my own classes, when the United States was rushing into its latest Iraq War in the aftermath of the September 11 attacks, students seemed rudderless to resist, unequipped to tap into their own moral compasses, too quick to mouth the culturally correct language of "support our troops," and too afraid to challenge authority and risk being labeled unpatriotic.

CONCLUSION

Spirituality and peace are both complex topics that become even more so when connected. Strong emotions are stirred and history is full of examples both bloody and inspired, when some used their "faith" to justify their attacks on innocents or when others called upon their "better angels" to help calm a conflict. In his inaugural address to Congress in 1861, Abraham Lincoln could not have known the enormity of the violence and loss that lie ahead. His words then are as valid today, and speak to the value of joining spirit and peace in our studies:

> We are not enemies, but friends. We must not be enemies. Though passion may have strained it must not break our bonds of affection. The mystic chords of memory, stretching from every battlefield and patriot grave to every living heart and hearthstone all over this broad land, will yet swell the chorus of the Union, when again touched, as surely they will be, by the better angels of our nature.

In my classes, I have attempted to raise awareness about alternatives to violence and point toward the knowledge and skills that can help students find constructive ways forward past conflicts and over barriers. The laboratory for our work is everywhere, in the residence halls, and between roommates, in classrooms where some voices dominate and many sit muffled, and out in the larger community where the needs and inequities are great. With study and practice, we can become our own "better angels."

REFERENCES

Allport, G. (1954) *The nature of prejudice.* Cambridge, MA: Addison-Wesley.

Bennett, M. (1998) Intercultural communication: A current perspective. In *Basic concepts of intercuotural communication* (pp. 1-34). Yarmouth, ME: Intercultural Press.

DeGroot, G. (2008, April) Rwanda's comeback. *The Christian Science Monitor, 28,* 9.

Gardner, H. (1999). *Intelligence reframed.* New York: Basic Books.

Moshia, M. E. (2006) *African village boy: poverty and Bantu education system of the Apartheid South Africa.* Bloomington, IN: AuthorHouse.

Moyers, W. (1999). *Facing the truth.* Princeton, NJ: Public Affairs Television, Films for the Humanities and Sciences.

Orr, D. (1994). *Earth in mind.* Washington, DC: Island Press

Orr, D. (2004) *The last refuge: Patriotism, politics and the environment in an age of terror.* Washington, DC: Island Press.

Timpson, W. (1999). *Metateaching and the instructional map.* Madison, WI: Atwood.

Timpson, W. (2002). *Teaching and learning peace.* Madison, WI: Atwood.

Timpson, W., Canetto, S., Borrayo, E., & Yang, R. (Eds.). (2003). *Teaching diversity: Challenges and complexities, identities and integrity.* Madison, WI: Atwood.

Timpson, W., & Doe, S. (2008). *Concepts and choices for teaching: Meeting the challenges in higher education* (2nd ed.). Madison, WI: Atwood.

Timpson, W., Dunbar, B., Kimmel, G., Bruyere, B., Newman, P., & Mizia, H. (2006). *147 tips for teaching sustainability: Connecting the environment, the economy and society.* Madison, WI: Atwood.

Timpson, W., Yang, R., Borrayo, E., & Canetto, S. (2005). *147 Tips for teaching diversity.* Madison, WI: Atwood.

Tutu, D. (1997). *No future without forgiveness.* New York: Doubleday.

Ury, W. (1999). *The third side.* New York: Penguin.

Wackernagel, M., & Rees, W. (1996) *Our ecological footprint.* Gabriola Island, BC: New Society Press.

CHAPTER 14

"SELF" RE-EDUCATION FOR TEACHERS

Gandhi, Deep Ecology, and Multicultural Peace Education

Edward J. Brantmeier

Part of the joy stems from consciousness of our intimate relation to something bigger than our ego; something which has endured for millions of years, and is worth continued life for many more millions of years.

—Arne Naess (1995)

INTRODUCTION

A limited sense of self creates a condition where "otherizing" is normalized and seemingly necessary for self identification. I define *my* reality in reference or in opposition to the *other's* reality. Such binary constructs of "I" and "other" can perpetuate potentially harmful division and are often integral to ethnocentrism, cultural conflict, the impetus of violence, and a legitimizing rationale for continued violence. A deeper "Self" re-education challenges the construct of "I" and "other" through positing a

Spirituality, Religion, and Peace Education, pp. 241–259

radical interconnectedness and interdependence of all life in which nondual existence becomes the perceptual and affective norm from which nonviolent behavior naturally follows. Using Galtung's (1969) constructs, the conditions of both negative peace, or the absence of direct physical violence or war, and positive peace, the absence of indirect and structural violence, emerge as desirable conditions from such "Self" realization. Exploration and expansion of the "limited self" (Brantmeier, 2003) emerges as a selective advantage in the cultivation of teachers who should exhibit multicultural competence and global understanding in schools that serve youth.

A critical issue that warrants the attention of teacher educators in the United States (and perhaps elsewhere around the world) is the growing cultural gap between a predominately homogenous, white, Euro-American teaching force and the youth who attend increasingly multicultural/multiracial schools (Howard, 2006). Teaching diverse learners requires increased cultural competence in teachers. According to Ladson-Billings (2006), culturally competent teachers:

> help students to recognize and honor their own cultural beliefs and practices while acquiring access to a wider culture, where they are likely to have a chance of improving their socioeconomic status and make informed decisions about the lives they wish to lead. (p. 36)

The challenge for teachers to affirm diversity as well as to provide awareness of mainstream cultural formations that will promote institutional access, opportunity, and the ability to self-actualize for historically marginalized students is critical. Banks et al. (2005) elaborate on culturally responsive teaching practices:

> Building a culturally responsive practice requires teachers to build a broad base of knowledge that grows and changes as students, contexts, and subject matters shift. Knowledge of self and others (students, parents, community) is an essential foundation for constructing, evaluating, and altering curriculum and pedagogy so that it is responsive to students. (p. 245)

Flexibility, fluidity, and contextual approaches to understanding "self" and other (individual students and their cultural backgrounds) emerge as paramount in teacher education. Teachers need to be able to learn from their students' cultural backgrounds (Zeichner, 1993).

The achievement gap reflects the irony of the intentions of the U.S. federal education policy No Child Left Behind (Darling-Hammond, 2007). Gross disparities exist among children of color and their White, Euro-American counterparts in relation to graduation rates, test scores, and disproportionately in punishments in schools (Banks et al., 2005).

Perhaps the "achievement" gap might be better labeled the "privilege" gap given the policies and practices of de-culturalization in regards to non-White populations in the United States via a history of structural, institutionalized inequality (Spring, 2006). Perhaps if teachers learn to pay attention to students cultural backgrounds and how they might be quite different from the culture of school, if they focus on understanding the privilege gap, this might refocus the burden of responsibility of standardized test failure from individual students or student groups to the system itself that reproduces inequality and inequity—a system that needs to learn to better engage future and present teachers in the use of culturally inclusive curriculum, in developing strategies for cultural responsive teaching, and in creating fair and inclusive tests.

One small step toward social justice might be found in attempts to decrease the cultural gap between teachers and their students; building intercultural empathy for peace becomes a crucial stepping stone for larger school reform efforts (Brantmeier, 2008). In efforts to both dismantle dominance paradigms (Howard, 2006) and transforming education for peace (Lin, Brantmeier, & Bruhn, 2008), the cultivation of the heart-mind capacities of teachers is critical; teacher educators and teachers themselves need to foster their capacities to understand the backgrounds of the diverse learners who enter their classrooms, to foster their capacities to empathize with their students, and to connect on intellectual, emotional, social, and spiritual levels. Teacher education institutions need to provide the tools necessary for prospective and in-service educators to move from moral exclusion to moral inclusion (Opotow, Gerson, & Woodside, 2005) where responsibility for all "others" and a deep, authentic inclusiveness are the norm.

This chapter is a step on a journey toward building a flexible conceptual framework for multicultural peace education—one that would help foster culturally competent and "spiritualized" educators. Through the philosophies and action orientations of M. K. Gandhi and of Arne Naess, the Norwegian eco-philosopher and founding member of the deep ecology movement, I will explore notions of a "self re-education" that encompass a more expansive identification which includes not only other human beings but also all flora and fauna on planet earth. Implications for teacher education, particularly developed for future multicultural peace education efforts, are suggested.

A PARADOX OF THE LIMITED AND UNIVERSAL: INSIGHTS FROM GANDHI AND DEEP ECOLOGY

"Self" re-education requires understanding a complex paradox; the self is both limited and universal. Previously, I have argued for the cultivation of four dimensions of "Self" for creating globalized teachers. Through reflection on a cross-cultural immersion student teaching program at Indiana University, the author explored a "Self" re-education model that asks teacher educators to urge preservice and in-service teachers to identify with a larger "Self," to cultivate meaning-building, to foster peacebuilding, and to cultivate adaptive capacities (Brantmeier, 2003). Referred to as the LAMP model for creating globalized teachers, the four dimensions of self to be cultivated follow: L = limited self; A = adaptive self; M = meaningful self; and P = peacebuilding self. The focal point of this present chapter is the first concept in the LAMP model, the "limited self."

The limited self is a paradox because it demands that an educator be able to toggle between the particular and the universal; he/she must see the "other" through both a culturally relative and universal human lens. In other words, one should see herself as limited and as unlimited. I am limited in that my own unique cultural vantage point is distinct from my Indian or Norwegian friend who holds a unique, valid, and historically shaped cultural views of the world. I am unlimited in that our fundamental human nature and many of our human needs are the same.

In the process of becoming culturally competent educators, teachers, both preservice and in-service, need to learn not to judge others based on their conscious and unconscious cultural standards. Recognition, understanding, and acceptance of differences in culturally responsive education cultivate a truly multicultural ethic and multicultural practices in the classrooms of our nations. Awareness of one's own cultural conditioning and validation of cultural diversity can promote a positive pluralism where honoring differences are the norm. A limited sense of self is helpful in the cultivation of "perspective consciousness," Hanvey's (1982) classic term defined as

> The recognition on the part of an individual that he or she has a view of world that is not universally shared, that this view of the world has been and continues to be shaped by influences that often escape conscious detection, and that others have views of the world that are profoundly different from one's own. (p. 3)

Understood from a culturally relative standpoint, the views, values, and ways of being in the world of both "self" and "other" emerge as distinct and are understood as conditioned and re-engineered in situated/nested cultural contexts.

However, a limited sense of self can pose problems if "radical otherness" (Haberman, 2002) creates an unbridgeable chasm of entrenched difference. A limited sense of self identity might create a condition where "otherizing" is normalized and in fact necessary for self identification; self and group identity constructs are reinforced via oppositional dynamics with "others." *I* define *my* reality in reference to the *other* reality of the *other.* One's more "rigid" self identity is thus defined in a dichotomous construct that posits mutual exclusiveness as the norm. The "lesser"—and thus devoid of equal status, value, and rights—"other" becomes the recipient of violence, be it physical violence or structural violence.

A deeper "Self" re-education challenges the rigid construct of "I" and "other" through positing a radical interconnectedness and interdependence of all life—human, animal, plant, and mineral. Through this re-education process, nondual existence becomes the perceptual and affective norm from which nonviolence and compassion naturally flow; violence against others (human and nonhuman) is considered violence against self. In the next section, the philosophical roots of Gandhian nonviolence will be contextualized in order to inform "Self" re-education toward moral inclusion.

Gandhi and Self Re-Education

Though Gandhi lived away from India much of his young adult life, Gandhian thought on self identity should not be divorced from his Indian cultural roots—specifically the *Vedantic* texts which he studied in great detail after returning to India from South Africa. David Haberman (2002), an expert on Hinduism, suggests:

> The primary aim of the *Upanisads* is to bring about a shift in identity from the transient ego self associated with the individual body to the eternal and infinite Self that is not different from the All. The ideal of human perfection for Vedantic Schools of Hinduism is the *jivanmukti,* one who remains in the world having realized his radical interconnectedness with everything. (India Studies Lecture, 10/17/02)

The "shift in identity" and the accompanying realization of the radical interconnectedness of everything are illustrated in the *Bhagavad Gita* when *Krsna* teaches *Arjuna* a valuable lesson in "Self" re-education:

> Arming himself with a discipline
> Seeing everything with an equal eye,
> He sees the self in all creatures
> And all creatures in the self. (Miller, 1986, p. 67, Verse 29)

Boundaries of a rigid self become fluid and inclusive when seeing oneself in all creatures. Self re-education occurs when experience shifts from isolated, atomized, or fragmented self-reference to an interrelatedness of being. Self re-education involves a perceptive and experiential shift from conceptions of the atomized individual to realization of the self as a node in interdependent processes and infinite webs of connectedness. Gandhi (1924) mirrors the essence of this radical inclusiveness and then alludes to a technique of nonviolence that naturally follows from such an insight:

> I believe in non-duality (*advaita*), I believe in the essential unity of man and, for that matter, of all that lives.... The rock bottom foundation of the technique for achieving the power of nonviolence is belief in the essential oneness of all life. (p. 390)

Both the *Bhagavad Gita* and Gandhi assert the need for a "Self" re-education—an identification of the self with the interconnected web of life. Through such a process, the guise of the autonomous and independent self give way to a more expansive and inclusive ontology, being in-relation or more acutely—being *as* relatedness. From this new inclusive and expanded positioning, a new action-orientation emerges; one acts nonviolently and selflessly for the benefit of others. Gandhi (1932) asserts Plato's time honored maxim and then provides an answer:

> The purpose of life is undoubtedly to know oneself. We cannot do it unless we learn to identify ourselves with all that lives. The sum total of all that life is God. Hence the necessity of realizing God living within every one of us. The instrument of this knowledge is boundless selfless service. (pp. 242-243)

Gandhi relays that the very purpose of life is to know the self as undifferentiated from all other sentient beings and to live in the world with the realization of the *Brahman* (God) within us all.[1] By stressing "that life" Gandhi is in effect saying that all life, human, plant, and animal, is a sacred part of the whole that needs to be recognized as having the spark of the divine—the same divine spark is in the buffalo and the black walnut tree.

We should identify ourselves with all life in the process of revealing our true natures—in re- "cognizing" our expansive Self. One might naturally contribute to the world through "boundless, selfless service." Thus, "Self" realization translates into enlightened social action. Gandhi suggests such a belief in the unity of all life serves as "the foundation of the technique for achieving the power of nonviolence." With this belief and understanding, one would conceive of violence against his/her neighbor, a creature, and a plant in the natural world as violence against the Self and therefore would be goaded to seek alternative nonviolent possibilities. Self re-education,

Gandhi style, requires identification with all forms of life and nonviolence seems the natural outcome.

Gandhi, Deep Ecology, and Self Re-Education

The connection of Gandhi's philosophy of nonviolent action to the deep ecology movement has been made by a few scholars (Haberman, 2002; Weber, 1999) and the connection of Gandhi to ecology by others Lal, 2000; Pimentel, 1996). Haberman (2002) situates the Vedantic view of self as one in the same with Gandhian thought and that of deep ecology and also poses the ethical implications that stem from such a view of a "radically interconnected self ": social justice, equality, and nonviolence (Haberman, 2002). Lal (2000) contests the notion of an explicit "Gandhian Ecology" by relaying that Gandhi wrote no texts on ecology or environmentalism; Gandhi's life itself was an "ecological symphony" composed of fasting, treating people and animals with equality, and other acts constituting simplicity of means and an embodied ecological ethic. In reviewing Khoshoo's book *Mahatma Gandhi: An Apostle of Applied Human Ecology*, Pimental argues that "it is obvious that Gandhi treasured nature and argued for biodiversity" (Pimental, 1996, p. 1). Though Pimental does not make direct connections between Gandhi and the deep ecology movement, he provides a quote from Gandhi that hints at the "rights of nature"—which is a cornerstone of deep ecological principles—"a human being has no power to create life, he has, therefore, no right to destroy life" (Gandhi cited in Khosoo, 1995, p. 4).

Alongside a quote by Arne Naess, Norwegian eco-philosopher and founding member of the deep ecology movement, we see the parallel between the principles of deep ecology and Gandhi's assertion of "live and let live,"

> One of the basic norms of deep ecology is that every life form has in principle a right to live and blossom … there is a basic intuition in deep ecology that we have no right to destroy other living beings without sufficient reason. (as cited in Sessions, 1995, pp. 28-29)

Weber (1999) maintains that Arne Naess's notion of "Self-Realization" can be understood and contextualized in Gandhian nonviolence and Self Realization.

During his lifetime, M. K. Gandhi's project in India was a spiritual, political, and social process that effectively created widespread change in the human world via a nonviolent philosophy of political action (*satyagraha*) and localized economics (*swadeshi*) that undoubtedly had positive environmental impact. The Indian *khadi* movement focused on local self-sufficiency and the production and consumption of local goods (*swadeshi* economics) which had considerably less environmental impact than a contemporary globalized economy that requires the transportation of products and goods from all spheres of the globe. Contemporary "be local" and "slow food" environmental/economic movements mirror the efforts of Gandhi who promoted localized, self-sufficiency via localized economics in India.

With several of my former students in 2000, I had the privilege of living at a Gandhian ashram in India that practices localized production and consumption of resources. Circular and communal production and consumption of resources was the norm; milk products, fruit and vegetable produce, cotton weaving, and silk spinning were integral to the localized, mostly self-sufficient economy. In this context, economic practices were a reflection of value system that focuses on nonviolent, self-realized action.

One of the foundational moral imperatives of deep ecology movement was/is to extend the right to live and prosper to ecosystems and the nonhuman inhabitants that live in them. This extension of moral rights to the nonhuman world goads individuals, groups, and societies to adapt an environmental ethic and economic practices that promote human and planetary sustainability, rather than overconsumption and linear consumption of finite natural resources.

Essentially, Arne Naess took the Vedantic notion of Self (a "radically interconnected Self") and more explicitly applied it to the nonhuman world. In his seminal essay titled "Self-Realization: An Ecological Approach to Being in the World," Naess suggests that the contemporary deep ecology movement requires a deepening of insight into the expansiveness of self, "Now is the time to share with all life on our maltreated Earth through a deepening identification with all life forms and the greater units: the ecosystems and Gaia, the fabulous old planet of ours" (as cited in Sessions, p. 235). Naess bridges the disconnect between humans and nature through expanding human identification to include both flora and fauna. Thus, interdependence is understood not only as relatedness of human beings to one another, but also as relatedness of all sentient and nonsentient beings to one another. Naess suggests that care for the environment naturally stems as a result of "widening" of the self, "The requisite care flows naturally if the "self" is widened and deepened so that protection of free nature is felt and conceived as protection of ourselves" (p. 236).

The roots of a new paradigm for peace require a widening of the self to include other inhabitants of the planet and other people; this surely is not a new idea originated in India and reinforced in Norway. A verse from a

Tom Early translation of the Chinese Taoist Lao Tsu's *Tao Te Ching* further accentuates a more universal call for Self re-education:

Recovering the root
Means just this:
The dynamics of peace—
Being recalled to our common fate
In the kinship of all creation. (as cited in Devall & Sessions, 1985, p 14)

What one does affects the ecological, the planetary whole. A deep ecological Self-realization emerges as the self is widened and deepened; an awareness and experience of connectedness becomes embodied and lived. Several of the world's great wisdom traditions, including Native American traditions, echo the profound insight of the radical interconnectedness of all life. In writing about deep ecology, Devall and Sessions (1985) echo and extend these sentiments:

But the deep ecology sense of self requires further maturity and growth, an identification that goes beyond humanity to include the nonhuman world…. This process of the full unfolding of Self can also be summarized by the phrase, "No one is saved until we are all saved," where the phrase "one" includes not only me, an individual human, but all humans, whales, grizzly bears, whole rain forest ecosystems, mountains, rivers, the tiniest of microbes in the soil, and so on. (p. 67)

Advancing an Environmental Ethic

Ascribing value to nonhuman organisms remains paramount and the development of a more fully evolved environmental ethic remains critical to globalizing teachers (discussed later) and to planetary sustainability. Barkdull (2000) distinguishes among three operating environmental ethics: anthropocentric, biocentric, and ecocentric. An anthropocentric environmental ethic considers how humans use the environment either positively or negatively and how that use impacts future generations. A biocentric environmental ethic considers the rights of animals in assessing environmental impact. An ecocentric environmental ethic assumes moral status for an ecological whole, be they bioregions or planetary ecosystems; "Gaia" is considered "a living breathing planetary system") (Barkdull, 2000, pp. 195-196). The assumption of moral status to creatures beyond homosapiens is critical to the cultivation of an environmental ethic that promotes planetary rights and sustainability.

Too often anthropocentrism guides human relationship with and action in the nonhuman world. The nonhuman world exists for the fulfillment of the desires of humans. More specifically, the maxim "Man has dominion over the earth" operates on many levels in post-industrial capitalistic societies. Human beings assume the right to use, exploit, and dominate the earth and her organisms. Humans allow environmental exploitation to be justified according to the "privileged" positions of human beings (and more so the global North in proportion to the global South) on the planet; nonhuman organisms are considered devoid of moral status and inherent rights. Such a hierarchy privileges humans over nonhumans, and some humans (many have white skin and are male—this depends on dominance paradigms in situated contexts however) over other humans. Such structural violence (i.e., economic, political, cultural systems that disadvantage some and privilege others) creates systemic inequality. Nonhuman organisms and certain marginalized populations (Sub-Saharan Africans, women, poor people in general) are exploited and suffer while others amount masses of material wealth. Shifting from an anthropocentric to an ecocentric environmental ethic that would dismantle certain aspects of the dynamics of this dominance paradigm might enable planetary justice and human sustainability.

Empathy and Ecological Sustainability

Empathy is critical to this process of "widening the self." Empathetic union, cojoining with another's thought patterns, emotions, and general disposition, emerges as essential in the cultivation of Self-realization. Perspective taking or shallow position-taking with the nonhuman world is not enough to make this shift of consciousness; the suffering of the earth must be deeply felt, as if that suffering was one's own. We need to learn to feel the tree being cut by chainsaws, we must feel the oil-slicked duck's slow death. We need to experience the grace of a dancing crane by dancing as a crane. We should experience the power of a turbulent thunderstorm; John Muir once climbed a pine tree during a torrential rainstorm to feel the power of nature intimately.

Empathy, not sympathy, need be the deeper response to the growing environmental problems of the planet. Empathy requires position-taking that goes beyond mere acknowledgement of perspective difference. In the field of intercultural communication, Milton Bennett (1998) makes a noteworthy distinction between sympathy and empathy; he suggests sympathy can be understood through the golden rule, "Therefore all things whatsoever ye would that men should do to you, do ye even so to them" (Matthew 7:12). Empathy is understood through the platinum rule, "Do unto others as they themselves would have you do unto them" (Bennett, 1998, p. 213). A sympathetic response comes from a detached and ego-centric relationship to environmental phenomenon. I feel sorry for the spotted-owl because it is losing its habitat. What a pity. An empathetic response comes from an interrelated positioning with the nonhuman world, a "Self-Realization" of how the "we," the sycamore, the spotted owl, the honeysuckle and I, are all in it together. We position-take to the point of empathetic union with a hackberry tree to understood how that hackberry tree lives in the world and how we and that hackberry trees share a common world. One could ask the question, "How do I, the hackberry tree, experience the world and need humans to relate to me?" Of course, this shifts the direction of the subject's action-orientation toward the object in reverse; the "object," a tree, then assumes rights—the right to live, prosper, and have moral status.

Providing empathetic skills and nurturing the capacity for empathy with the nonhuman world emerge as critical to the development of eco-logically consciousness residents of planet Earth, residents whose "limited self" has expanded to include nonhuman life forms. Robert Aitken Roshi, writing from the Zen tradition, says similar things about empathy in a different way,

> The practice of "being with them" converts the third person, *they, it, she, he,* into the first person, *I* and *we.* For Dogen Zenji, the others who are "non other than myself" include mountains, rivers, and the great earth. (as cited Devall & Sessions, 1985, p. 234)

SELF RE-EDUCATION: MULTICULTURAL PEACE EDUCATION[2] FOR TEACHERS

> The ultimate objective of education should be, Gandhi said, to help create not only a balanced and harmonious individual but also a balanced and har-monious society where true justice prevails, where there is no unnatural divi-sion between the "haves" and the "have-nots," and where everybody is assured of a living wage and the right to live and the right to freedom.
>
> —Arun Gandhi (2001, p. 15)

Power, Multicultural Peace Education, and Deep Ecology

Banks and Banks (2001) define multiculturalism as:

> A philosophical position and movement that assumes that the gender, eth-nic, racial, and cultural diversity of a pluralistic society should be reflected in all of the institutionalized structures of educational institutions, including staff, the norms and values, the curriculum, and the student body. (p. 447)

Two assumptions in the above quote are that pluralism *is fair and just* and that perhaps pluralism can be *beneficial for all*. The affirmation of "diversity as fair" in multiculturalism and the deconstruction of the privilege of some and under-privilege of others illuminates unequal power relationships and unfair access and opportunity for some (in the United States— African Americans, Latinos, women, children with disabilities, the poor, etc.) in human educational environments. Multicultural education aims to expose, examine, and socially reconstruct society to transform power relationships and inequalities to create more egalitarian and inclusive educational and social environments for all (Sleeter & Grant, 1994).

A critical analysis of the forces in schooling that promote diversity, homogeneity, liberation, or oppression is necessary. In a turn of the century French context, Emile Durkheim argued that schooling should homogenize the general population and that the teacher should act as a moral agent for the state in the homogenizing process. The power to influence society, the power that schools and teachers wield, should be used to create homogeneity—sameness. Durkheim argues:

> Society can survive only if there exists among its members a sufficient degree of homogeneity; education perpetuates and reinforces this homogeneity; education perpetuates and reinforces this homogeneity by fixing children, from the beginning, the essential similarities that collective life demands. (Hurn, 1993, p. 78)

In contrast, the contemporary multicultural education movement argues for heterogeneity in schooling—in institutional structuring, in staffing, in pedagogy, in curriculum, and in assessment. Multiculturalism promotes strong ethnic identities in the spirit of a positive pluralism and it simultaneously works to create more inclusive and collective identities (national, regional, global, human).

Power dynamics in formal schooling continue to be an important topic for academic inquiry. The nature of power in human relationship with the nonhuman world is equally as complex to understand. With technological innovation, it is arguable that humans indeed do have "dominion over nature," though we are repeatedly humbled by the raw power of earthquakes, volcanic eruptions, floods, and other natural disasters. Humans do have considerable power over the natural world; DNA cloning projects, automobiles, and nuclear weapons illustrate how much human knowledge and effort have advanced this domination. We do have considerable potential to take life away, and a seedling potential to recreate life (i.e., DNA cloning). Human "dominion over nature" is apparent on many levels in human societies, particular post-industrial capitalistic societies.

The hegemonic worldview of "humans have dominion over the world," which has roots in a Christian religious framework, is contested by deep ecologists who call upon Chief Seattle's maxim of "The earth does not belong to man, man belongs to the earth." One position posits ownership and therefore domination; the other posits relatedness and therefore service and stewardship. When we contemplate the decay that happens to various life forms after death, we understand who ultimately belongs to whom.

Redistributed power that promotes access and opportunity for *all* seem to be the common thread between the multicultural education and the deep ecology movements. Though multiculturalism operates within the human domain and deep ecology operates with the assumption that the nonhuman world has inherent value, both seem to suggest that new configurations of power, defined in a fluid and dynamic sense, need be cultivated in our hearts and our institutions. The nature of power, structures of domination, oppression, marginalization, and exploitation need be critically examined to dismantle the obstacles to others' (humans and nonhumans) rights to survival and to encourage the actualization of a self-defined happiness. Cultivating both negative peace (the absence of war/direct physical violence that has catastrophic, negative environmental impact) and positive peace (the absence of structural, indirect, and inner violence) emerge as integral to this endeavor. Understanding and transforming anthropocentrism, racism, sexism, environmental racism, environmental exploitation and numerous other divisive blemishes in the mind and in society appear to be a step in the right direction.

Promoting Diversity Affirmation in Teacher Education

Naess (1995) asserts a diversity affirmative orientation by stating that one's identification with a bountiful diversity enhances with the realization of diverse life forms:

> Self-realization is that realization of the potentialities of life. Organisms that differ from each other in three ways give us less diversity than organisms that differ from each other in one hundred ways. Therefore, the self-realization we experience when we identify with the universe is heightened by an increase in the number of ways in which individuals, societies, and even species and life forms realize themselves. The greater the diversity, the greater the Self-Realization. (as cited in Sessions, p. 30)

Diversity multiples and widens the Self that is identified with everything. This subtle, and very refined diversity affirmative position implies identification with the diversity of the universe and not homogenizing the universe into a projection of one's narrow, ego-centric self. Rather, the more heterogeneity of personalities, of cultures, of organisms and the more each achieves their potentials (actualization) the more this leads to the deeper unfoldment of Self—the undifferentiated Totality of which seemingly separate organisms are the exemplars. If through the human practice of *ahimsa* (nonviolence) in relationship with the nonhuman world, all sentient beings have the right to self-actualize and realize their fullest potentials, the Self-realization of all will be enhanced. Diversity then leads to greater Self-realization.

Through actualizing our own human potentials and allowing other nonhuman beings to actualize theirs, we are coparticipating in the evolution and unfolding of the universe. Such participation in the actualization of the universe becomes a walking delight of awe and wonder. In Naess' (1995) elaboration of Ecosophy T, the name for his philosophy of deep ecology, he suggests that "Self-Realization" is the ultimate norm of deep ecology (as cited in Sessions, p. 80). He proposes "Maximize (long-range, universal) diversity" as a call to maximize the diversity of life forms on the planet, "A corollary is that the higher the levels of Self-realization attained by any person, the more any further increase depends upon the Self-realization of others" (p.80). Self-realization is contingent on and interdependent with the realization of diverse life forms; thus humans and nonhumans are mutually bound in a process of Self-realization. We understand that human, cultural, biological, and ecological diversity is beneficial for all.

Making the parallel between diversity affirmation and nonviolence, Harris (1995-1996) maintains:

> A multicultural approach to knowledge teaches that all different cultures have important insights into truth. A nonviolent approach to conflict resolution in a diverse world requires that all voices be respected and urged to come to the table to create a dialogue that would build a consensus about how to create positive peace. In order to appreciate the diversity of life on this planet, students should be taught global awareness, where they learn to respect different cultures. (p. 264)

Validating multiple insights into truth, respect of and fairness to multiple voices, awareness of global connectedness and cultural difference provide a foundation on which equality and equity can be built. Valuing diversity can be achieved through various educational means. Diversity affirmation can become part of reform in curriculum, instruction, assessment, state and federal educational policies, social and power structures of educational institutions, and staffing. *Ahimsa*, or nonviolence, can become an integral means toward diversity affirmation in schooling.

Understanding the inherent value of diversity is fundamental in both multicultural peace education and in deep ecology. Diversity can result in a collective gain for all involved. Gandhi embraced this idea, "I do not want my house to be walled in on all sides and my windows stuffed. I want the cultures of all lands to be blown about my house as freely as possible (Kripalani, 1992, p. 143 as cited in Harris, 1996).

Gandhi's association with people from various religions, races, and nationalities in South Africa, India, England, Italy, and elsewhere provide evidence of his valuing diversity. His ongoing struggle to unite Hindus and Muslims in common solidarity in India attest to his value of diversity; he worked with multiple sides. Building solidarity, not division, was part of Gandhi's master plan,

> Nothing can be farther from my thought than that we should become exclusive or erect barriers. But I do respectfully contend that an appreciation of other cultures can fitly follow, never precede, an appreciation and assimilation of our own. (Kripilani, 1992, p. 143 quoted in Harris, 1996)

Gandhi understood the insight of how deeply knowing self leads to increased appreciation of others. The common thread in Gandhi's ideas, the deep ecology movement, and the multicultural education movement is that social and planetary justice need be actualized through fairness to all (humans and nonhumans) and through affirmation of diversity. Nonviolence in means and ends becomes integral to a new soft infrastructure—a value transformation that embodies diversity and an identification with all.

RE-EDUCATION FOR TEACHERS: INFUSING PRACTICE WITH VISION

Informed by Gandhi's philosophy of nonviolence, principles of deep ecology, and both multicultural and peace education, a multicultural, eco-peace education for teachers draws out from learners:

- Awareness and contextualized appreciation of fundamental differences in individuals, groups, societies, cultures, species, ecosystems (i.e., Hanvey's "perspective consciousness").
- Recognition that diversity is beneficial for all; diversity multiplies potentialities for survival, sustainability, creativity, and innovation.
- Awareness of the fundamental unity of all life—human and nonhuman.
- Desire to build intercultural empathy for peace via common ground among people with distinctive primary cultures
- Capacities for empathetic union with humans and nonhumans.

- Awareness of inequality and inequity in power dynamics (discrepancies in opportunity and access as well) within the human world and within the relationship of humans to the nonhuman world.
- A commitment toward access, opportunity, fairness, and the right to self-actualize for all.
- Validation of multiple insights into truth, respect of and fairness to multiple voices—human and nonhuman.
- Determination to create awareness about inequality and to build a more egalitarian world for marginalized and oppressed people, nonhuman organisms, and ecosystems through educational means.
- Awareness of how an environmental ethics can contribute to violence, domination, or exploitation of the nonhuman world and how an ecocentric environmental ethic is desirable.
- Insight into the complexity of unity and diversity and the concept of interdependence.
- Action toward positive change for uplifting marginalized and oppressed human beings and nonhuman organisms and ecosystems.
- Commitment to engage in the transformation of institutional and structural arrangements that privilege some at the exclusion of others.

These are merely flexible suggestions for contemplation, not a rigid blueprint, for cultivating multicultural peace educators.

Why the focus on teacher education in this paper? The potential for the multiplication of "Self" re-education and learning in general in teacher education programs is great. In turn, highly attuned teachers can have great effects on children's learning opportunities in schools. Preservice and in-service teacher need to recognize their own cultural assumptions, conditioning, and the limits of their knowledge paradigms. They also need to learn how they can learn from their students and their rich, diverse backgrounds. Cultivating capacities to empathize with, connect to, and to empower colearners fosters positive relationships—a necessary foundation for engaging students in transformative education experiences. But first, the journey begins with educating the educators in dialogic ways that draw out capacities for reflection and action.

Learning need not be an imposition of knowledge or an instilling of ideas and values because some expert said so. It can be an elicitation of communally defined desirable values, ideas, and action-orientations. Naess suggests that an ecocentric environmental ethic should be embraced for its validity alone, and not on the basis of vested human self-interest:

But such an ethic would surely be more effective if it were acted upon by people who believe in its validity, rather than its usefulness. This, I think, will come to be understood more and more by those in charge of educational policies. Quite simply, it is indecent for a teacher to proclaim an ethic for tactical reasons only. (as cited in Session, p. 67)

Deeper moral commitment needs to replace instrumental means to an end. Teachers can introduce their students to new ideas that may allow alternative, equitable, and sustainable possibilities (positive peace) to replace a world steeped in violence and oppression. The degree of harm we do to one another, animals, plants and ecosystems can significantly be reduced through new educational, lifestyle, and relational practices. Self-re-education involves peeling through the layers of conditioning to examine core assumptions, knowledge paradigms, and conceptions of self and other. Self-re-education urges us to "be in the world ever anew."

When one tugs at a single thing in nature, he [she] finds it attached to the rest of the world.

—John Muir

NOTES

1. Notice, Gandhi says the "Sum total of all that life is God." For those who feel uncomfortable with "God," maybe substitute "interdependence."
2. The term "multicultural peace education" emerged from my collaborations with Dr. Antonette Aragon at Colorado State University.

REFERENCES

Aitken, R. (1985). Gandhi, dogen, and deep ecology. In B. Devall & G. Sessions (Eds.), *Deep ecology: Living as if nature mattered*. Salt Lake City, UT: Peregrine Smith Books.

Banks, J., Cochran-Smith, M., Moll, L., Richert, A., Zeichner, K., LePage, P., Darling-Hammong, et al. (2005). Teaching diverse learners. In L. Darling-Hammond & J. Bransford (2005). *Preparing teachers for a changing world: What teachers should learn and be able to do*. San Francisco: Jossey-Bass.

Banks, J. A., & McGee Banks, C. (2001). *Multicultural education: Issues and Perspectives*. New York: Wiley.

Barkdull, J. (2000). Why environmental ethics matters to international relations. In R. M. Jackson (Ed.), *Annual Editions: Global Issues 02/03*. Connecticut: McGraw-Hill.

Brantmeier, E. J. (2003, June). *"Self" Education for an Interdependent World: Core Concepts for Creating Globalized Teachers*. Presented at UNESCO Conference on

Intercultural Education, Human Rights, and a Culture of Peace. Jyvaskyla, Finland. Published in Conference Proceedings.

Brantmeier, E. J. (2008) Building empathy for intercultural peace: Teacher involvement in peace curricula development at a U.S. Midwestern High School. In J. Lin, E. J. Brantmeier, & C. Bruhn (Eds.), *Transforming education for peace* (pp. 67-89). Greenwich, CT: Information Age Publishing.

Bennett, M. J. (1998). Overcoming the Golden Rule: Sympathy and empathy. In *Basic Concepts of Intercultural Communication*. Yarmouth, ME. Intercultural Press.

Darling-Hammond, L. (2007). Race, inequality, and educational accountability: The irony of "No Child Left Behind." *Race, Ethnicity, and Education, 10*(3), 245-260.

Devall, B., & Sessions, G. (1985). *Deep ecology: Living as if nature mattered.* Salt Lake City: Peregrine Smith Books.

Galtung, J. (1969). Violence, peace, and peace research. *Journal of Peace Research, 3,* 167-192

Gandhi, A. (2002). Gandhian education: The difference between knowledge and wisdom. *Encounter, 15*(2), 14.

Gandhi, M. K. (1924) Young India. *Collected Works, 25,* 390.

Gandhi, M. K. (1932). Essential writings of Mahatma Gandhi. A Letter. *Mahadevbhaini Diary, I,* 242-2433.

Haberman, D. (2002, Oct. 17). *Gandhi and deep ecology: Living with the Vedantic view of self.* India Studies Lecture, Indiana University.

Hanvey, R. G. (1982). An attainable global perspective. *Theory in to Practice. 21*(3), 162-167.

Harris, I. (1995-1996). Nonviolence in Education. *Proceedings of the Midwest Philosophy of Education Society. 255-274.*

Howard, G. (2006). *We can't teach what we don't know: White teachers, multiracial school.* New York: Teachers College Press.

Hurn, C. J. (1993). *The limits and possibilities of schooling: An introduction to the sociology of education* (3rd ed.). Boston: Allyn & Bacon.

Khosoo, T. N. (1995). *Mahatma Gandhi: An apostle of applied human ecology.* New Dehli, India. Tata Energy Research Institute.

Kripalani, K. (Ed.). (1992). *Mahatma Gandhi: All men are brothers.* New York: Continuum.

Lal, V. (2000). *Gandhian ecology.* Retrieved September 26, 2003, from http://www.sscnet.ucla.edu/southasia/History/Gandhi/Gandhian_ecology.html

Ladson-Billings, G. (2006). Yes, But How Do We Do It? In J. Landsman & C. W. Lewis (Eds.), *White teachers, diverse classrooms a guide to building inclusive schools, promoting high expectations, and eliminating racism* (pp. 29-42). Sterling, Va: Stylus.

Lin, J., Brantmeier, E. J., Bruhn, C. (Eds.). (2008). *Transforming education for peace.* Greenwich, CT: Information Age Publishing.

Miller, S. B. (Trans.). (1986). *Bhagavad-Gita: Krishna's counsel in a time of war.* New York: Bantam Classics.

Naess, A. (1995). Self realization: An ecological approach to being in the world. In G. Sessions (Ed.), *Deep ecology for the 21st century: Readings on the philosophy and practice of the new environmentalism* (pp. 225-239). Boston: Shambhala.

Optowo, S., Gerson, J., & Woodside, S. (2005) From moral exclusion to moral inclusion: Theory for teaching peace. *Theory Into Practice, 44*(4), 303-318.

Pimentel, D. (1996). Gandhi and nature. *Bioscience, 46*(8), 626-628.

Sessions, G. (Ed.). (1995). *Deep ecology for the 21st century: Readings on the philosophy and practice of the new environmentalism.* Boston: Shambhala.

Sleeter, C. E., & Grant, C. (1994). *Making choices for multicultural education: Five approaches to race, class, and gender* (2nd ed.). New York: Merrill.

Spring, J. (2006). *Deculturalization and the struggle for equality: A brief history of the education of dominated cultures in the United States* (5th ed.). Boston: McGraw-Hill Humanities/Social Sciences/Languages.

Weber, T. (1999). Gandhi, deep ecology, peace research, and Buddhist economics. *Journal of Peace Research.* 36 (3)

Zeichner, K. (1993). *Educating teachers for cultural diversity* (NCRTL Special Report). East Lansing, MI: National Center for Research on Teacher Learning.

CHAPTER 15

EDUCATING FOR WISDOM

John P. Miller

The focus of most schools and universities is on the development of marketable skills. Departments and Ministries of Education support this focus by stating that these skills are needed if citizens are to compete in the global marketplace. We have heard this mantra since the early 80s with documents as a *Nation at Risk* which eventually led to programs such as No Child Left Behind with its emphasis on standardized testing. Has this emphasis achieved its goals? In some cases test scores have gone up but has this focus made the world a better place to live in? In the fall of 2008 the world experienced a financial meltdown that began in the United States where investment banks and the banking system in general were engaged in high risk investment strategies. Many of the individuals running these institutions were educated in the best universities in the United States. Clearly there was little wisdom in their decisions that led to the financial mess. We also live in a world where each day there is more evidence of climate change that could very soon make much of the world uninhabitable. Yet governments and world leaders refuse to seriously address the problem.

It is time that schools and universities focus on the development of wisdom if humanity is to survive. Matthew Fox quotes a Native American

Spirituality, Religion, and Peace Education, pp. 261–275
Copyright © 2010 by Information Age Publishing

elder who said: "Only a madman thinks with his head" Fox (2006) goes on to write:

> I might add, only a mad civilization thinks with its head … or educates people to think their heads. A healthy individual and a healthy educational system learn to think with heart as well as with head. Such a civilization thinks wisely. (p. 102)

Our education system needs to focus on the development of wisdom or what the ancients called the "thinking heart" (Miller, 2008).

WISDOM

What is wisdom? It is not the collection of information but a deeper knowing that is characterized by *insight, humility, and love.*

Insight

Wisdom involves seeing into the nature of things. Both science and religion have helped us in this quest. Science and particularly ecology has shown us the interdependence and interconnectedness of nature. Yet various religions have also shared this insight at a more personal level. In Christianity there is the proverb "as a man thinkth so he or she is" clarifying the effect that our thoughts have on our life. In Buddhism there is the following statement:

> The thought manifests as the word,
> The word manifests as the deed,
> The deed develops into habit,
> And the habit hardens into character.
> So watch the thought
> And its ways with care,
> And let it spring from love
> Born out of respect for all beings.
> (as cited in Miller, 2007. p. 191)

Seeing how our thoughts impact ourselves and others is an insight that can eventually change our behavior so that we live more wisely.

Another insight into the nature of things is that universe is constantly changing and evolving. We see this in our own lives as we go through infancy, childhood, adolescence, adulthood, and old age and we witness it in nature with the change of the seasons. In Buddhism this is the principle of *impermanence* as things are constantly in a state of flux. Because of this fact different religions encourage us not to grasp but let go. Hinduism encourages nonattachment to the results of our work. Hinduism is not the only faith to advocate nonattachment. St. John of the Cross wrote: "The soul that is attached to anything, however much good there may be in it, will not arrive at the liberty of divine union" (as cited in Huxley, 1970, p. 105). Chuang Tzu, the Taoist master, stated: "And so it is with man. If he could only pass empty through life, who would be able to injure him?" (p.106) Finally there is a Sufi Aphorism which says: "When the heart weeps for what it has lost, the spirit laughs for what it has found" (p.106).

As we see how we are interconnected and how we are part of a dynamic process of change, we lose the sense of self-importance that our egos crave. Instead we can see our place in the cosmos.

Humility

Seeing our place in nature is a humbling process. By humbling I do not mean demeaning, in fact, it can lead to a sense that each of us has a unique role to fill in the universe. Yet this sense should not lead us to egoism but an awareness that we are part of a whole. The *Tao Te Ching* constantly reinforces this message and suggests that the best leaders are the ones who in their wisdom bring out the best in people and do not feel the need to control others. One quotation (#59) for the Tao Te Ching states "Know your position and understand the Mother" (Kaufman, 1998, p. 122)

Emerson (1990) comments on how humans separate themselves from nature:

> These roses under my window make no reference to former roses or to bet-ter ones; they are for what they are; they exist with God to-day. There is no time to them. There is simply the rose; it is perfect in every moment of its existence. Before a leaf-bud has burst, its whole life acts; in the full-blown flower there is no more; in the leafless root there is no less. Its nature is sat-isfied and it satisfies nature in all moments alike. But man postpones or remembers; he does not live in the present, but with reverted eye laments the past, or, heedless of the riches that surround him, stand on tiptoe to foresee the future. He cannot be happy and strong until he too lives with nature in the present, above time. (p. 160)

As a result of having not seen ourselves as part of nature, we have inflicted environmental damage on the planet. Rather than humility there has been an arrogance that has led to the subjugation of indigenous peoples, needless wars (e.g., Vietnam and Iraq) and poverty. Through wisdom and seeing our place in the cosmos, we could begin heal the planet.

Nature helps us see our place in the universe and to also embrace the mystery at the heart of the cosmos. Confronting this mystery leads to sense of not-knowing and humility. Zen and Taoism emphasize this element. For example, Ray Grigg (1994) cites the following Zen saying "The most dangerous thing in the world is to think you understand something" (p. 247). He then follows with a quotation from Taoism "Knowing is the way of fools" (p. 247). Both these quotations point to how experience cannot be explained away. Grigg argues that this wisdom leads to a "perpetual preparedness" where the person approaches each situation with a readiness and openness. He states: "Each individual person becomes the balanced and shapeless center of the universe, dancing alone with the unpredictable order that swirls everywhere" (p. 247).

Susan Murphy (2006), a Zen teacher writes of not knowing our own goodness:

> The *Tao Te Ching* speaks of the "people of old" (or people closer to our own original simplicity) as being good without knowing that they were good, and being just without knowing that they were just. When we stop supposing that this or that and freely become what we actually are, we leave generous room for the other to be free to be exactly what they are. What a gift!" (p. 161)

Love

> A commitment to spiritual life necessarily means we embrace the eternal principle that love is all, everything, our true destiny. Despite overwhelming pressure to conform to the culture of lovelessness, we still seek to know love. That seeking is itself a manifestation of divine spirit. (hooks, 2000, p. 78)

Like hooks (2000), King and Gandhi believed that love was at the centre of the cosmos and underlies all that we strive for. Wisdom acknowledges this and nourishes all forms of love.

I find hooks' (2000) arguments particularly compelling because she suggests that those who fight for social justice and equity often ignore the importance of love in their struggles. She sees love as "the primary way we end domination and oppression" (p. 76). Through love we see how as human beings we all want happiness and well being. Of course, the shape of this happiness can differ in various contexts but still we share this desire to be happy and not suffer.

Gandhi and King would not let themselves hate their opponents but instead saw them through the eye of compassion. Mandela also had this quality. When he was in prison, he would look for small acts of kindness from the guards and this awareness kept him going for the 27 years he was in prison. When he was heading up the commission for reconciliation, he made sure that wardens from his prison were included.

When love disappears then we see the other as object and no longer as a human being. Unfortunately much political discourse today in the United States is characterized by name calling and lack of mutual respect. Paul Krugman (2009) calls this behavior "The Big Hate."

Love, or compassion, is also missing in our education. How often do we hear education officials or academics speak of love? Dzogchen Ponlop Rinpoche (1999) states:

> that the development of compassion is what is most missing from schools today. Perhaps it is that our teachers are not compassionate, or maybe it is the students who are not compassionate. But it is clear—something is wrong. We are not learning properly. I feel that we are not learning properly because we are not open to each other. Compassion, however, is what opens the heart. (p. 59)

I turn now to how we can develop wisdom-based learning in our schools.

WISDOM BASED LEARNING

If insight is one of the key aspects of wisdom, then how can we foster this in our schools? I have argued in other contexts that *the curriculum should focus primarily on relationships and connections so that the student can become aware of the interdependence of life* (Miller, 2007). Unfortunately the school curriculum tends to be fragmented as we break information down into courses, units, and lessons with little emphasis on how knowledge is connected. Instead, the curriculum should be developed around several key connections and I have identified six. They include:

1. Subject connections
2. Earth connections
3. Community connections
4. Thinking connections
5. Body mind connections
6. Soul connections.

The first three tend to be more external while the last three are more internal to the individual. Let me describe each of the six and give an example of how each connection might be manifested in the classroom.

Subject Connections

There are different ways of making these connections. One way is called *multidisciplinary*. Here the curriculum retains separate subjects, but establishes linkages between the separate subjects. For example, the history teacher might reference the literature and art of a specific historical period and explore how the art was representative of that period. Another approach is *interdisciplinary* level as two or three subjects are integrated around a theme or problem. For example, in examining the problem of city traffic and other problems of urban planning, subjects such as economics, political science, design technology and mathematics can be brought together and integrated. A third approach is *transdisciplinary* where several subjects are integrated around a broad theme. Issues such as poverty and violence in society lend themselves to this broadly integrative approach. James Beane (1997) is an advocate of this approach and describes how teachers can implement it in his book *Curriculum Integration*. In all these approaches knowledge is not kept within a particular subject but linked to other subjects and themes. An outcome for students is that they see relationships and how these relationships can impact their life and society at large.

Earth Connections

Here students see their relationship to the earth and its processes. They can start by reading indigenous people's literature from around the world. I particularly like a book titled *Touch the Earth* (McLuhan, 1972). For example, below are the words of Walking Buffalo, a Stoney Indian:

> Hills are always more beautiful than stone buildings, you know. Living in a city is an artificial existence. Lots of people hardly ever feel real soil under their feet, see plants grow except in flower pots, or get far enough beyond the street light to catch the enchantment of a night sky studded with stars. When people live far from scenes of the Great Spirit's making, it's easy for them to forget his laws.
>
> We saw the great Spirit's work in almost everything: sun, moon, trees, wind, and mountains. Sometimes we approached him through these things. Was that so bad? I think we have a true belief in the supreme being, a stronger faith than that of most whites who have called us pagans.... Indians living close to nature and nature's ruler are not living in darkness.
>
> Did you know that trees talk? Well they do. They talk to each other, and they'll talk to you if you listen. Trouble is, white people don't listen. They never learned to listen to the Indians so I don't suppose they'll listen to other

voices in nature. But I have learned a lot from trees: sometimes about the weather, sometimes about animals, sometimes about the Great Spirit. (p. 23)

Even more important is to have direct experiences with the earth. Schools are using gardens for this purpose. Kiefer and Kemple (1998) in their book, *Digging Deeper*, describe how youth gardens can be integrated with schools and communities. They identify their vision at the beginning of the book:

> Growing gardens with children is a living testament to how to restore our ancient ties to the natural rhythms of the earth itself. It is in the learning of this lesson—flower by flower, child by child, season by season—that we will be able to reclaim the heritage that is rightfully ours: as the caretakers of a natural paradise where all species thrive. (p.xiii)

Kiefer and Kemple argue that growing a garden has several benefits for children:

- seeing the results of growing food with their own hands;
- working in harmony with the forces of nature;
- learning basic academic skills in science, math, language, and social studies;
- learning to work cooperatively with others.

The book is part of the "Garden in Every School Campaign" that began in 1995 and has spread throughout North America. The process does not just involve schools and children but includes "elders to share their experience, stories and practical wisdom; local historians, naturalist, farmers, artisans and other professionals willing to contribute their expertise"(p.xiv) as well parents and families.

Community Connections

Children need to develop connections to each other, to adults, to the community at large and the global community. Ideally the classroom should be community where students feel safe and loved. The teacher sets this tone of trust and acceptance through their care and authenticity. Strategies as cooperative learning (Johnson & Johnson, 1994) and Tribes (Gibbs, 1987) can also help in this process.

King developed his vision of the Beloved Community for society and I believe this vision can also be applied to the school. King (1968) believed that "We are tied together in the single garment of destiny, caught in an inescapable network of mutuality" (p. 168). Students need to see how their well being is connected to the well being of others in the school. This vision runs counter to the one that is fostered by the current emphasis on testing and competition. This kind of mutuality can be developed through school wide projects. The film *Paper Clips* shows how a school came together through a project that collected a paper clip for each person who died in the holocaust.

As the children mature they can also see how they are part of wider community that extends to the entire planet. Awareness that we are not separate from people suffering on other continents should gradually emerge as the students sense of interconnectedness grows and expands.

Thinking Connections

In her book, *A Stroke of Insight,* Jill Bolte Taylor (2009), a brain scientist, describes her stroke experience and how it made her aware of the importance of right brained thinking. Her stroke affected her left brain which is the seat of logical thought and language. She refers to this "brain chatter" or that "calculating intelligence that knows when you have to do your laundry" (p. 31). It is also home of our "ego center." The right hemisphere sees things in relationship and in the large context of the whole:

> our right mind perceives each of us as equal members of the human family. It identifies our similarities and recognizes our relationship with this marvelous planet, which sustains our life. It perceives the big picture, how everything is related, and how we all join together to make up the whole. Our ability to be empathic, to walk in the shoes of another and feel their feelings is a product of our right frontal cortex. (p. 30)

Taylor also suggests that it is the place where we experience inner peace. For a time her life was dominated by the right brain and here she experienced moments of deep peace and feeling of being connected to the cosmos. Before the stroke, like most people living in the industrialized world, Taylor was caught up in "do-do-doing lots of stuff at a very fast pace" (p. 70). This stressful existence also led to frustration and anger. Her stroke allowed her to experience a different world. She writes "In absence of my left hemisphere's negative judgment, I perceived myself as perfect, whole, and beautiful just the way I was" (p. 74).

Through rehabilitation therapy Taylor has recovered the use of her left brain but she has learned to use both sides of the brain to live more fully and realize a deeper happiness. Now when she begins to feel stress she "shifts right" and thus slows down and now listens to her body and trusts her instincts. She breathes deeply and repeats to herself "*In this moment I reclaim my JOY, or In this moment I am perfect, whole, and beautiful, or I am an innocent and peaceful child of the universe"* I shift back into the consciousness of right mind" (p. 178).

Our students need to use both the right and left brain. They need to able to think clearly and analyze information but they also need to see relationships and feel the kind of peace that Taylor and all of us can experience. I believe that the use of imagery and metaphor in the classroom can stimulate the right side of the brain while various approaches to critical thinking can support the left side (Miller, 2007).

The work of Howard Gardner (1983) provides a broader conception of human intelligence than has been used within most educational settings. His intelligences theory provides a framework for exploring various modes of thinking. The eight intelligences include: *linguistic* (language development, abstract reasoning, use of symbols), *logical/mathematical* (scientific thinking, use of abstract symbols, and recognizing patterns), *visual/spatial* (visual arts, architecture, imagery, visual discrimination), *bodily/kinesthetic* (sports activities, body movement and expression, dance), *musical* (perceiving and interpreting sound), *interpersonal* (working cooperatively with others, feeling empathy for others, responding to the needs of others), *intrapersonal* (awareness of internal states, intuition, and reflection) and *natural* (awareness of the environment). Since the development of his work there have been many applications of this model to education. For example, the Pittsburgh Public Schools and the Educational Testing Service have collaborated with Gardner on a project called Arts PROPEL. This project has focused on assessment so as to move beyond what Gardner refers to as "the often wooden standardized instruments" (p. 238) that have been used so inappropriately in the arts. The project has also involved the development of a curriculum in the arts (Gardner, 1991).

David Lazear (1991a, 1991b) has also applied Gardner's work to an educational setting. Lazear has developed a number of classroom activities that teachers can use to develop the various intelligences.

Body-Mind Connections

We have lost touch with our bodies. The evidence that supports this view is the data on the high percentage of people that are overweight in North America (see data available at http://www.reuters.com/article/lifestyleMolt/idUSL0778048620070807). These data include young people as well. This problem is in part due to a tendency to live in our heads with little connection to body and soul. Abrams (1996) points to Descartes' work as contributing to our alienation from the body. He believes this has lead to our disconnection from the environment instead of recognizing that the body and the earth are intimately connected. Indigenous people have made this connection. Abrams describes how the native peoples of Australia would walk the routes of their ancestors and in this process the body and the land would become one. Abrams states: "he virtually *becomes* the journeying Ancestor, and thus the storied earth is born afresh" (p. 170).

Annie Klein (1997) in her discussion of women's embodiment argues to feel "we are located in and even confined to our bodies, yet at the same time alienated from them, is ingrained in modern identity and the individualism that is part and parcel of it" (p. 144).

Some teachers are addressing this problem by introducing yoga into the classroom. Yoga and other body disciplines such as *Qi Gong* and *Tai Chi* focus on mindful movement so that we begin to listen to our bodies. One teacher, Ana Neves (2009), describes how she has yoga with her elementary school students in her thesis. She provided yoga classes twice a week as part of the daily physical activity program required by the Ontario Ministry of Education. She taught the students how to be mindful of their movements as they did the various poses. Students were also taught awareness of their breathing as they practiced the yoga. Ana writes: "Similarly yoga practice requires the practitioner to develop increased self-awareness and concentration. One must focus one's attention on the breath, survey the mind and body and make adjustments as necessary so that the pose is most effective" (p. 77). She noticed that yoga helped improved their hand-eye coordination and concentration as well as becoming more relaxed. I have had other teachers report similar results (Miller, 2007, p. 122).

Soul Connections

Emerson (1990) wrote that "Education is the drawing out of the soul," yet the term soul is rarely heard in educational discourse. Soul is defined here as a vital and mysterious energy that gives meaning and purpose to one's life. In my book *Education and the Soul* (2000) I have described my understanding of soul and how it can be nurtured in students, our schools, and ourselves.

Awareness of the soul in education means that we are sensitive to the inner life of the student and attempt to nourish this life in various ways. I have called for a *curriculum for the inner life* which can include journal writing where students explore their thoughts and feelings, writing their own autobiography, visualization, dream work, and meditation.

Another valuable approach to soul connections is what Maria Montessori (1992) called *cosmic education*. Montessori's son, Mario, describes cosmic education when he writes: "Cosmic education seeks to offer the young, at the appropriate sensitive period, the stimulation and help they need to develop their minds, their vision, and their creative power, whatever the level or range of their personal contributions may be" (p. 101). Her son wrote that the child needs to have a "prior interest in the whole" so he or she can make sense of individual facts. This can be done in part by introducing students to ecological principles that focus on the interdependence of living and non-living things. Mario Montessori gives the example of students studying the life cycle of salmon and its relationship with the environment.

Aline Wolf (2004) has recently written about Montessori's vision of cosmic education. She argues that

> Essentially Montessori's cosmic education gives the child first an all-encompassing sense of the universe with its billions of galaxies. Then it focuses on our galaxy, the Milky Way, our solar system, planet Earth and its geological history, the first specimens of life, all species of plants and animals and finally human beings. Inherent in the whole study is the interconnectedness of all creation, the oneness of things. (p. 6)

Wolf also makes reference to the work of Brian Swimme and the Universe story. Cosmic education helps the children place themselves within the total framework of the universe. The image of the universe presented by Montessori and Swimme is one of order and purpose. Since human beings are part of the universe, it gives us a common reference point beyond the boundaries created by nations and religions. Wolf also points out the cosmic education can help children develop a sense of reverence for life and care for the earth. Seeing the miracle of life on life on earth within the vastness of the universe can help students appreciate more deeply life and the earth itself. Cosmic education can also give students a deep sense of gratitude as well.

> As examples, when we see a beautiful valley nestled in the mountains, we can reflect on the fact that it was formed by water that labored thousands of years to wear down the mountainous terrain, when we enter a car or train, we can look back and feel grateful to the first human being who constructed a wheel. Awareness of the long-term cosmic pattern, of which we are only an infinitesimal part, calls us to a deep humility and reverence for all the labors of nature and the work of human beings that preceded us. (p.16)

Wolf suggests that cosmic education can give children a sense of meaning, place, and purpose in their lives. Montessori felt that within the person lay a *spiritual embryo* which needs to be respected and nourished so that students can eventually find their purpose on earth.

WISE TEACHERS

To foster wisdom in students we need wise teachers. To foster their own insight, love and humility, teachers need to be engaged to practices that nurture these qualities. One of these practices is meditation. In the past 20 years I have introduced meditation practices to over 2000 teachers taking graduate courses at the Ontario Institute for Studies in Education. Students are introduced to six different types of meditation which include: meditation on the breath, counting the breath, lovingkindness (sending thoughts of well being to self and others), mantra (meditation on sound or phrase), movement (e.g., walking), visualization, and contemplation on poetry or sacred texts. Some students work out their own forms and integrate meditation with their own spiritual and religious practice. Although sitting meditation is encouraged, some students do movement meditation. For example, one student swam every day as he approached swimming with mindful awareness. Whatever form students choose, meditation can be seen as letting go of the calculating mind and opening to the listening mind that tends to be characterized by a relaxed alertness.

Most of the students are women (80%) in their late 20s 30s or 40s. While most of the students come from Ontario, there have also been students from Brazil, China, India, Indonesia, Iran, Italy, Jamaica, Lebanon, Japan, Kenya, Korea, Malta, Malaysia, and Somalia. Most of the students are teachers taking graduate courses in education. In the last few years, however, I have also been introducing meditation to students in teacher education programs for individuals seeking certification as teachers. These students are mostly in their mid- to late 20s.

Students are asked to meditate each day for 6 weeks. In the beginning, they meditate for about 10 to 15 minutes a day and by the end of the 6 weeks they are encouraged to meditate 20-30 minutes. Students are required to keep a journal which focuses on how the process of meditation is going (e.g., how the concentration and focus are going, how the body is feeling, etc.). The journals also focus on how meditation has affected them. Some of themes have included

- Giving themselves permission to be alone and enjoy their own company;
- Increased listening capacities;
- Feeling increased energy;
- Being less reactive to situations and generally experiencing greater calm and clarity.

At the end of the process they write a reflective summary of the experience. Below is an excerpt from one of these summaries.

I find it difficult to express how the meditation experience has been for me, … I find it difficult to use language to describe what's happened to over the course of the last few weeks…. What amazed me the most was how concentrating intensely on loving kindness and its implications for myself, my friends, my family my neighbors, my teachers, my colleagues, my acquaintances, the people who pass me on the street, the people who upset me, the people who participate and perpetuate structures that I oppose-that projecting lovingkindness to them resulted in a tangible concrete shift in my relationships-without my necessarily knowing, or intending it. We always think we have to "do" something in order to effect change, without realizing that we are acting, we are effecting change by attuning to our self, to our capacity for compassion and understanding and reflection. Mindfulness practice, similarly, I do believe effects change. For me at least it enables me to pause a moment before I react, before I blindly go about responding or acknowledging as I walk through my daily experiences without every really needing to be there. I felt the effects-I felt a shift-I felt it most when it would suddenly occur to me that I'm feeling good as a result of relating to people-and I don't mean my friends and family. I felt it most when I related to strangers, when I looked at them and saw them for the first time, when I thought about them as co-creators, as parts of myself…. What I mean is that … it is a matter of me not seeing a distinction between myself and them.

Another teacher's description of how the practices impacted her teaching shows her wisdom:

However, my thinking is expanding somewhat to stretch into a new sense of what it means to know someone, student or colleague, in a way that facilitates true and effective learning and growth. To teach from an intuitive source is to submit myself to an ocean of largeness of possibility that roars and flows with its own greatness and power quite outside the realm of my orchestration and planning and timing. It is to let go of the illusion of my own control and expertness, recognizing instead that to limit my students to the meager feelings of my ego is to miss the hugeness and importance of authentic educative growth. I am reminded here of my earlier teaching days, furiously pouring over the little section on China in the Social Studies binder, pathetically planning what glorious reams of knowledge I might impart, only to realize with horror that two-thirds of my class were *born* there. Who do I think I am? Teaching from the ego is ultimately a crash-course in humiliation. It is only when I submit to the truth of my smallness as one who is learning and struggling along a humble growth road with these brothers and sisters who are my students that I come closest to teaching in truth.

So crucial and authentic was the experience of "teaching through living" with my students, that I have since found myself questioning the validity of some of my former practice. I am beginning to see my students and myself as ultimately one growing, changing organism continuing to become. I am only beginning this journey; there is so much that is new and unknown to me about the scope and breadth of holistic teaching and living. I only know that it is becoming my passion and perhaps my life-work to teach and to live from the fireside, to "be quiet and listen and see what we hear."

This teacher shows insight, humility, and love in this passage. For example, she realizes that many of her students probably have more knowledge of China than she does since they were born there. She has the insight that she cannot *control* the educational experiences of her students. Finally, she feels love for her students as she sees "my students and myself as ultimately one growing, changing organism continuing to become." I am convinced that wisdom can come from teachers working on themselves through various mind and body practices. These practices allow the teacher to move from just teaching from their head to teaching with their whole being. From this wholeness wisdom can arise in our schools and classrooms.

REFERENCES

Abrams, D. (1996). *The spell of the sensuous.* New York: Vintage.

Beane, J. (1997). *Curriculum integration: Designing the core of democratic education.* New York: Teachers College Press.

Emerson, R. W. (1990). *Selected essays, lectures, and poems.* New York: Bantam.

Fox, M. (2006). *The A. W. E.: Reinventing education, Reinventing the human.* Kelowna, BC: Copper House.

Gardner, H. (1983). *Frames of mind: The theory of multiple intelligences.* New York: Basic Books.

Gardner, H. (1991). *The unschooled mind: How children think and how schools should teach.* New York: Basic Books.

Gibbs, J. (1987). *Tribes: A process for social development and cooperative learning.* Santa Rosa, CA: Center Source.

Grigg, R. (1994). *The Tao of Zen.* Boston: Charles E. Tuttle.

hooks, b. ((2000). *All about love.* New York: Harper Perennial.

Huxley, A. (1970). *The perennial philosophy.* New York: Harper Colophon.

Johnson, R.T., & Johnson, D. W. (1994) An overview of cooperative learning. In J. Thousand, A, Villa, & A. Nevin (Eds.), *Creativity and collaborative learning* (pp. 1-23) Baltimore, MD: Brookes Press.

Kaufman, S. F. (1998) *The living Tao: Meditations on the Tao Te Ching to empower your life.* Boston: Charles Tuttle.

Kiefer, J., & Kemple, M. (1998) *Digging deeper: Integrating youth gardens into schools & communities.* Montpelier, VT: Foodworks.

King, M. L. (1968, May). *Negro History Bulletin, 31,* 12

Klein, A. (1997). *Ground and opening.* Boston: Shambhala.

Krugman, P. (2009, June 12). The big hate. *New York Times,* p. A27

Lazear, D. (1991a). *Seven ways of knowing: Teaching for multiple intelligences.* Pallatine. IL: Skylight.

Lazear, D. (1991b). *Seven ways of teaching: The artistry of teaching with multiple intelligences.* Pallatine, IL: Skylight.

Miller, J. (2000). *Education and the soul: Toward a spiritual curriculum.* Albany, NY: SUNY Press.

Miller, J. (2007) *The holistic curriculum.* Toronto: University of Toronto Press.

Miller, J. (2008). The thinking heart. In C. M. Huat & T. Kerry (Eds.), *Issues in education: Integrating theory and practice* (pp. 62-76), London: Continuum.

McLuhan, T. C. (1972). *Touch the Earth: A self-portrait of Indian existence.* New York: Pocket Books

Montessori, M. (1992). *Education for human development: Understanding Montessori.* Oxford, England: Clio

Murphy, S. (2006). *Upside down zen: Finding the marvelous in the ordinary.* Boston: Wisdom.

Neves, A. (2009). *A holistic approach to the Ontario curriculum: Moving to a more coherent curriculum.* MA thesis at University of Toronto.

Ponlop Rinpoche, D. (1999). Buddhist education: The path of wisdom and knowledge. In S. Glazer (Ed.), *The heart of learning.* New York: Putnam.

Taylor, J. B. (2009). *My stroke of insight: A brain scientist's personal journey.* New York: Plume.

Wolf, A. (2004, October 7-10). *Maria Montessori cosmic education as a non-sectarian framework for nurturing children's spirituality.* Paper presented at the ChildSpirit Conference, Pacific Grove, CA.

ABOUT THE AUTHORS

Michelle Ayaz is from Los Angeles, California, the daughter of Iranian immigrants. Although born into a family that practiced Sufism, Michelle did not begin studying Sufism in earnest until her early adulthood. Michelle recieved her bachelor's degree in business management from California State University, Northridge in 2003. She earned her master's degree in 2008 from the University of Maryland, College Park in international education policy. Her areas of research were spirituality and peace education, and study abroad and peace education. Michelle currently works at the University of Maryland, College Park as the coordinator of the Persian Studies Department in the School of Languages, Literatures, and Cultures.

Dr. Edward J. Brantmeier is an assistant professor in the School of Education and School of Teacher Education and Principal Preparation at Colorado State University. He serves as cochair of the Interdisciplinary Program in Peace and Reconciliation Studies at CSU. He teaches multicultural education and foundations courses at the undergraduate and graduate level. He has authored or coauthored articles in the following select journals: *Theory and Research in Social Education; Journal of Peace Education; Journal of American Indian Education; International Education; Forum on Public Policy;* and *Infactis Pax*. He coedited a book titled *Transforming Education for Peace* (2008) and coauthored a book titled *147 Tips for Teaching Peace and Reconciliation* (2009). In the fall of 2009, he was awarded a Fulbright-Nehru Scholar grant in peace studies to lecture in India.

Mr. D. Brent Edwards is a doctoral student in the International Education Policy program in the Department of Education Leadership, Higher Education, and International Education at the University of Maryland, College Park. His research interests are many and include decentralization and democratization of education governance, education policy formation processes in international contexts, critical pedagogy, and education for and through personal transformation. His regional focus is Latin America, where he has traveled and worked extensively. He holds a MS Ed from the University of Pennsylvania, as well as degrees in finance, Spanish, and Latin American Studies from the University of Maryland, College Park

Ian Harris is professor emeritus at the Department of Educational Policy & Community Studies, University of Wisconsin-Milwaukee. Dr. Harris, is the author of two books—*Peace Education* (Jefferson, NC: McFarland & Co., 1988) and *Messages Men Hear: Constructing Masculinities* (London: Taylor & Francis, 1995) and coauthor (with Paul Denise) of *Experiential Education for Community Development* (New York: Greenwood Press, 1999); (with Linda Forcey) of *Peacebuilding for Adolescents: Strategies for Educators and Community Leaders* (New York: Peter Lang, 1999); and (with Mary Lee Morrison) of *Peace Education, Second Edition* (Jefferson, NC: McFarland & Co., (2003).

Four Arrows, although of Cherokee and Irish ancestry, follows the path of the Oglala, though the story is too long to tell here. Formerly dean of education at Oglala Lakota College and then a tenured professor at Northern Arizona University, he now proudly serves as faculty with the College of Educational Leadership and Change at Fielding Graduate University. With doctorates in health psychology and in curriculum and instruction, he is the author of 19 books, and numerous chapters and articles on such diverse topics as wellness, neuropsychology, critical inquiry character education, and Indigenous worldviews. In 2004, he was awarded the Moral Courage Award from the Martin Springer Institute. A Vietnam era Marine Corps officer, he cofounded the Veterans for Peace chapter in Northern Arizona. He lives in Canada and Mexico, depending on the season, with his wife and pets. His website is www.teachingvirtues.net.

Reuben Jacobson is a PhD student in education policy at the University of Maryland—College Park. He also serves as a consultant to the Coalition for Community Schools. Previously, he taught elementary school in the Washington DC public school system and worked as a research analyst at the American Institutes for Research. He received his MA policy from the George Washington University. Jacobson and Rabbi Steigmann are cousins and grew up together in Milwaukee, WI.

Nathalie Kees, EdD is an associate professor of counseling and career development in the School of Education at Colorado State University. Her teaching and research focuses on individual and group counseling, spirituality and counseling, and diversity and gender issues in counseling. She served as guest editor for special issues on women in counseling for *The Journal of Counseling and Development* and *The Journal for Specialists in Group Work.* She is coauthor of the book *Manager as Facilitator* and coeditor of the book *147 Tips for Teaching Peace and Reconciliation.* Dr. Kees is the founder of ACA's Women's Interest Network and has over 20 years of experience as an educator and advocate for peaceful resolutions to daily conflict.

Xin Li (PhD University of Toronto) is professor in the Department of Teacher Education at California State University-Long Beach, and cofounder and current chair for the Confucianism, Taoism, and Education Special Interest Group of the American Education Research Association. She teaches graduate students in the areas of multicultural education, language diversity, and curriculum studies. Dr. Li's research focuses on Daoist philosophy in curriculum theories and development, encompassing narrative inquiry of cross-cultural education, curriculum studies of multicultural education, global education, and peace education. Dr. Li has published her research in many journal articles and book chapters, and is the author of *The Tao of Life Stories: Chinese Language, Poetry, and Culture in Education* (2002), and the first author of *Shifting Polarized Positions: A Narrative Approach in Teacher Education* (2009).

Dr. Jing Lin is professor of international education policy at University of Maryland, College Park. She is the author of four books on Chinese education: *The Red Guard's Path to Violence* (1991), *Education in Post-Mao China* (1993), *The Opening of the Chinese Mind* (1994), and *Social Transformation and Private Education in China* (1999). Her recent research focuses on higher education expansion and the pursuit of world class excellence in China. The findings from the project will be published in a coauthored book entitled *Portraits of 21st Century Chinese Universities: In the Move to Mass Higher Education.* Jing Lin's second strand of research concentrates on peace education, environmental education, religion, and spirituality in education. She published *Love, Peace and Wisdom in Education: Vision for Education in the 21st Century* in 2006. A book that she coedited titled *Transforming Education for Peace* was published in 2008.

Jia Luo taught in the Tibetan Language and Culture Department at the Northwest University for Minorities in China. As a visiting scholar invited by OISE at the University of Toronto, he produced the first *Tibetan Culture Readings,* a bilingual text book on traditional knowledge for Tibetan children. His second one was published in Tibetan and distributed throughout Tibetan areas. His interests cover cultural dilemmas in modernization and indigenous education, a Tibetan peace perspective, and he cowrote a chapter in the *Global Issues in Education: A Reader.* He currently is a doctoral candidate at OISE/UT and is developing a theory of human peace from a global perspective.

John (Jack) Miller has been working in the field of holistic education for over 30 years. He is author/editor of more than a dozen books on holistic learning and contemplative practices in education which include *Education and the Soul, The Holistic Curriculum, and Educating for Wisdom and Compassion.* His writing has been translated into eight languages. *The Holistic Curriculum* has provided the framework for the curriculum at the Whole Child School in Toronto where Jack has served on the advisory board. Jack has worked extensively with holistic educators in Japan and Korea for the past decade and has been visiting professor at two universities in Japan. Jack was one of 25 scholars invited to a UNESCO conference on cultural diversity and transversal values held in Kyoto and Tokyo in 2007. He teaches courses on holistic education and spirituality in education at the Ontario Institute for Studies in Education at the University of Toronto where he is professor.

Mary Lee Morrison is the founding director and president of Pax Educare, Inc., the Connecticut Center for Peace Education in Hartford, Connecticut. Pax Educare, as a not for profit, seeks to build public understanding of peace education and to promote and advocate for the importance of integrating peace and sustainability principles and concepts into every aspect of education, both formal and informal. A former practicing clinical social worker, Dr. Morrison has taught educational foundations and courses in global social work and sociology at several universities, has authored books and articles on peace education and has been providing consultation and trainings for schools and community groups for the past 18 years.

Sarfaroz Niyozov did his BA in Middle Eastern Studies (Arabic) from Tajik State University (Tajikistan) in 1983, his postgraduate studies in Arabic thought and literature in 1991, his master's in education from the Aga Khan University in Karachi (Pakistan) in 1995 and his PhD in education from OISE/University of Toronto in 2001. He worked as a translator in Middle East for a number of years and as an instructor at State Universities in Tajikistan, and the Aga Khan University in Karachi. From 2001 to July 2005 Niyozov served as a Research Fellow and Coordinator of the Central Asian Studies at the Institute of Ismaili Studies (IIS) in London, England. Since 2005, Sarfaroz Niyozov is an assistant professor at the Ontario Institute for Studies in Education (OISE), University of Toronto. Currently he is a codirector of the Center for Comparative, International and Development Education (CIDE) at the OISE. He offers courses in "Issues in International, Global Education," "Introduction to Comparative, International and Development Education" "Teacher Development in Comparative and Cross-cultural Perspectives," and "Perspectives on Muslim Education."

Rebecca Oxford is professor of cross-cultural relations at the Air University, where she teaches military officers to understand values, beliefs, and behaviors of people from different cultural backgrounds. She is currently researching global jihad and has edited a book titled *Language of Peace in a Global Society.* She wrote a seminal article, "Gender and the Trinity," for *Theology Today* (Princeton University Press), studied ecumenism, and cotaught world religions with Jing Lin at the University of Maryland. She made presentations in 35 countries and received the Distinguished Scholar-Teacher Award at the University of Maryland and the Lifetime Achievement Award from the language field.

Zahra Punja graduated with her PhD in curriculum, teaching and learning at the Ontario Institute for Studies in Education at the University of Toronto in 2007. She then worked at the Northern Ontario School of Medicine in Sudbury, the Royal College of Physicians and Surgeons of Canada in Ottawa and the Canadian Memorial Chiropractic College in Toronto. She also worked with Professor Niyozov on developing a paper on Ismaili Muslim teachers in Central Asia.

Rabbi Moishe Steigmann is the associate rabbi of the Westchester Jewish Center in Mamaroneck, NY. He was ordained as a rabbi and received his master's in education in 2006 from the Jewish Theological Seminary of America in New York. He is also a graduate of the University of Wisconsin-Madison. In addition to his role as a synagogue rabbi, Rabbi Steigmann has taught in both formal and informal educational settings and designed curricula that have been used throughout the country in various synagogues. He is constantly seeking out new and creative ways to make education part of his rabbinic work.

Dr. William M. Timpson is a professor in the School of Education at Colorado State University and cochair of the Interdisciplinary Studies Program in Peace and Reconciliation. He has written or coauthored 14 books including several that address issues of peace and reconciliation, diversity, and sustainability: *147 Tips for Teaching Peace and Reconciliation* (2009), *147 Tips for Teaching Sustainability* (2006), *147 Tips for Teaching Diversity* (2005), *Teaching Diversity* (2003), and *Teaching and Learning Peace* (2002). In 2006 he served as a Fulbright Senior Specialist for peace and reconciliation studies at the UNESCO Centre in Northern Ireland.

Priyankar Upadhyaya is a professor of peace studies and director of the Malaviya Centre for Peace Research at the Banaras Hindu University in Varanasi, India. He has served as the adjunct/visiting professor at various universities in Europe and North America and has authored/coauthored several books and research articles in reputed international journals.

Yingji Wang is doctoral candidate from the College of Education at University of Maryland, College Park. She is interested in peace education, holistic education, spirituality and education, and other related fields that help nurture whole beings in education. Her previous research involves integrating peace education into second language education. Currently, her dissertation is an exploration of the experiences of Chinese language teachers in the United States, which reveals a connection between Chinese language education and peace-building. She herself aspires to follow the footsteps of spiritual teachers, cultivating love and peace from within so as to serve others.

INDEX

Breinigsville, PA USA
28 October 2010
248212BV00003B/13/P

9 781617 350580